FOURTEEN BRITISH & AMERICAN POETS

ROWLAND L. COLLINS

INDIANA UNIVERSITY

THE MACMILLAN COMPANY

Dedicated to my father and mother,
John Leland and Velma Jones Collins

Third Printing, 1970

Library of Congress catalog card number: 64–16864

THE MACMILLAN COMPANY
866 THIRD AVENUE, NEW YORK, NEW YORK 10022
COLLIER-MACMILLAN CANADA, LTD., TORONTO, ONTARIO

Printed in the United States of America

ACKNOWLEDGMENTS

EMILY DICKINSON
"Success Is Counted Sweetest," "I Never Hear the Word 'Escape,' " "Sur-
geons Must Be Very Careful," "Bring Me the Sunset in a Cup," "A
Wounded Deer Leaps Highest," "Two Swimmers Wrestled on the Spar,"

"I Taste a Liquor Never Brewed," " 'Hope' Is the Thing with Feathers," "There's a Certain Slant of Light," "I Felt a Funeral in My Brain," "I Know Some Lonely Houses off the Road," "The Soul Selects Her Own Society," "A Bird Came down the Walk," "After Great Pain, a Formal Feeling Comes," "It Might Be Lonelier," "I Died for Beauty," "I Heard a Fly Buzz When I Died," " 'Twas Warm at First, Like Us," "I Took My Power in My Hand," "I've Seen a Dying Eye," "I Gave Myself to Him," "I Like to See It Lap the Miles," "Pain Has an Element of Blank," "They Say That 'Time Assuages,' " "Because I Could Not Stop for Death," "She Rose to His Requirement," "Remorse Is Memory Awake," "The Wind Began to Knead the Grass," "Ample Make This Bed," "We Outgrow Love Like Other Things," "A Narrow Fellow in the Grass," "I Never Saw a Moor," "The Last Night That She Lived," "Immortal Is an Ample Word," "As Imperceptibly as Grief," "Of God We Ask One Favor," "My Life Closed Twice Before Its Close." Reprinted by permission of the publishers and the Trustees of Amherst College from Thomas H. Johnson, editor, THE POEMS OF EMILY DICKINSON, Cambridge, Mass.: The Belknap Press of Harvard University Press, Copyright, 1951, '55, by The President and Fellows of Harvard College.

"After Great Pain, a Formal Feeling Comes." Copyright 1929, © 1957 by Mary L. Hampson, reprinted by permission of Little, Brown and Co. "It Might Have Been Lonelier." Copyright 1935, © 1963 by Martha Dickinson Bianchi, reprinted by permission of Little, Brown and Co. "I Never Hear the Word 'Escape,' " "I've Never Seen a Dying Eye," reprinted by courtesy of Little, Brown and Co.

GERARD MANLEY HOPKINS

"Heaven-Haven," "The Habit of Perfection," "God's Grandeur," "Spring," "The Windhover," "Pied Beauty," "The Loss of the Eurydice," "At the Wedding March," "Felix Randal," "Brothers," "Spring and Fall," "Inversnaid," " (Carrion Comfort) ," "No Worst, There Is None," "To Seem the Stranger Lies My Lot, My Life," "I Wake and Feel the Fell of Dark, Not Day," "Patience, Hard Thing!" From *Poems of Gerard Manley Hopkins*, Third Edition, edited by W. H. Gardner. Copyright 1948 by Oxford University Press, Inc. Reprinted by permission.

WILLIAM BUTLER YEATS

"Down by the Salley Gardens," "The Pity of Love," "When You Are Old," "The Lake Isle of Innisfree," "The Sorrow of Love," "A Dream of Death." Reprinted with permission of the publisher from COLLECTED POEMS by W. B. Yeats. Copyright 1906 by The Macmillan Company, Renewed 1934 by William Butler Yeats. "To a Friend Whose Work Has Come to Nothing," "The Magi." Reprinted with permission of the publisher from COLLECTED POEMS by W. B. Yeats. Copyright 1916 by The Macmillan Company, Renewed 1944 by Bertha Georgie Yeats. "An Irish Airman Foresees His Death," "The Scholars," "A Deep-Sworn Vow." Reprinted with permission of the publisher from COLLECTED POEMS by W. B. Yeats. Copyright 1919 by The Macmillan Company, Renewed 1946 by Bertha Georgie Yeats. "Easter 1916," "The Second Coming." Reprinted with permission of the publisher from COLLECTED POEMS by W. B. Yeats. Copyright 1924 by The Macmillan Company, Renewed 1952 by Bertha Georgie Yeats. "Sailing to Byzantium," "Leda and the Swan," "Two Songs

from a Play," "Among School Children." Reprinted with permission of the
publisher from COLLECTED POEMS by W. B. Yeats. Copyright 1928 by
The Macmillan Company, Renewed 1956 by Georgie Yeats. "Byzantium,"
"Crazy Jane and Jack the Journeyman," "Crazy Jane Talks with the
Bishop," "A Last Confession," "After Long Silence," "A First Confession,"
"Crazy Jane on God." Reprinted with permission of the publisher from
COLLECTED POEMS by W. B. Yeats. Copyright 1933 by The Macmillan
Company, Renewed 1961 by Bertha Georgie Yeats. "Lapis Lazuli," "Poli-
tics." Reprinted with permission of The Macmillan Company from COL-
LECTED POEMS by W. B. Yeats. Copyright 1940 by Georgie Yeats.
    Permission extended to the Philippine Islands by Mrs. W. B. Yeats and
A. P. Watt & Son.

ROBERT FROST

"Mending Wall," "The Death of the Hired Man," "After Apple-Picking,"
"The Road Not Taken," "Meeting and Passing," "The Oven Bird,"
"Birches," "The Hill Wife," "Fire and Ice," "Stopping by Woods on a
Snowy Evening," "Plowmen," "Once by the Pacific," "Bereft," "Acquainted
with the Night," "Two Tramps in Mud Time," "Desert Places," "The
Strong Are Saying Nothing," "Come In," "A Semi-Revolution," "Revela-
tion." From COMPLETE POEMS OF ROBERT FROST. Copyright 1916,
1921, 1923, 1928, 1930, 1934, 1939 by Holt, Rinehart and Winston, Inc.
Copyright 1936, 1942 by Robert Frost. Copyright renewed 1944, 1951, ©
1956, 1962 by Robert Frost. Reprinted by permission of Holt, Rinehart and
Winston, Inc.

THOMAS STEARNS ELIOT

"The Love Song of J. Alfred Prufrock," "Aunt Helen," "Cousin Nancy,"
"Gerontion," "Whispers of Immortality," "Sweeney Among the Nightingales,"
"The Hollow Men," "Journey of the Magi." From COLLECTED POEMS
OF T. S. ELIOT, copyright, 1936, by Harcourt Brace & World, Inc. and
reprinted with their permission.

PREFACE

Anthologies can never be constructed according to absolutely objective criteria. The editor's taste often invades even the most elementary decisions. I have tried, however, to include no poet who could peacefully be labeled "minor." Some critics may refuse official majority to Herbert, Keats, Dickinson, or Hopkins, but these poets could never be ranked below the best in any grouping. My choice of poems has heavily involved the lyric, for obvious reasons of length. Within these limitations, I have attempted to include no poem that represents only personal caprice and to exclude as few as possible that have strong critical favor.

The anthology that includes a fairly large selection of writings from a rather small number of writers no longer needs to be justified to the teacher of English. Several such collections have appeared in recent years and have been found useful as texts in a variety of courses, whether in the general introduction to literature, the historical survey of literature, the specific introduction to poetry, or critical analysis. Naturally, any anthologist hopes his selection makes a valid and enjoyable volume for any careful reader.

Needless to say, I have tried to include only the most authoritative texts of each author. I have modernized the spelling, capitalization, and punctuation of the texts of Shakespeare, Donne, Herbert, Milton, and Blake. The spelling has been more liberally modernized than the punctuation, but in no instance has spelling been changed so as to modify syllabification or to mar rhyme. Consequently, a few inconsistencies of modernization remain. In the case of Emily Dickinson, the authoritative texts established by Thomas H. Johnson are, of course, used. As Mr. Johnson suggests, Miss Dickinson's punctuation can stand rather free regularization. Recent scholarship, however, demonstrates that many of Miss Dickinson's manuscript marks indicate the inflections with which the poem should be read, not punctuation for printed editions. In my adaptation of the frequent dash in Johnson's text (he uses the dash for a variety of manuscript markings), I have tried to keep in mind the relationship between our modern punctuation marks and the appropriate oral delivery of the poems.

Annotation in this anthology has been strictly limited. Information that the student can easily glean from the standard desk dictionaries is not included. This principle has been carefully tested with *Webster's New World Dictionary* and *Webster's Collegiate Dictionary*. Coined compounds by Hopkins and created place-names by Blake and others have also remained unglossed. On the other hand, no interpretations are attempted in the notes. The student and teacher are left free from encumbering commentary but provided with essential factual supplements to the poems. A general chronological order is attempted in the arrangement of the poems of each author; this order is not strictly maintained, however, and should not be relied on.

In the long process of compiling this anthology, I have become indebted, often indirectly, to many of my colleagues here at Indiana University and to friends at other universities. Several have been particularly kind in advising me on special problems. I am happy to thank Mr. Gates K. Agnew and Professors Charles R. Forker, Robert Gross, James Halporn, James H. Justus, Mark Musa, David E. Smith, Stuart M. Sperry, and, especially, Wallace E. Williams for timely and careful advice. Miss Joan M. Durstine gave several helpful suggestions for the Blake section. Miss Judith Fetterley, Mrs. Pauline Veach, and Mrs. Winifred Wertz assisted with numerous secretarial tasks. Mr. J. G. Case of The Macmillan Company has been of extraordinary help at many points. Errors and lapses, of course, remain my own.

ROWLAND L. COLLINS

CONTENTS

❧ WILLIAM SHAKESPEARE ❧

❦ JOHN DONNE ❧

❦ GEORGE HERBERT ❧

∽ WILLIAM WORDSWORTH ∽

∽ JOHN KEATS ∽

∽ ALFRED, LORD TENNYSON ∽

⌁ WALT WHITMAN ⌁

⌁ EMILY DICKINSON ⌁

∽ GERARD MANLEY HOPKINS ∽

∽ WILLIAM BUTLER YEATS ∽

∽ ROBERT FROST ∽

∾   **THOMAS STEARNS ELIOT**   ∾

₵ WILLIAM SHAKESPEARE was born of prosperous parents in the peaceful village of Stratford-on-Avon in Warwickshire. Although our records of his early life are scant, we know that he married Anne Hathaway late in November or early in December, 1582, and that their first child was baptized about six months later.

William Shakespeare

[1564-1616]

Shakespeare moved to London, probably in the late 1580's, and became associated with the theatrical world; by the autumn of 1594 he was in the Lord Chamberlain's Men. He had already written and produced at least nine plays, and with this new company he went on to *Romeo and Juliet, A Midsummer Night's Dream, Richard II, The Merchant of Venice,* and the two parts of *Henry IV*.

Disputes about business affairs led the company to build its own playhouse, the Globe, in 1598. Shakespeare must have prospered considerably from his writing by this time, somewhat earlier he had purchased a handsome home in Stratford and had set himself up in fine style. After the Globe was opened, Shakespeare produced *Henry V, Julius Caesar, Much Ado About Nothing, As You Like It, Twelfth Night, Hamlet,* and *Troilus and Cressida*.

When King James succeeded Queen Elizabeth in 1603, he showed great favor to Shakespeare's company, causing them to take the name King's Men. In the early years of James' reign, Shakespeare wrote his so-called somber comedies, *All's Well That Ends Well* and *Measure for Measure;* the four great tragedies, *Othello, King Lear, Macbeth,* and *Antony and Cleopatra;* and the lesser tragedy *Coriolanus.* The rise of smaller private theaters led the King's Men to acquire a second playhouse and to compete with the new styles of dramatic entertainment as well as with the old. Shakespeare contributed four plays to the genre of tragicomedy: *Pericles, Cymbeline, The Winter's Tale,* and *The Tempest*.

Shakespeare's nondramatic poetry dates from the 1590's. *Venus and Adonis,* an immediate success, was published in 1593, and was followed in 1594 by *The Rape of Lucrece.* Composition of the famous sequence of sonnets was probably begun in 1593. Portions of the sequence were apparently circulated in manuscript form among a rather intimate literary coterie, in accordance with the practice then used by such contemporary sonneteers as Spenser, Sidney, Drayton, Daniel, and Lodge. Publication of the sonnets followed in 1609.

SONGS FROM THE PLAYS

Who Is Silvia?

Who is Silvia? what is she?
    That all our swains commend her?
Holy, fair, and wise is she;
    The heavens such grace did lend her,
    That she might admired be.   5

Is she kind as she is fair?
    For beauty lives with kindness:
Love doth to her eyes repair,
    To help him of his blindness;
    And, being help'd, inhabits there.   10

Then to Silvia let us sing,
    That Silvia is excelling;
She excels each mortal thing
    Upon the dull earth dwelling;
    To her let us garlands bring.   15

The Two Gentlemen of Verona, IV, 2

Spring

When daisies pied and violets blue,
And lady-smocks all silver-white,
And cuckoo-buds of yellow hue,
Do paint the meadows with delight,
The cuckoo then, on every tree,   5
Mocks married men; for thus sings he,
                                "Cuckoo;
Cuckoo, cuckoo!" O, word of fear,
Unpleasing to a married ear!

When shepherds pipe on oaten straws,   10
And merry larks are ploughmen's clocks,
When turtles tread, and rooks, and daws,
And maidens bleach their summer smocks,

The cuckoo then, on every tree,
Mocks married men; for thus sings he,   15
       "Cuckoo;
Cuckoo, cuckoo!" O, word of fear,
Unpleasing to a married ear!

     Love's Labour's Lost, V, 2

Winter

When icicles hang by the wall,
And Dick the shepherd blows his nail,
And Tom bears logs into the hall,
And milk comes frozen home in pail,
When blood is nipp'd, and ways be foul,   5
Then nightly sings the staring owl,
       "Tu-who!
To-whit, tu-who!"—a merry note,
While greasy Joan doth keel the pot.

When all aloud the wind doth blow,   10
And coughing drowns the parson's saw,
And birds sit brooding in the snow,
And Marian's nose looks red and raw,
When roasted crabs hiss in the bowl,
Then nightly sings the staring owl,   15
       "Tu-who!
To-whit, tu-who!"—a merry note,
While greasy Joan doth keel the pot.

    Love's Labour's Lost, V, 2

Tell Me, Where Is Fancy Bred

Tell me, where is fancy bred,
Or in the heart or in the head?
How begot, how nourished?
   Reply, reply.
It is engender'd in the eyes,   5
With gazing fed; and fancy dies
In the cradle where it lies.

Let us all ring fancy's knell:
I'll begin it,—Ding, dong, bell.
Ding, dong, bell.　　　　　　　　　　　　10

The Merchant of Venice, III, 2

O Mistress Mine!

O mistress mine! where are you roaming?
O, stay and hear; your true love's coming,
　That can sing both high and low.
Trip no further, pretty sweeting;
Journeys end in lovers meeting,　　　　　　5
　Every wise man's son doth know.

What is love? 'tis not hereafter;
Present mirth hath present laughter;
　What's to come is still unsure:
In delay there lies no plenty;　　　　　　　10
Then come kiss me, sweet and twenty,
　Youth's a stuff will not endure.

Twelfth Night, II, 3

Come Away, Come Away, Death

Come away, come away, death,
　And in sad cypress let me be laid;
Fly away, fly away, breath;
　I am slain by a fair cruel maid.
My shroud of white, stuck all with yew,　　5
　O! prepare it.
My part of death, no one so true
　Did share it.

Not a flower, not a flower sweet,
　On my black coffin let there be strown;　　10
Not a friend, not a friend greet
　My poor corse, where my bones shall be thrown.
A thousand thousand sighs to save,
　Lay me, O! where

Sad true lover never find my grave,   15
    To weep there.

Twelfth Night, II, 4

Take, O Take Those Lips Away

Take, O take those lips away,
    That so sweetly were forsworn;
And those eyes, the break of day,
    Lights that do mislead the morn:
But my kisses bring again, bring again,   5
Seals of love, but seal'd in vain, seal'd in vain.

Measure for Measure, IV, 1

Hark, Hark! The Lark

Hark, hark! the lark at heaven's gate sings,
    And Phœbus 'gins arise,
His steeds to water at those springs
    On chalic'd flowers that lies;
And winking Mary-buds begin   5
    To ope their golden eyes.
With every thing that pretty is,
    My lady sweet, arise:
      Arise, arise!

Cymbeline, II, 3

Fear No More the Heat o' the Sun

Fear no more the heat o' the sun,
    Nor the furious winter's rages;
Thou thy worldly task hast done,
    Home art gone, and ta'en thy wages;
Golden lads and girls all must,   5
As chimney-sweepers, come to dust.

Fear no more the frown o' the great,
    Thou art past the tyrant's stroke.

Care no more to clothe and eat;
    To thee the reed is as the oak.
The sceptre, learning, physic, must
All follow this, and come to dust.

Fear no more the lightning-flash,
    Nor th' all-dreaded thunder-stone;
Fear not slander, censure rash;
    Thou hast finish'd joy and moan.
All lovers young, all lovers must
Consign to thee, and come to dust.

No exorciser harm thee!
    Nor no witchcraft charm thee!
Ghost unlaid forbear thee!
    Nothing ill come near thee!
Quiet consummation have;
And renowned be thy grave!

Cymbeline, IV, 2

Full Fathom Five

Full fathom five thy father lies;
    Of his bones are coral made:
Those are pearls that were his eyes:
    Nothing of him that doth fade,
But doth suffer a sea-change
Into something rich and strange.
Sea-nymphs hourly ring his knell:
    Ding-dong.
Hark! now I hear them,—
    Ding-dong, bell.

The Tempest, I, 2

Where the Bee Sucks, There Suck I

Where the bee sucks, there suck I:
In a cowslip's bell I lie;
There I couch when owls do cry.
On the bat's back I do fly

After summer merrily.   5
Merrily, merrily shall I live now
Under the blossom that hangs on the bough.

The Tempest, V, 1

Orpheus with His Lute

Orpheus with his lute made trees,
And the mountain tops that freeze
    Bow themselves when he did sing:
To his music plants and flowers
Ever sprung; as sun and showers   5
    There had made a lasting spring.

Every thing that heard him play,
Even the billows of the sea,
    Hung their heads, and then lay by.
In sweet music is such art,   10
Killing care and grief of heart
    Fall asleep, or hearing, die.

King Henry VIII, III, 1

SONNETS

2. *When Forty Winters Shall Besiege Thy Brow*

When forty winters shall besiege thy brow
And dig deep trenches in thy beauty's field,
Thy youth's proud livery, so gazed on now,
Will be a tottered weed of small worth held:
Then being asked where all thy beauty lies,   5
Where all the treasure of thy lusty days,
To say within thine own deep-sunken eyes
Were an all-eating shame and thriftless praise.
How much more praise deserved thy beauty's use
If thou couldst answer, "This fair child of mine   10
Shall sum my count and make my old excuse,"
Proving his beauty by succession thine!

This were to be new made when thou art old
And see thy blood warm when thou feel'st it cold.

12. When I Do Count the Clock That Tells the Time

When I do count the clock that tells the time
And see the brave day sunk in hideous night,
When I behold the violet past prime
And sable curls all silvered o'er with white,
When lofty trees I see barren of leaves,   5
Which erst from heat did canopy the herd,
And summer's green all girded up in sheaves
Borne on the bier with white and bristly beard;
Then of thy beauty do I question make
That thou among the wastes of time must go,   10
Since sweets and beauties do themselves forsake
And die as fast as they see others grow;
    And nothing 'gainst Time's scythe can make defense
    Save breed, to brave him when he takes thee hence.

2. *brave:* splendid, excellent.

15. When I Consider Everything That Grows

When I consider everything that grows
Holds in perfection but a little moment,
That this huge stage presenteth nought but shows
Whereon the stars in secret influence comment;
When I perceive that men as plants increase,   5
Cheered and checked even by the selfsame sky,
Vaunt in their youthful sap, at height decrease,
And wear their brave state out of memory:
Then the conceit of this inconstant stay
Sets you most rich in youth before my sight,   10
Where wasteful Time debateth with Decay
To change your day of youth to sullied night;
    And, all in war with Time for love of you,
    As he takes from you, I ingraft you new.

9. *conceit:* concept, idea; *stay:* duration.

18. Shall I Compare Thee to a Summer's Day?

Shall I compare thee to a summer's day?
Thou art more lovely and more temperate.
Rough winds do shake the darling buds of May,
And summer's lease hath all too short a date.
Sometime too hot the eye of heaven shines,   5
And often is his gold complexion dimmed;
And every fair from fair sometime declines,
By chance, or nature's changing course, untrimmed:
But thy eternal summer shall not fade
Nor lose possession of that fair thou ow'st,   10
Nor shall Death brag thou wand'rest in his shade
When in eternal lines to time thou grow'st.
    So long as men can breathe or eyes can see,
    So long lives this, and this gives life to thee.

8. *untrimmed:* stripped of trimming.

19. Devouring Time, Blunt Thou the Lion's Paws

Devouring Time, blunt thou the lion's paws,
And make the earth devour her own sweet brood;
Pluck the keen teeth from the fierce tiger's jaws
And burn the long-lived phœnix in her blood;
Make glad and sorry seasons as thou fleet'st,   5
And do whate'er thou wilt, swift-footed Time,
To the wide world and all her fading sweets,
But I forbid thee one most heinous crime:
O, carve not with thy hours my love's fair brow,
Nor draw no lines there with thine antique pen;   10
Him in thy course untainted do allow
For beauty's pattern to succeeding men.
    Yet do thy worst, old Time: despite thy wrong,
    My love shall in my verse ever live young.

10. *antique:* can mean either "old" or "antic," i.e., capricious.

29. When, in Disgrace with Fortune and Men's Eyes

When, in disgrace with Fortune and men's eyes,
I all alone beweep my outcast state,

And trouble deaf heaven with my bootless cries,
And look upon myself and curse my fate,
Wishing me like to one more rich in hope,   5
Featured like him, like him with friends possessed,
Desiring this man's art, and that man's scope,
With what I most enjoy contented least;
Yet in these thoughts myself almost despising,
Haply I think on thee, and then my state,   10
Like to the lark at break of day arising
From sullen earth, sings hymns at heaven's gate;
  For thy sweet love rememb'red such wealth brings
  That then I scorn to change my state with kings.

33. Full Many a Glorious Morning Have I Seen

Full many a glorious morning have I seen
Flatter the mountain tops with sovereign eye,
Kissing with golden face the meadows green,
Gilding pale streams with heavenly alchemy;
Anon permit the basest clouds to ride   5
With ugly rack on his celestial face,
And from the forlorn world his visage hide,
Stealing unseen to west with this disgrace:
Even so my sun one early morn did shine
With all-triumphant splendor on my brow;   10
But, out alack! he was but one hour mine,
The region cloud hath masked him from me now.
  Yet him for this my love no whit disdaineth;
  Suns of the world may stain when heaven's sun staineth.

12. *region cloud:* cloud of the upper atmosphere.

55. Not Marble nor the Gilded Monuments

Not marble nor the gilded monuments
Of princes shall outlive this pow'rful rime,
But you shall shine more bright in these contents
Than unswept stone, besmeared with sluttish time.
When wasteful war shall statues overturn,   5
And broils root out the work of masonry,
Nor Mars his sword nor war's quick fire shall burn

The living record of your memory.
'Gainst death and all oblivious enmity
Shall you pace forth; your praise shall still find room   10
Even in the eyes of all posterity
That wear this world out to the ending doom.
  So, till the judgment that yourself arise,
  You live in this, and dwell in lovers' eyes.

64. *When I Have Seen by Time's Fell Hand Defaced*

When I have seen by Time's fell hand defaced
The rich proud cost of outworn buried age,
When sometime lofty towers I see down-razed
And brass eternal slave to mortal rage;
When I have seen the hungry ocean gain   5
Advantage on the kingdom of the shore,
And the firm soil win of the wat'ry main,
Increasing store with loss and loss with store;
When I have seen such interchange of state,
Or state itself confounded, to decay,   10
Ruin hath taught me thus to ruminate,
That Time will come and take my love away.
  This thought is as a death, which cannot choose
  But weep to have that which it fears to lose.

10. *confounded:* reduced.

73. *That Time of Year Thou Mayst in Me Behold*

That time of year thou mayst in me behold
When yellow leaves, or none, or few, do hang
Upon those boughs which shake against the cold,
Bare ruined choirs where late the sweet birds sang.
In me thou seest the twilight of such day   5
As after sunset fadeth in the west,
Which by and by black night doth take away,
Death's second self that seals up all in rest.
In me thou seest the glowing of such fire
That on the ashes of his youth doth lie,   10
As the deathbed whereon it must expire,
Consumed with that which it was nourished by.

This thou perceiv'st, which makes thy love more strong,
To love that well which thou must leave ere long.

77. Thy Glass Will Show Thee How Thy Beauties Wear

Thy glass will show thee how thy beauties wear,
Thy dial how thy precious minutes waste;
The vacant leaves thy mind's imprint will bear,
And of this book this learning mayst thou taste.
The wrinkles which thy glass will truly show,
Of mouthèd graves will give thee memory.
Thou by thy dial's shady stealth mayst know
Time's thievish progress to eternity.
Look what thy memory cannot contain,
Commit to these waste blanks, and thou shalt find   1
Those children nursed, delivered from thy brain,
To take a new acquaintance of thy mind.
   These offices, so oft as thou wilt look,
   Shall profit thee and much enrich thy book.

1. *glass:* mirror.

87. Farewell: Thou Art Too Dear for My Possessing

Farewell! thou art too dear for my possessing,
And like enough thou know'st thy estimate.
The charter of thy worth gives thee releasing;
My bonds in thee are all determinate.
For how do I hold thee but by thy granting,
And for that riches where is my deserving?
The cause of this fair gift in me is wanting,
And so my patent back again is swerving.
Thyself thou gav'st, thy own worth then not knowing,
Or me, to whom thou gav'st it, else mistaking;   1
So thy great gift, upon misprision growing,
Comes home again, on better judgment making.
   Thus have I had thee as a dream doth flatter—
   In sleep a king, but waking no such matter.

2. *estimate:* worth, value.
4. *determinate:* terminated.
8. *patent:* legal claim.

116. *Let Me Not to the Marriage of True Minds*

Let me not to the marriage of true minds
Admit impediments; love is not love
Which alters when it alteration finds
Or bends with the remover to remove.
O, no! it is an ever-fixèd mark   5
That looks on tempests and is never shaken;
It is the star to every wand'ring bark,
Whose worth's unknown, although his height be taken.
Love's not Time's fool, though rosy lips and cheeks
Within his bending sickle's compass come.   10
Love alters not with his brief hours and weeks,
But bears it out even to the edge of doom.
   If this be error, and upon me proved,
   I never writ, nor no man ever loved.

124. *If My Dear Love Were but the Child of State*

If my dear love were but the child of state,
It might for Fortune's bastard be unfathered,
As subject to Time's love or to Time's hate,
Weeds among weeds, or flowers with flowers gathered.
No, it was builded far from accident;   5
It suffers not in smiling pomp, nor falls
Under the blow of thrallèd discontent,
Whereto th' inviting time our fashion calls:
It fears not Policy, that heretic
Which works on leases of short-numb'red hours,   10
But all alone stands hugely politic,
That it nor grows with heat nor drowns with show'rs.
   To this I witness call the fools of Time,
   Which die for goodness, who have lived for crime.

1. *child of state*: i.e., had its origins in the material world.
2. *for*: as; *be unfathered*: be denied a father.

129. *Th' Expense of Spirit in a Waste of Shame*

Th' expense of spirit in a waste of shame
Is lust in action; and, till action, lust

Is perjured, murd'rous, bloody, full of blame,
Savage, extreme, rude, cruel, not to trust;
Enjoyed no sooner but despisèd straight;
Past reason hunted, and no sooner had,
Past reason hated as a swallowed bait
On purpose laid to make the taker mad:
Mad in pursuit, and in possession so;
Had, having, and in quest to have, extreme;
A bliss in proof, and proved, a very woe;
Before, a joy proposed; behind, a dream.
    All this the world well knows; yet none knows well
    To shun the heaven that leads men to this hell.

130. My Mistress' Eyes Are Nothing Like the Sun

My mistress' eyes are nothing like the sun;
Coral is far more red than her lips' red;
If snow be white, why then her breasts are dun;
If hairs be wires, black wires grow on her head.
I have seen roses damasked, red and white,
But no such roses see I in her cheeks;
And in some perfumes is there more delight
Than in the breath that from my mistress reeks.
I love to hear her speak; yet well I know
That music hath a far more pleasing sound:
I grant I never saw a goddess go;
My mistress, when she walks, treads on the ground.
    And yet, by heaven, I think my love as rare
    As any she belied with false compare.

138. When My Love Swears That She Is Made of Truth

When my love swears that she is made of truth
I do believe her, though I know she lies,
That she might think me some untutored youth,
Unlearnèd in the world's false subtilties.
Thus vainly thinking that she thinks me young,
Although she knows my days are past the best,
Simply I credit her false-speaking tongue:

1. *truth*: fidelity.

On both sides thus is simple truth suppressed.
But wherefore says she not she is unjust?
And wherefore say not I that I am old?   10
O, love's best habit is in seeming trust,
And age in love loves not to have years told.
   Therefore I lie with her and she with me,
   And in our faults by lies we flattered be.

146. Poor Soul, the Center of My Sinful Earth

Poor soul, the center of my sinful earth,
Foiled by these rebel pow'rs that thee array,
Why dost thou pine within and suffer dearth,
Painting thy outward walls so costly gay?
Why so large cost, having so short a lease,   5
Dost thou upon thy fading mansion spend?
Shall worms, inheritors of this excess,
Eat up thy charge? Is this thy body's end?
Then, soul, live thou upon thy servant's loss,
And let that pine to aggravate thy store;   10
Buy terms divine in selling hours of dross;
Within be fed, without be rich no more:
   So shalt thou feed on Death, that feeds on men,
   And Death once dead, there's no more dying then.

2. *Foiled by:* the first edition is obviously corrupt; a frequent conjecture is
"Fooled by."
10. *aggravate:* enlarge.

147. My Love Is As a Fever, Longing Still

My love is as a fever, longing still
For that which longer nurseth the disease,
Feeding on that which doth preserve the ill,
Th' uncertain sickly appetite to please.
My reason, the physician to my love,   5
Angry that his prescriptions are not kept,
Hath left me, and I desperate now approve
Desire is death, which physic did except.

2. *longer nurseth:* extends.

Past cure I am, now reason is past care,
And frantic-mad with evermore unrest;
My thoughts and my discourse as madmen's are,
At randon from the truth vainly expressed:
    For I have sworn thee fair, and thought thee bright,
    Who art as black as hell, as dark as night.

12. *At randon:* at random, *viz.*, separate.

❨ JOHN DONNE was the son of a well-to-do Catholic merchant who, at his early death, left his widow and six children in reasonably prosperous circumstances. Young John was admitted to Hart Hall, Oxford, when he was only twelve. Ultimately he left Oxford without a degree, probably because of conflict between his Catholic tenets and the rules of the establishment. After leaving college, he probably traveled on the continent before being admitted to Lincoln's Inn in 1592. In his early London years Donne became closely concerned with religious doctrines and

John Donne

[1572-1631]

took a strong interest in public affairs. In 1596 he became secretary to the Lord Keeper of the Great Seal, but in his spare time he turned to poetry. Donne's epistles, satires, and elegies circulated widely among his courtly associates. When Donne secretly married Anne, the daughter of Sir George More, her father's outrage quickly spoiled Donne's promising career.

Although he tried in vain to advance his cause at the court of Queen Elizabeth, it was only after James I was on the throne that Donne once again began to attract attention. His religious beliefs had gradually become Anglican and in 1607 the King offered him the deanery of Gloucester. Still hoping for a proper civil post, the poet reluctantly declined the deanship. Although his court connections led to his writing several official poems to commemorate royal weddings and deaths, his "divine poems" still found greater favor.

When all other avenues for advancement appeared closed, Donne at last consented to take holy orders. At once James made him court chaplain. His general preferment was rapid. Ecclesiastical livings were offered; he became divinity reader at Lincoln's Inn and ultimately Dean of St. Paul's. Donne soon was the most famous preacher in London. Modern readers recognize his eminence in both sermon literature and poetry.

LOVE'S USURY

For every hour that thou wilt spare me now,
    I will allow,
Usurious God of Love, twenty to thee,
When with my brown, my gray hairs equal be;
Till then, Love, let my body reign, and let   5
Me travel, sojourn, snatch, plot, have, forget,
Resume my last year's relict: think that yet
    We'had never met.

Let me think any rival's letter mine,
    And at next nine   10
Keep midnight's promise; mistake by the way
The maid, and tell the lady of that delay;
Only let me love none, no, but the sport;
From country grass, to comfitures of Court,
Or city's quelque choses, let report   15
    My mind transport.

This bargain's good; if when I'am old, I be
    Inflam'd by thee,
If thine own honor, or my shame, or pain,
Thou covet most, at that age thou shalt gain.   20
Do thy will then, then subject and degree,
And fruit of love, Love I submit to thee;
Spare me till then, I'll bear it, though she be
    One that loves me.

   8. *We'had:* most probably Donne pronounced this contraction somewhere
between the modern monosyllabic "we'd" and the clearly disyllabic "we had."
15. *quelque choses:* dainties, fancy trifles.

THE CANONIZATION

For Godsake hold your tongue, and let me love,
    Or chide my palsy, or my gout,
My five gray hairs, or ruin'd fortune flout,
    With wealth your state, your mind with arts improve,
      Take you a course, get you a place,   5
      Observe his honor, or his grace,

Or the King's reall, or his stamped face
   Contemplate, what you will, approve,
   So you will let me love.

Alas, alas, who's injur'd by my love?   10
   What merchants' ships have my sighs drown'd?
Who says my tears have overflow'd his ground?
   When did my colds a forward spring remove?
      When did the heats which my veins fill
      Add one more to the plaguy bill?   15
Soldiers find wars, and lawyers find out still
   Litigious men, which quarrels move,
   Though she and I do love.

Call us what you will, we are made such by love;
   Call her one, me another fly,   20
We'are tapers too, and at our own cost die,
   And we in us find the'eagle and the dove.
      The phœnix riddle hath more wit
      By us, we two being one, are it.
So, to one neutral thing both sexes fit,   25
   We die and rise the same, and prove
   Mysterious by this love.

We can die by it, if not live by love,
   And if unfit for tombs and hearse
Our legend be, it will be fit for verse;   30
   And if no piece of chronicle we prove,
      We'll build in sonnets pretty rooms;
      As well a well wrought urn becomes
The greatest ashes, as half-acre tombs,
   And by these hymns, all shall approve   35
   Us *Canoniz'd* for Love:

And thus invoke us; You whom reverend love
   Made one another's hermitage;
You, to whom love was peace, that now is rage;
   Who did the whole world's soul contract, and drove   40
      Into the glasses of your eyes
      (So made such mirrors, and such spies,
That they did all to you epitomize,)
   Countries, towns, Courts: Beg from above
   A pattern of your love!   45

SONG

Sweetest Love, I Do Not Go

Sweetest Love, I do not go,
    For weariness of thee,
Nor in hope the world can show
    A fitter Love for me;
        But since that I   5
Must die at last, 'tis best,
To use my self in jest
        Thus by feign'd deaths to die;

Yesternight the Sun went hence,
    And yet is here today,   10
He hath no desire nor sense,
    Nor half so short a way:
        Then fear not me,
But believe that I shall make
Speedier journeys, since I take   15
        More wings and spurs than he.

O how feeble is man's power,
    That if good fortune fall,
Cannot add another hour,
    Nor a lost hour recall!   20
        But come bad chance,
And we join to'it our strength,
And we teach it art and length,
        Itself o'er us to'advance.

When thou sigh'st, thou sigh'st not wind,   25
    But sigh'st my soul away,
When thou weep'st, unkindly kind,
    My life's blood doth decay.
        It cannot be
That thou lov'st me, as thou say'st,   30
If in thine my life thou waste,
        That art the best of me.

Let not thy divining heart
    Forethink me any ill,
Destiny may take thy part, 35
    And may thy fears fulfill;
      But think that we
Are but turn'd aside to sleep;
They who one another keep
    Alive, ne'r parted be. 40

LOVE'S GROWTH

I scarce believe my love to be so pure
    As I had thought it was,
    Because it doth endure
Vicissitude, and season, as the grass;
Methinks I lied all winter, when I swore, 5
My love was infinite, if spring make'it more.
But if this medicine, love, which cures all sorrow
With more, not only be no quintessence,
But mixed of all stuffs, paining soul, or sense,
And of the sun his working vigor borrow, 10
Love's not so pure, and abstract, as they use
To say, which have no mistress but their Muse,
But as all else, being elemented too,
Love sometimes would contemplate, sometimes do.

And yet no greater, but more eminent, 15
    Love by the spring is grown;
    As, in the firmament,
Stars by the sun are not enlarg'd, but shown.
Gentle love deeds, as blossoms on a bough,
From love's awakened root do bud out now. 20
If, as in water stir'd more circles be
Produc'd by one, love such additions take,
Those like so many spheres, but one heaven make,
For, they are all concentric unto thee.
And though each spring do add to love new heat, 25
As princes do in times of action get
New taxes, and remit them not in peace,
No winter shall abate the spring's increase.

THE FLEA

Mark but this flea, and mark in this,
How little that which thou deny'st me is;
It suck'd me first, and now sucks thee,
And in this flea, our two bloods mingled be;
Thou know'st that this cannot be said   5
A sin, nor shame, nor loss of maidenhead,
    Yet this enjoys before it woo,
    And pamper'd swells with one blood made of two,
    And this, alas, is more than we would do.

Oh stay, three lives in one flea spare,   10
Where we almost, yea more than married are.
This flea is you and I, and this
Our marriage bed, and marriage temple is;
Though parents grudge, and you, w'are met,
And cloister'd in these living walls of jet.   15
    Though use make you apt to kill me,
    Let not to that, self murder added be,
    And sacrilege, three sins in killing three.

Cruel and sudden, hast thou since
Purpled thy nail in blood of innocence?   20
Wherein could this flea guilty be,
Except in that drop which it suck'd from thee?
Yet thou triumph'st, and sayst that thou
Find'st not thyself, nor me the weaker now;
    'Tis true, then learn how false fears be;   25
    Just so much honor, when thou yield'st to me,
    Will waste, as this flea's death took life from thee.

A NOCTURNAL UPON ST. LUCY'S DAY,

Being the Shortest Day *

Tis the year's midnight, and it is the day's,
Lucy's, who scarce seven hours herself unmasks,

---

* St. Lucy's Day is observed on 13 December; it marked the winter solstice in
the unreformed calendar.

The Sun is spent, and now his flasks
Send forth light squibs, no constant rays;
   The world's whole sap is sunk: 5
The general balm th'hydroptic earth hath drunk,
Whither, as to the bed's-feet, life is shrunk,
Dead and interr'd; yet all these seem to laugh,
Compar'd with me, who am their epitaph.

Study me then, you who shall lovers be   10
At the next world, that is, at the next spring:
   For I am every dead thing,
   In whom love wrought new alchemy.
     For his art did express
A quintessence even from nothingness,   15
From dull privations, and lean emptiness
He ruin'd me, and I am re-begot
Of absence, darkness, death; things which are not.

All others, from all things, draw all that's good,
Life, soul, form, spirit, whence they being have;   20
   I, by Love's limbeck, am the grave
   Of all, that's nothing. Oft a flood
     Have we two wept, and so
Drown'd the whole world, us two; oft did we grow
To be two chaoses, when we did show   25
Care to ought else; and often absences
Withdrew our souls, and made us carcasses.

But I am by her death, (which word wrongs her)
Of the first nothing, the elixir grown;
   Were I a man, that I were one,   30
   I needs must know; I should prefer,
     If I were any beast,
Some ends, some means; Yea plants, yea stones detest,
And love; All, all some properties invest;
If I an ordinary nothing were,   35
As shadow, a light and body must be here.

But I am none; nor will my Sun renew.
You lovers, for whose sake, the lesser Sun
   At this time to the Goat is run

21. *limbeck*: apparatus for distillation.
39. *Goat*: Capricornus, the tenth sign of the Zodiac.

To fetch new lust, and give it you,   40
    Enjoy your summer all;
Since she enjoys her long night's festival,
Let me prepare towards her, and let me call
This hour her vigil, and her Eve, since this
Both the year's, and the day's deep midnight is.   45

A VALEDICTION: FORBIDDING
MOURNING

As virtuous men pass mildly away,
    And whisper to their souls, to go,
Whilst some of their sad friends do say,
    The breath goes now, and some say, no:

So let us melt, and make no noise,   5
    No tear-floods, nor sigh-tempests move,
T'were profanation of our joys
    To tell the laity our love.

Moving of th'earth brings harms and fears,
    Men reckon what it did and meant,   10
But trepidation of the spheres,
    Though greater far, is innocent.

Dull sublunary lovers' love
    (Whose soul is sense) cannot admit
Absence, because it doth remove   15
    Those things which elemented it.

But we by a love, so much refin'd,
    That ourselves know not what it is,
Inter-assured of the mind,
    Careless eyes, lips, and hands to miss.   20

Our two souls therefore, which are one,
    Though I must go, endure not yet
A breach, but an expansion,
    Like gold to airy thinness beat.

11. *trepidation of the spheres*: in the Ptolemaic astronomy, the sequence of
equinoxes was caused by vibrations in the ninth sphere.

If they be two, they are two so   25
    As stiff twin compasses are two,
Thy soul the fix'd foot, makes no show
    To move, but doth, if the'other do.

And though it in the center sit,
    Yet when the other far doth roam,   30
It leans, and hearkens after it,
    And grows erect, as that comes home.

Such wilt thou be to me, who must
    Like th'other foot, obliquely run;
Thy firmness draws my circle just,   35
    And makes me end, where I begun.

THE ECSTASY

Where, like a pillow on a bed,
    A pregnant bank swell'd up, to rest
The violet's reclining head,
    Sat we two, one another's best.
Our hands were firmly cemented   5
    With a fast balm, which thence did spring,
Our eye-beams twisted, and did thread
    Our eyes, upon one double string;
So to'intergraft our hands, as yet
    Was all the means to make us one,   10
And pictures in our eyes to get
    Was all our propagation.
As 'twixt two equal armies, Fate
    Suspends uncertain victory,
Our souls, (which to advance their state,   15
    Were gone out,) hung 'twixt her, and me.
And whil'st our souls negotiate there,
    We like sepulchral statues lay;
All day, the same our postures were,
    And we said nothing, all the day.   20
If any, so by love refin'd,
    That he soul's language understood,
And by good love were grown all mind,
    Within convenient distance stood,

He (though he knew not which soul spake,   25
    Because both meant, both spake the same)
Might thence a new concoction take,
    And part far purer than he came.
This ecstasy doth unperplex
    (We said) and tell us what we love,   30
We see by this, it was not sex,
    We see, we saw not what did move:
But as all several souls contain
    Mixture of things, they know not what,
Love, these mix'd souls, doth mix again,   35
    And makes both one, each this and that.
A single violet transplant,
    The strength, the color, and the size,
(All which before was poor, and scant,)
    Redoubles still, and multiplies.   40
When love, with one another so
    Interinanimates two souls,
That abler soul, which thence doth flow,
    Defects of loneliness controls.
We then, who are this new soul, know,
    Of what we are compos'd, and made,
For, the'atomies of which we grow,
    Are souls, whom no change can invade.
But O alas, so long, so far
    Our bodies why do we forbear?   50
They are ours, though they are not we. We are
    The intelligences, they the spheres.
We owe them thanks, because they thus,
    Did us, to us, at first convey,
Yielded their forces, sense, to us,   55
    Nor are dross to us, but allay.
On man heaven's influence works not so,
    But that it first imprints the air,
So soul into the soul may flow,
    Though it to body first repair.   60
As our blood labors to beget
    Spirits, as like souls as it can,
Because such fingers need to knit
    That subtle knot, which makes us man:

So must pure lovers' souls descend   65
    T'affections, and to faculties,
Which sense may reach and apprehend,
    Else a great Prince in prison lies.
To'our bodies turn we then, that so
    Weak men on love reveal'd may look;   70
Love's mysteries in souls do grow,
    But yet the body is his book.
And if some lover, such as we,
    Have heard this dialogue of one,
Let him still mark us, he shall see   75
    Small change, when we'are to bodies gone.

56. *allay*: alloy.

LOVE'S DEITY

I long to talk with some old lover's ghost,
    Who died before the god of Love was born:
I cannot think that he, who then lov'd most,
    Sunk so low, as to love one which did scorn.
But since this god produc'd a destiny,   5
And that vice-nature, custom, lets it be,
    I must love her, that loves not me.

Sure, they which made him god, meant not so much,
    Nor he, in his young godhead practic'd it.
But when an even flame two hearts did touch,   10
    His office was indulgently to fit
Actives to passives. Correspondency
Only his subject was; It cannot be
    Love, till I love her, that loves me.

But every modern god will now extend   15
    His vast prerogative, as far as Jove.
To rage, to lust, to write to, to commend,
    All is the purlieu of the god of Love.
Oh were we wak'ned by this Tyranny
To ungod this child again, it could not be   20
    I should love her, who loves not me.

Rebel and atheist too, why murmur I,
   As though I felt the worst that love could do?
Love might make me leave loving, or might try
   A deeper plague, to make her love me too,   25
Which, since she loves before, I'am loath to see;
Falsehood is worse than hate; and that must be,
If she whom I love, should love me.

THE BLOSSOM

   Little think'st thou, poor flower,
     Whom I have watch'd six or seven days,
And seen thy birth, and seen what every hour
Gave to thy growth, thee to this height to raise,
And now dost laugh and triumph on this bough,   5
     Little think'st thou
That it will freeze anon, and that I shall
Tomorrow find thee fall'n, or not at all.

   Little think'st thou poor heart
     That labour'st yet to nestle thee,   10
And think'st by hovering here to get a part
In a forbidden or forbidding tree,
And hop'st her stiffness by long siege to bow:
     Little think'st thou,
That thou tomorrow, ere that Sun doth wake,   15
Must with this Sun, and me a journey take.

   But thou which lov'st to be
     Subtle to plague thyself, wilt say,
Alas, if you must go, what's that to me?
Here lies my business, and here I will stay: 20
You go to friends, whose love and means present
     Various content
To your eyes, ears, and tongue, and every part.
If then your body go, what need you a heart?

   Well then, stay here; but know,
     When thou hast stay'd and done thy most,   25
A naked thinking heart, that makes no show,
Is to a woman, but a kind of ghost;

How shall she know my heart; or having none,
　　　Know thee for one? 　　　　　　　　30
Practice may make her know some other part,
But take my word, she doth not know a heart.

　　Meet me at London, then,
　　　Twenty days hence, and thou shalt see
Me fresher, and more fat, by being with men, 　35
Than if I had stay'd still with her and thee.
For God's sake, if you can, be you so too:
　　　　I would give you
　　There, to another friend, whom we shall find
As glad to have my body, as my mind. 　　40

A LECTURE UPON THE SHADOW

Stand still, and I will read to thee
A Lecture, love, in Love's philosophy.
　　　These three hours that we have spent,
　　　Walking here, two shadows went
Along with us, which we ourselves produc'd; 　5
But, now the sun is just above our head,
　　　We do those shadows tread;
　　　And to brave clearness all things are reduc'd.
　　So whilst our infant loves did grow,
　　Disguises did, and shadows, flow, 　　10
　　From us, and our cares; but, now 'tis not so.

That love hath not attain'd the high'st degree,
Which is still diligent lest others see.

Except our loves at this noon stay,
We shall new shadows make the other way. 　15
　　　As the first were made to blind
　　　Others, these which come behind
Will work upon ourselves, and blind our eyes.
If our loves faint, and westwardly decline,
　　　To me thou, falsely, thine, 　　20
　　　And I to thee mine actions shall disguise.
　　The morning shadows wear away,

But these grow longer all the day,
But oh, love's day is short, if love decay.

Love is a growing, or full constant light;   25
And his first minute, after noon, is night.

ELEGY ON HIS MISTRESS

By our first strange and fatal interview,
By all desires which thereof did ensue,
By our long starving hopes, by that remorse
Which my words' masculine persuasive force
Begot in thee, and by the memory   5
Of hurts, which spies and rivals threat'ned me,
I calmly beg: But by thy father's wrath,
By all pains, which want and divorcement hath,
I conjure thee, and all the oaths which I
And thou have sworn to seal joint constancy,   10
Here I unswear, and overswear them thus,
Thou shalt not love by ways so dangerous.
Temper, O fair Love, love's impetuous rage,
Be my true mistress still, not my feign'd page;
I'll go, and, by thy kind leave, leave behind   15
Thee, only worthy to nurse in my mind,
Thirst to come back; O if thou die before,
My soul from other lands to thee shall soar.
Thy (else Almighty) beauty cannot move
Rage from the Seas, nor thy love teach them love,   20
Nor tame wild Boreas' harshness; Thou hast read
How roughly he in pieces shivered
Fair Orithea, whom he swore he lov'd.
Fall ill or good, 'tis madness to have prov'd
Dangers unurg'd; feed on this flattery,   25
That absent lovers one in th'other be.
Dissemble nothing, not a boy, nor change
Thy body's habit, nor mind's; be not strange
To thyself only; all will spy in thy face
A blushing womanly discovering grace;   30
Richly cloth'd apes, are call'd apes, and as soon

Eclips'd as bright we call the moon the moon.
Men of France, changeable chameleons,
Spittles of diseases, shops of fashions,
Love's fuellers, and the rightest company   35
Of players, which upon the world's stage be,
Will quickly know thee, and no less, alas!
Th'indifferent Italian, as we pass
His warm land, well content to think thee page,
Will hunt thee with such lust, and hideous rage,   40
As Lot's fair guests were vex'd. But none of these
Nor spongy hydroptic Dutch shall thee displease,
If thou stay here. O stay here, for, for thee
England is only a worthy gallery,
To walk in expectation, till from thence   45
Our greatest King call thee to his presence.
When I am gone, dream me some happiness,
Nor let thy looks our long hid love confess,
Nor praise, nor dispraise me, nor bless nor curse
Openly love's force, nor in bed fright thy nurse   50
With midnight's startings, crying out, oh, oh
Nurse, O my love is slain, I saw him go
O'er the white Alps alone; I saw him I,
Assail'd, fight, taken, stabb'd, bleed, fall, and die.
Augur me better chance, except dread *Jove*   55
Think it enough for me to'have had thy love.

ELEGY TO HIS MISTRESS
GOING TO BED

Come, Madam, come, all rest my powers defy,
Until I labor, I in labor lie.
The foe oft-times having the foe in sight,
Is tir'd with standing though he never fight.
Off with that girdle, like heaven's zone glistering,   5
But a far fairer world encompassing.
Unpin that spangled breastplate which you wear,
That th'eyes of busy fools may be stopp'd there.

Unlace yourself, for that harmonious chime,
Tells me from you, that now it is bed time.   10
Off with that happy busk, which I envy,
That still can be, and still can stand so nigh.
Your gown going off, such beauteous state reveals,
As when from flow'ry meads th'hill's shadow steals.
Off with that wiry coronet and show   15
The hairy diadem which on you doth grow:
Now off with those shoes, and then safely tread
In this love's hallow'd temple, this soft bed.
In such white robes, heaven's Angels us'd to be
Receiv'd by men; Thou, Angel, bringst with thee   20
A heaven like Mahomet's Paradise; and though
Ill spirits walk in white, we eas'ly know,
By this these Angels from an evil sprite,
Those set our hairs, but these our flesh upright.

    License my roving hands, and let them go,   25
Before, behind, between, above, below.
O my America! my new-found-land,
My kingdom, safeliest when with one man man'd,
My mine of precious stones, my empery,
How blest am I in this discovering thee!   30
To enter in these bonds, is to be free;
Then where my hand is set, my seal shall be.

    Full nakedness! All joys are due to thee,
As souls unbodied, bodies uncloth'd must be,
To taste whole joys. Gems which you women use   35
Are like Atlanta's balls, cast in men's views,
That when a fool's eye lighteth on a gem,
His earthly soul may covet theirs, not them.
Like pictures, or like books' gay coverings made
For lay-men, are all women thus array'd;   40
Themselves are mystic books, which only we
(Whom their imputed grace will dignify)
Must see reveal'd. Then since that I may know,
As liberally, as to a midwife, show
Thyself: cast all, yea, this white linen hence,   45
Here is no penance, much less innocence.

    To teach thee, I am naked first; why then
What needst thou have more covering than a man?

ELEGY ON THE LADY MARCKHAM *

Man is the World, and Death th'Ocean,
    To which God gives the lower parts of man.
This Sea environs all, and though as yet
    God hath set marks, and bounds, twixt us and it,
Yet doth it roar, and gnaw, and still pretend,   5
    And breaks our banks, when e'er it takes a friend.
Then our land waters (tears of passion) vent;
    Our waters, then, above our firmament,
(Tears which our Soul doth for her sins let fall)
    Take all a brackish taste, and funeral,   10
And even these tears, which should wash sin, are sin.
    We, after God's *Noe*, drown our world again.
Nothing but man of all envenom'd things
    Doth work upon itself, with inborn stings.
Tears are false spectacles, we cannot see   15
    Through passion's mist, what we are, or what she.
In her this sea of death hath made no breach,
    But as the tide doth wash the slimy beach,
And leaves embroider'd works upon the sand,
    So is her flesh refin'd by death's cold hand.   20
As men of China,'after an age's stay,
    Do take up porcelain, where they buried clay;
So at this grave, her limbeck, which refines
    The diamonds, rubies, sapphires, pearls, and mines,
Of which this flesh was, her soul shall inspire   25
    Flesh of such stuff, as God, when his last fire
Annuls this world, to recompense it, shall,
    Make and name then, th'elixir of this all.
They say, the sea, when it gains, loseth too;
    If carnal Death (the younger brother) do   30
Usurp the body, our soul, which subject is
    To th'elder death, by sin, is freed by this;
They perish both, when they attempt the just;
    For, graves our trophies are, and both deaths' dust.

* Lady Marckham, née Bridget Harrington (1579–1609), was the wife of
Sir Anthony Marckham of Sedgebrook, Nottinghamshire.

So, unobnoxious now, she'hath buried both;   3
    For, none to death sins, that to sin is loath,
Nor do they die, which are not loath to die;
    So hath she this, and that virginity.
Grace was in her extremely diligent,
    That kept her from sin, yet made her repent.   4(
Of what small spots pure white complains! Alas,
    How little poison cracks a crystal glass!
She sinn'd, but just enough to let us see
    That God's word must be true; all sinners be.
So much did zeal her conscience rarefy,   45
    That, extreme truth lack'd little of a lie,
Making omissions, acts; laying the touch
    Of sin, on things that sometimes may be such.
As *Moses'* Cherubins, whose natures do
    Surpass all speed, by him are wingèd too: 50
So would her soul, already'in heaven, seem then,
    To climb by tears, the common stairs of men.
How fit she was for God, I am content
    To speak, that Death his vain haste may repent.
How fit for us, how even and how sweet,   55
    How good in all her titles, and how meet,
To have reform'd this forward heresy,
    That women can no parts of friendship be;
How moral, how divine shall not be told,
    Lest they that hear her virtues, think her old: 60
And lest we take Death's part, and make him glad
    Of such a prey, and to his triumph add.

12. *Noe:* Noah.

FROM THE *HOLY SONNETS*

5. I Am a Little World Made Cunningly

I am a little world made cunningly
Of elements, and an Angelike sprite,
But black sin hath betray'd to endless night

My world's both parts, and (oh) both parts must die.
You which beyond that heaven which was most high   5
Have found new spheres, and of new lands can write,
Pour new seas in mine eyes, that so I might
Drown my world with my weeping earnestly,
Or wash it if it must be drown'd no more:
But oh it must be burnt! alas the fire   10
Of lust and envy have burnt it heretofore,
And made it fouler; Let their flames retire,
And burn me O Lord, with a fiery zeal
Of thee and thy house, which doth in eating heal.

7. At the Round Earth's Imagin'd Corners, Blow

At the round earth's imagin'd corners, blow
Your trumpets, Angels, and arise, arise
From death, you numberless infinities
Of souls, and to your scatt'red bodies go,
All whom the flood did, and fire shall o'erthrow,   5
All whom war, dearth, age, agues, tyrannies,
Despair, law, chance, hath slain, and you whose eyes,
Shall behold God, and never taste death's woe.
But let them sleep, Lord, and me mourn a space,
For, if above all these, my sins abound,   10
'Tis late to ask abundance of thy grace,
When we are there; here on this lowly ground,
Teach me how to repent; for that's as good
As if thou'hadst seal'd my pardon, with thy blood.

9. If Poisonous Minerals, and If That Tree

If poisonous minerals, and if that tree,
Whose fruit threw death on else immortal us,
If lecherous goats, if serpents envious
Cannot be damn'd, Alas, why should I be?
Why should intent or reason, born in me,   5
Make sins, else equal, in me more heinous?
And mercy being easy, and glorious
To God, in his stern wrath, why threatens he?

But who am I, that dare dispute with thee?
O God, Oh! of thine only worthy blood,   10
And my tears, make a heavenly Lethean flood,
And drown in it my sins black memory;
That thou remember them, some claim as debt,
I think it mercy, if thou wilt forget.

10. Death Be Not Proud, Though Some Have Called Thee

Death be not proud, though some have called thee
Mighty and dreadful, for, thou art not so;
For, those whom thou think'st thou dost overthrow,
Die not, poor death, nor yet canst thou kill me.
From rest and sleep, which but thy pictures be,   5
Much pleasure; then from thee, much more must flow,
And soonest our best men with thee do go,
Rest of their bones, and soul's delivery.
Thou art slave to Fate, Chance, kings, and desperate men,
And dost with poison, war, and sickness dwell,   10
And poppy, or charms can make us sleep as well,
And better than thy stroke; why swell'st thou then?
One short sleep past, we wake eternally,
And death shall be no more; death, thou shalt die.

11. Spit in My Face You Jews, and Pierce My Side

Spit in my face you Jews, and pierce my side,
Buffet, and scoff, scourge, and crucify me,
For I have sinn'd, and sinn'd, and only he,
Who could do no iniquity, hath died:
But by my death can not be satisfied   5
My sins, which pass the Jews' impiety:
They kill'd once an inglorious man, but I
Crucify him daily, being now glorified.
Oh let me then, his strange love still admire:
Kings pardon, but he bore our punishment.   10
And *Jacob* came cloth'd in vile harsh attire
But to supplant, and with gainful intent:
God cloth'd himself in vile man's flesh, that so
He might be weak enough to suffer woe.

14. Batter My Heart, Three Person'd God

Batter my heart, three person'd God; for, you
As yet but knock, breathe, shine, and seek to mend;
That I may rise, and stand, o'erthrow me, and bend
Your force, to break, blow, burn and make me new.
I, like an usurp'd town, to'another due,   5
Labor to'admit you, but Oh, to no end,
Reason your viceroy in me, me should defend,
But is captiv'd, and proves weak or untrue.
Yet dearly I love you, and would be loved fain,
But am betroth'd unto your enemy: 10
Divorce me, untie, or break that knot again,
Take me to you, imprison me, for I
Except you'enthral me, never shall be free,
Nor ever chaste, except you ravish me.

17. Since She Whom I Lov'd Hath Paid Her Last Debt

Since she whom I lov'd hath paid her last debt
To Nature, and to hers, and my good is dead,
And her soul early into heaven ravished,
Wholly on heavenly things my mind is set.
Here the admiring her my mind did whet   5
To seek thee God; so streams do show the head;
But though I have found thee, and thou my thirst hast fed,
A holy thirsty dropsy melts me yet.
But why should I beg more Love, when as thou
Dost woo my soul for hers; off'ring all thine: 10
And dost not only fear lest I allow
My Love to Saints and Angels, things divine,
But in thy tender jealousy dost doubt
Lest the World, Flesh, yea Devil put thee out.

GOOD FRIDAY, 1613, RIDING WESTWARD

Let man's Soul be a sphere, and then, in this,
The intelligence that moves, devotion is,

And as the other spheres, by being grown
Subject to foreign motions, lose their own,
And being by others hurried every day,   5
Scarce in a year their natural form obey:
Pleasure or business, so, our souls admit
For their first mover, and are whirl'd by it.
Hence is't, that I am carried towards the West
This day, when my Soul's form bends toward the East.   10
There I should see a Sun, by rising set,
And by that setting endless day beget;
But that Christ on this Cross, did rise and fall,
Sin had eternally benighted all.
Yet dare I almost be glad, I do not see   15
That spectacle of too much weight for me.
Who sees God's face, that is self life, must die;
What a death were it then to see God die?
It made his own Lieutenant Nature shrink,
It made his footstool crack, and the Sun wink.   20
Could I behold those hands which span the poles,
And tune all spheres at once, pierc'd with those holes?
Could I behold that endless height which is
Zenith to us, and to our Antipodes,
Humbled below us? or that blood which is   25
The seat of all our Souls, if not of his,
Make dirt of dust, or that flesh which was worn
By God, for his apparel, ragg'd, and torn?
If on these things I durst not look, durst I
Upon his miserable mother cast mine eye,   30
Who was God's partner here, and furnish'd thus
Half of that sacrifice, which ransom'd us?
Though these things, as I ride, be from mine eye,
They'are present yet unto my memory,
For that looks towards them; and thou look'st towards me,   35
O Saviour, as thou hang'st upon the tree;
I turn my back to thee, but to receive
Corrections, till thy mercies bid thee leave.
O think me worth thine anger, punish me,
Burn off my rusts, and my deformity,   40
Restore thine image, so much, by thy grace,
That thou may'st know me, and I'll turn my face.

A HYMN TO CHRIST

At the Author's Last Going into Germany

In what torn ship soever I embark,
That ship shall be my emblem of thy Ark;
What sea soever swallow me, that flood
Shall be to me an emblem of thy blood;
Though thou with clouds of anger do disguise   5
Thy face; yet through that mask I know those eyes,
    Which, though they turn away sometimes,
        They never will despise.

I sacrifice this Island unto thee,
And all whom I lov'd there, and who lov'd me;   10
When I have put our seas 'twixt them and me,
Put thou thy sea betwixt my sins and thee.
As the tree's sap doth seek the root below
In winter, in my winter now I go,
    Where none but thee, th'eternal root   15
        Of true Love I may know.

Nor thou nor thy religion dost control,
The amorousness of an harmonious soul,
But thou would'st have that love thyself: As thou
Art jealous, Lord, so I am jealous now,   20
Thou lov'st not, till from loving more, thou free
My soul: Whoever gives, takes liberty:
    O, if thou car'st not whom I love
        Alas, thou lov'st not me.

Seal then this bill of my Divorce to All,   25
On whom those fainter beams of love did fall;
Marry those loves, which in youth scattered be
On Fame, Wit, Hopes (false mistresses) to thee.
Churches are best for prayer, that have least light:
To see God only, I go out of sight: 30
    And to 'scape stormy days, I choose
        An everlasting night.

A HYMN TO GOD THE FATHER

1

Wilt thou forgive that sin where I begun,
  Which is my sin, though it were done before?
Wilt thou forgive those sins, through which I run,
  And do run still: though still I do deplore?
    When thou hast done, thou hast not done,   5
      For, I have more.

2

Wilt thou forgive that sin by which I'have won
  Others to sin, and, made my sin their door?
Wilt thou forgive that sin which I did shun
  A year, or two, but wallowed in, a score?   10
    When thou hast done, thou hast not done,
      For, I have more.

3

I have a sin of fear, that when I have spun
  My last thread, I shall perish on the shore;
Swear by thyself, that at my death thy son   15
  Shall shine as he shines now, and heretofore;
    And, having done that, Thou hast done,
      I fear no more.

❝ GEORGE HERBERT is one of the few great English poets who came from the ranks of the nobility. He received a careful education, first from his mother, then at the Westminster School. In 1609 he went to Trinity College, Cambridge, where he had received a scholarship. His academic career there was distinguished: he received the B.A. and M.A. and was made a fellow of the college. Although his scholarly and musical accomplishments insured his general favor in the university community, he gradually turned to theological studies. The need for money and a

George Herbert

[1593-1633]

very real attraction to public affairs led Herbert to compete for the position of Public Orator at Cambridge. He gained this sinecure and, as a result, frequently associated with the men of the court. Herbert gained particular favor with King James I and several of his high-ranking associates. With the death of the King in 1625, Herbert could again turn to the church without the constant and immediate attraction of possible secular preferment.

His first ecclesiastical charge was but a few miles from Little Gidding, the home of Nicholas Ferrar, a former acquaintance at Cambridge and a theologian of growing importance. Now their mutual theological interests drew them close together, for the circle of Ferrar's friends was deeply concerned with the forms of religious devotions, particularly with the *Spiritual Exercises* of St. Ignatius. Ferrar's influence was deep and Herbert's ultimate commitment to the religious life doubtless owes much to this association. Although they met rarely in later years, Herbert and Ferrar continued a warm correspondence.

Even though threatened with tuberculosis, Herbert married in 1629. Shortly thereafter he was presented the rectory of Fugglestone and Bemerton, Wiltshire, by Charles I. After an initial hesitation, he was instituted and finally ordained. At Bemerton he showed an unusually strong devotion to his priestly duties, and there he wrote most of his well-known sacred poems. Herbert published none of his poetry other than a few Latin poems. On his deathbed he asked that a slim manuscript volume of poems be sent to Ferrar. These were published in 1633, shortly after his death, as *The Temple: Sacred Poems and Private Ejaculations.*

THE ALTAR

A broken ALTAR, Lord, thy servant rears,
Made of a heart, and cemented with tears:
    Whose parts are as thy hand did frame;
    No workman's tool hath touch'd the same.
            A HEART alone   5
            Is such a stone,
            As nothing but
            Thy pow'r doth cut.
            Wherefore each part
            Of my hard heart   10
            Meets in this frame,
            To praise thy Name:
    That, if I chance to hold my peace,
    These stones to praise thee may not cease.
O let thy blessed SACRIFICE be mine,   15
And sanctify this ALTAR to be thine.

GOOD FRIDAY

        O my chief good,
    How shall I measure out thy blood?
    How shall I count what thee befell,
        And each grief tell?

        Shall I thy woes   5
    Number according to thy foes?
    Or, since one star show'd thy first breath,
        Shall all thy death?

        Or shall each leaf,
    Which falls in Autumn, score a grief?   10
    Or can not leaves, but fruit, be sign
        Of the true vine?

        Then let each hour
    Of my whole life one grief devour;
    That thy distress through all may run,   15
        And be my sun.

Or rather let
My several sins their sorrows get;
That as each beast his cure doth know,
　　Each sin may so.   20

Since blood is fittest, Lord, to write
Thy sorrows in, and bloody fight;
My heart hath store, write there, where in
One box doth lie both ink and sin:

That when sin spies so many foes,   25
Thy whips, thy nails, thy wounds, thy woes,
All come to lodge there, sin may say,
No room for me, and fly away.

Sin being gone, oh fill the place,
And keep possession with thy grace;   30
Lest sin take courage and return,
And all the writings blot or burn.

CHURCH-MONUMENTS

While that my soul repairs to her devotion,
Here I intomb my flesh, that it betimes
May take acquaintance of this heap of dust;
To which the blast of death's incessant motion,
Fed with the exhalation of our crimes,   5
Drives all at last. Therefore, I gladly trust

My body to this school, that it may learn
To spell his elements, and find his birth
Written in dusty heraldry and lines;
Which dissolution sure doth best discern,   10
Comparing dust with dust, and earth with earth.
These laugh at jet and marble put for signs,

To sever the good fellowship of dust,
And spoil the meeting. What shall point out them,
When they shall bow, and kneel, and fall down flat   15
To kiss those heaps, which now they have in trust?
Dear flesh, while I do pray, learn here thy stem
And true descent; that when thou shalt grow fat,

And wanton in thy cravings, thou mayst know,
That flesh is but the glass, which holds the dust   2
That measures all our time; which also shall
Be crumbled into dust. Mark here below
How tame these ashes are, how free from lust,
That thou mayst fit thy self against thy fall.

AVARICE

Money, thou bane of bliss, and source of woe,
    Whence com'st thou, that thou art so fresh and fine?
    I know thy parentage is base and low:
Man found thee poor and dirty in a mine.
Surely thou didst so little contribute   5
    To this great kingdom, which thou now hast got,
    That he was fain, when thou wert destitute,
To dig thee out of thy dark cave and grot:
Then forcing thee by fire he made thee bright:
    Nay, thou hast got the face of man; for we   10
    Have with our stamp and seal transferr'd our right:
Thou art the man, and man but dross to thee.
    Man calleth thee his wealth, who made thee rich;
    And while he digs out thee, falls in the ditch.

UNGRATEFULNESS

Lord, with what bounty and rare clemency
        Hast thou redeem'd us from the grave!
            If thou had'st let us run,
            Gladly had man ador'd the sun,
        And thought his god most brave;
Where now we shall be better gods than he.

Thou hast but two rare cabinets full of treasure,
        The *Trinity*, and *Incarnation*:
            Thou hast unlock'd them both,
            And made them jewels to betroth   10
            The work of thy creation
Unto thyself in everlasting pleasure.

The statelier cabinet is the *Trinity,*
  Whose sparkling light access denies;
   Therefore, thou dost not show   15
  This fully to us, till death blow
   The dust into our eyes:
For by that powder thou wilt make us see.

But all thy sweets are pack'd up in the other;
  Thy mercies thither flock and flow: 20
   That as the first affrights,
  This may allure us with delights;
   Because this box we know;
For we have all of us just such another.

But man is close, reserv'd, and dark to thee: 25
  When thou demandest but a heart,
   He cavils instantly.
  In his poor cabinet of bone
   Sins have their box apart,
Defrauding thee, who gavest two for one.   30

COLOSSIANS III:3

Our Life Is Hid with Christ in God.

My words and thoughts do both express this notion,
That *Life* hath with the sun a double motion.
The first *Is* straight, and our diurnal friend,
The other *Hid* and doth obliquely bend.
One life is wrapt *In* flesh, and tends to earth: 5
The other winds towards *Him,* whose happy birth
Taught me to live here so, *That* still one eye
Should aim and shoot at that which *Is* on high:
Quitting with daily labor all *My* pleasure,
To gain at harvest an eternal *Treasure.*   10

VIRTUE

Sweet day, so cool, so calm, so bright,
  The bridal of the earth and sky:

The dew shall weep thy fall tonight;
　　　　　For thou must die.

Sweet rose, whose hue angry and brave
Bids the rash gazer wipe his eye:
Thy root is ever in its grave,
　　　　　And thou must die.

Sweet spring, full of sweet days and roses,
A box where sweets compacted lie:
My music shows ye have your closes,
　　　　　And all must die.

Only a sweet and virtuous soul,
Like season'd timber, never gives;
But though the whole world turn to coal,
　　　　　Then chiefly lives.

LIFE

I made a posie, while the day ran by:
Here will I smell my remnant out, and tie
　　　　　My life within this band.

But Time did beckon to the flowers, and they
By noon most cunningly did steal away,
　　　　　And wither'd in my hand.

My hand was next to them, and then my heart:
I took, without more thinking, in good part
　　　　　Time's gentle admonition:

Who did so sweetly death's sad taste convey,
Making my mind to smell my fatal day;
　　　　　Yet sug'ring the suspicion.

Farewell dear flowers, sweetly your time ye spent,
Fit, while ye liv'd, for smell or ornament,
　　　　　And after death for cures.

I follow straight without complaints or grief,
Since if my scent be good, I care not if
　　　　　It be as short as yours.

MORTIFICATION

How soon doth man decay!
When clothes are taken from a chest of sweets
   To swaddle infants, whose young breath
      Scarce knows the way;
   Those clouts are little winding sheets,   5
Which do consign and send them unto death.

   When boys go first to bed,
They step into their voluntary graves,
   Sleep binds them fast; only their breath
      Makes them not dead: 10
   Successive nights, like rolling waves,
Convey them quickly, who are bound for death.

   When youth is frank and free,
And calls for music, while his veins do swell,
   All day exchanging mirth and breath   15
      In company;
   That music summons to the knell,
Which shall befriend him at the hour of death.

   When man grows staid and wise,
Getting a house and home, where he may move   20
   Within the circle of his breath,
      Schooling his eyes;
   That dumb inclosure maketh love
Unto the coffin, that attends his death.

   When age grows low and weak,   25
Marking his grave, and thawing ev'ry year,
   Till all do melt, and drown his breath
      When he would speak;
   A chair or litter shows the bier,
Which shall convey him to the house of death.   30

   Man, ere he is aware,
Hath put together a solemnity,
   And dress'd his hearse, while he has breath
      As yet to spare:

    Yet Lord, instruct us so to die,   3

That all these dyings may be life in death.

CONFESSION

      O what a cunning guest

Is this same grief! within my heart I made

    Closets; and in them many a chest;

    And, like a master in my trade,

In those chests, boxes; in each box, a till:

Yet grief knows all, and enters when he will.

      No screw, no piercer can

Into a piece of timber work and wind,

    As God's afflictions into man,

    When he a torture hath design'd   1

They are too subtle for the subtlest hearts;

And fall, like rheums, upon the tend'rest parts.

      We are the earth; and they,

Like moles within us, heave, and cast about:

    And till they foot and clutch their prey,   1

    They never cool, much less give out.

No smith can make such locks but they have keys:

Closets are halls to them; and hearts, high-ways.

      Only an open breast

Doth shut them out, so that they cannot enter;   2

    Or, if they enter, cannot rest,

    But quickly seek some new adventure.

Smooth open hearts no fastening have; but fiction

Doth give a hold and handle to affliction.

      Wherefore my faults and sins,   2

Lord, I acknowledge; take thy plagues away:

    For since confession pardon wins,

    I challenge here the brightest day,

The clearest diamond: let them do their best,

They shall be thick and cloudy to my breast.   3

THE HOLDFAST

I threatened to observe the strict decree
    Of my dear God with all my power and might.
    But I was told by one, it could not be;
Yet I might trust in God to be my light.
Then will I trust, said I, in him alone.
    Nay, ev'n to trust in him, was also his:
    We must confess that nothing is our own.
Then I confess that he my succour is:
But to have nought is ours, not to confess
    That we have nought, I stood amaz'd at this,   10
    Much troubled, till I heard a friend express,
That all things were more ours by being his.
    What Adam had, and forfeited for all,
    Christ keepeth now, who cannot fail or fall.

THE COLLAR

I struck the board, and cried. No more.
            I will abroad.
    What? shall I ever sigh and pine?
My lines and life are free; free as the road,
    Loose as the wind, as large as store.   5
        Shall I be still in suit?
Have I no harvest but a thorn
To let me blood, and not restore
What I have lost with cordial fruit?
          Sure there was wine   10
Before my sighs did dry it: there was corn
        Before my tears did drown it.
    Is the year only lost to me?
        Have I no bays to crown it?
No flowers, no garlands gay? all blasted?   15
        All wasted?
    Not so, my heart: but there is fruit,
        And thou hast hands.

11. *corn:* grain.

Recover all thy sigh-blown age
On double pleasures: leave thy cold dispute   2
Of what is fit, and not. Forsake thy cage,
                    Thy rope of sands,
Which petty thoughts have made, and made to thee
                Good cable, to enforce and draw,
                        And be thy law,   2
            While thou didst wink and wouldst not see.
                    Away; take heed:
                    I will abroad.
Call in thy death's head there: tie up thy fears.
                    He that forbears   3
                To suit and serve his need,
                    Deserves his load.
But as I rav'd and grew more fierce and wild
                    At every word,
Me thoughts I heard one calling, *Child!*   3
                And I replied, *My Lord.*

THE PULLEY

When God at first made man,
Having a glass of blessings standing by;
Let us (said he) pour on him all we can:
Let the world's riches, which dispersed lie,
            Contract into a span.

            So strength first made a way;
Then beauty flow'd, then wisdom, honor, pleasure:
When almost all was out, God made a stay,
Perceiving that alone of all his treasure
            Rest in the bottom lay.   1

            For if I should (said he)
Bestow this jewel also on my creature,
He would adore my gifts instead of me,
And rest in Nature, not the God of Nature:
            So both should losers be.   1

            Yet let him keep the rest,
But keep them with repining restlessness:

Let him be rich and weary, that at least,
If goodness lead him not, yet weariness
    May toss him to my breast.   20

BITTER-SWEET

Ah my dear angry Lord,
Since thou dost love, yet strike;
Cast down, yet help afford;
Sure I will do the like.

I will complain, yet praise;   5
I will bewail, approve:
And all my sour-sweet days
I will lament, and love.

THE FOIL

      If we could see below
The sphere of virtue, and each shining grace
      As plainly as that above doth show;
This were the better sky, the brighter place.

      God hath made stars the foil   5
To set off virtues; griefs to set off sinning:
      Yet in this wretched world we toil,
As if grief were not foul, nor virtue winning.

LOVE

Love bade me welcome: yet my soul drew back,
      Guilty of dust and sin.
But quick-ey'd Love, observing me grow slack
      From my first entrance in,
Drew nearer to me, sweetly questioning,   5
      If I lack'd any thing.

A guest, I answer'd, worthy to be here:
      Love said, You shall be he.

I, the unkind, ungrateful? Ah my dear,
        I cannot look on thee.   10
Love took my hand, and smiling did reply,
        Who made the eyes but I?

Truth, Lord, but I have marr'd them: let my shame
        Go where it doth deserve.
And know you not, says Love, who bore the blame?   15
        My dear, then I will serve.
You must sit down, says Love, and taste my meat:
        So I did sit and eat.

❦ JOHN MILTON was the son of a prosperous scrivener who saw to his son's proper education. From St. Paul's School, London, the young scholar went to Christ's College, Cambridge, where he continued his studies with some diligence and was distinguished not only for a certain primness of character but for a few misdemeanors which resulted in his temporary suspension. After he took the M.A. degree he retired to his father's country estate, where he wrote a number of poems including *Comus,* a noble masque, and "Lycidas," an elegy occasioned by the death of a

John Milton

[1608-1674]

fellow student and poet, Edward King. In 1638 and 1639 he took the "grand tour" of major European cities. Not long after his return Milton became involved with the conflicts between Parliament and Charles I. He contributed admirable tracts to the reform movement, both before and after the formation of the Cromwellian government. Ultimately Milton was asked to take a responsible position in the Commonwealth—Secretary for Foreign Tongues to the Council of State. He devoted himself wholly to his public duties, even after the complete loss of his sight.

Throughout his governmental service Milton never relaxed his conviction that his ultimate career was in poetry. In 1646 he published his collected "minor" poems in Latin and English, most of which had been completed several years before. This demonstrable interest in his poetry came only a year after the publication of the pamphlets *Of Education* and *Areopagitica,* and not far from the time that he began two major prose works, the *History of Britain* and *De Doctrina Christiana.* When the monarchy was restored in 1660, Milton was, of course, definitely unwelcome in government circles. Thus for the first time in many years he could devote himself without interference to poetry. Although he had at one time considered doing an epic on an Arthurian theme, he settled on the Bible as his chief source. Blind since 1652, he composed his major works by dictating to hired amanuenses. In 1667 his great epic *Paradise Lost* was first published. Four years later he brought out its companion piece, *Paradise Regained,* and his classical verse drama *Samson Agonistes.*

SONG

On May Morning

Now the bright morning star, day's harbinger,
Comes dancing from the east, and leads with her
The flow'ry May, who from her green lap throws
The yellow cowslip, and the pale primrose.
    Hail bounteous May that dost inspire   5
    Mirth and youth and warm desire.
    Woods and groves are of thy dressing,
    Hill and dale doth boast thy blessing.
Thus we salute thee with our early song,
And welcome thee, and wish thee long.   10

O NIGHTINGALE, THAT ON YON BLOOMY SPRAY

O Nightingale, that on yon bloomy spray
Warbl'st at eve, when all the woods are still,
Thou with fresh hope the lover's heart dost fill,
While the jolly hours lead on propitious May.
Thy liquid notes that close the eye of day,   5
First heard before the shallow cuckoo's bill
Portend success in love; O if Jove's will
Have link'd that amorous power to thy soft lay,
Now timely sing, ere the rude bird of hate
Foretell my hopeless doom in some grove nigh: 10
As thou from year to year hast sung too late
For my relief; yet hadst no reason why,
Whether the Muse, or Love call thee his mate,
Both them I serve, and of their train am I.

ON SHAKESPEARE

What needs my Shakespeare for his honor'd bones,
The labor of an age in piled stones,
Or that his hallow'd relics should be hid

Under a star-ypointing pyramid?
Dear son of memory, great heir of Fame,   5
What need'st thou such weak witness of thy name!
Thou in our wonder and astonishment
Hast built thy self a live-long monument.
For whilst to th'shame of slow-endeavoring art,
Thy easy numbers flow, and that each heart   10
Hath from the leaves of thy unvalued book,
Those Delphic lines with deep impression took,
Then thou our fancy of itself bereaving,
Dost make us marble with too much conceiving;
And so sepulcher'd in such pomp dost lie,   15
That Kings for such a tomb would wish to die.

4. *ypointing*: pointing.

ON THE UNIVERSITY CARRIER

Who sickn'd in the time of his vacancy, being forbid to go to London,
by reason of the Plague

Here lies old Hobson, Death hath broke his girt,
And here alas, hath laid him in the dirt,
Or else the ways being foul, twenty to one,
He's here stuck in a slough, and overthrown.
'Twas such a shifter, that if truth were known,   5
Death was half glad when he had got him down;
For he had any time this ten years full,
Dodg'd with him, betwixt Cambridge and the Bull.
And surely, Death could never have prevail'd,
Had not his weekly course of carriage fail'd;   10
But lately finding him so long at home,
And thinking now his journey's end was come,
And that he had ta'en up his latest Inn,
In the kind office of a Chamberlin
Shew'd him his room where he must lodge that night,   15
Pull'd off his boots, and took away the light:
If any ask for him, it shall be said,
Hobson has supp'd and's newly gone to bed.

1. *girt*: girth.
8. *the Bull*: the Bull Inn, Bishopsgate Street, London.

AN EPITAPH ON THE MARCHIONESS
OF WINCHESTER*

This rich marble doth inter
The honor'd Wife of Winchester
A Viscount's daughter, an Earl's heir,
Besides what her virtues fair
Added to her noble birth,
More than she could own from Earth.
Summers three times eight save one
She had told, alas too soon,
After so short time of breath,
To house with darkness, and with death.   10
Yet had the number of her days
Been as complete as was her praise,
Nature and fate had had no strife
In giving limit to her life.
Her high birth, and her graces sweet,   15
Quickly found a lover meet;
The Virgin choir for her request
The God that sits at marriage feast;
He at their invoking came
But with a scarce-well-lighted flame;   20
And in his garland as he stood,
Ye might discern a cypress bud.
Once had the early matrons run
To greet her of a lovely son,
And now with second hope she goes,   25
And calls Lucina to her throes;
But whether by mischance or blame
Atropos for Lucina came;
And with remorseless cruelty,
Spoil'd at once both fruit and tree: 30
The hapless Babe before his birth

* Jane Savage, wife of John Paulet, fifth Marquis of Winchester; she died in
April, 1631.

26. *Lucina:* The Roman goddess of childbirth.
28. *Atropos:* one of the Fates, who cut short the threads of life.

Had burial, yet not laid in earth,
And the languish'd Mother's womb
Was not long a living tomb.
So have I seen some tender slip   35
Sav'd with care from Winter's nip,
The pride of her carnation train,
Pluck'd up by some unheedy swain,
Who only thought to crop the flow'r
New shot up from vernal show'r;   40
But the fair blossom hangs the head
Side-ways as on a dying bed,
And those pearls of dew she wears,
Prove to be presaging tears
Which the sad morn had let fall   45
On her hast'ning funeral.
Gentle Lady, may thy grave
Peace and quiet ever have;
After this thy travail sore
Sweet rest seize thee evermore,   50
That to give the world increase,
Short'ned hast thy own life's lease;
Here, besides the sorrowing
That thy noble House doth bring,
Here be tears of perfect moan   55
Wept for thee in Helicon,
And some flowers, and some bays,
For thy hearse to strew the ways,
Sent thee from the banks of Came,
Devoted to thy virtuous name;   60
Whilst thou, bright Saint, high sit'st in glory,
Next her much like to thee in story,
That fair Syrian Shepherdess,
Who after years of barrenness,
The highly favor'd Joseph bore   65
To him that serv'd for her before,
And at her next birth, much like thee,

46. *funeral:* death.
59. *Came:* Cam, the river which flows through Cambridge.
  63. *Syrian Shepherdess:* Rachel, second wife of Jacob and mother of Joseph
and Benjamin.

Through pangs fled to felicity,
Far within the bosom bright
Of blazing majesty and light,   70
There with thee, new welcome Saint,
Like fortunes may her soul acquaint,
With thee there clad in radiant sheen,
No Marchioness, but now a Queen.

HOW SOON HATH TIME, THE SUBTLE THIEF OF YOUTH

How soon hath time, the subtle thief of youth,
Stol'n on his wing my three and twentieth year!
My hasting days fly on with full career,
But my late spring no bud or blossom shew'th.
Perhaps my semblance might deceive the truth,   5
That I to manhood am arriv'd so near,
And inward ripeness doth much less appear,
That some more timely-happy spirits endu'th.
Yet be it less or more, or soon or slow,
It shall be still in strictest measure ev'n,   10
To that same lot, however mean or high,
Toward which Time leads me, and the will of Heav'n;
All is, if I have grace to use it so,
As ever in my great task-Master's eye.

L'ALLEGRO

Hence loathed Melancholy
    Of Cerberus, and blackest midnight born,
In Stygian Cave forlorn.
    'Mongst horrid shapes, and shrieks, and sights unholy,
Find out some uncouth cell,   5
    Where brooding darkness spreads his jealous wings
And the night-raven sings;
    There under Ebon shades, and low-brow'd rocks,
As ragged as thy locks,
    In dark Cimmerian desert ever dwell.   10
But come thou Goddess fair and free,

In Heav'n yclep'd Euphrosyne,
And by men, heart-easing Mirth,
Whom lovely Venus at a birth
With two sister Graces more   15
To ivy-crowned Bacchus bore;
Or whether (as some sager sing)
The frolic wind that breathes the spring,
Zephir with Aurora playing,
As he met her once a-Maying,   20
There on beds of violets blue,
And fresh-blown roses wash'd in dew,
Fill'd her with thee a daughter fair,
So buxom, blithe, and debonair.
Haste thee nymph, and bring with thee   25
Jest and youthful Jollity,
Quips and cranks, and wanton wiles,
Nods, and becks, and wreathèd smiles
Such as hang on Hebe's cheek,
And love to live in dimple sleek: 30
Sport that wrinkled Care derides,
And Laughter holding both his sides.
Come, and trip it as you go
On the light fantastic toe,
And in thy right hand lead with thee,   35
The mountain nymph, sweet Liberty;
And if I give thee honor due,
Mirth, admit me of thy crew
To live with her, and live with thee,
In unreproved pleasures free;   40
To hear the lark begin his flight,
And singing startle the dull night,
From his watch-tow'r in the skies,
Till the dappled dawn doth rise;
Then to come in spite of sorrow,   45
And at my window bid good morrow,
Through the sweet-briar, or the vine,
Or the twisted eglantine;

12. *yclep'd*: called.
24. *debonair*: courteous, gentle.
45. *in spite of sorrow*: in contempt for sorrow.

While the cock with lively din,
Scatters the rear of darkness thin,   50
And to the stack, or the barn door,
Stoutly struts his dames before;
Oft list'ning how the hounds and horn
Cheerly rouse the slumb'ring morn,
From the side of some hoar hill,   55
Through the high wood echoing shrill.
Sometime walking not unseen
By hedge-row elms, on hillocks green,
Right against the eastern gate,
Where the great sun begins his state,   60
Rob'd in flames, and amber light,
The clouds in thousand liveries dight,
While the plowman near at hand,
Whistles o'er the furrow'd land,
And the milkmaid singeth blithe,   65
And the mower whets his scythe,
And every shepherd tells his tale
Under the hawthorn in the dale.
Straight mine eye hath caught new pleasures
Whilst the lantskip round it measures,   70
Russet lawns, and fallows gray,
Where the nibbling flocks do stray,
Mountains on whose barren breast
The laboring clouds do often rest:
Meadows trim with daisies pied,   75
Shallow brooks, and rivers wide.
Towers and battlements it sees
Bosom'd high in tufted trees,
Where perhaps some beauty lies,
The cynosure of neighboring eyes.   80
Hard by, a cottage chimney smokes,
From betwixt two aged oaks,
Where Corydon and Thyrsis met,
Are at their savory dinner set
Of herbs, and other country messes,   85
Which the neat-handed Phillis dresses;

70. *lantskip:* landscape.

And then in haste her bow'r she leaves,
With Thestylis to bind the sheaves;
Or if the earlier season lead
To the tann'd haycock in the mead,   90
Sometimes with secure delight
The up-land hamlets will invite,
When the merry bells ring round,
And the jocund rebecks sound
To many a youth, and many a maid,   95
Dancing in the chequer'd shade;
And young and old come forth to play
On a sunshine holiday,
Till the live-long daylight fail,
Then to the spicy nut-brown ale,   100
With stories told of many a feat
How Færy Mab the junkets eat,
She was pinch'd and pull'd, she said,
And he, by Friar's lanthorn led,
Tells how the drudging goblin sweat,   105
To earn his cream-bowl duly set,
When in one night, ere glimpse of morn,
His shadowy flail hath thresh'd the corn,
That ten day-laborers could not end;
Then lies him down the lobber fiend.   110
And stretch'd out all the chimney's length,
Basks at the fire his hairy strength;
And crop-full out of doors he flings,
Ere the first cock his Matin rings,
Thus done the tales, to bed they creep,   115
By whispering winds soon lull'd asleep.
Tow'red cities please us then,
And the busy hum of men,
Where throngs of Knights and Barons bold,
In weeds of peace high triumphs hold,   120
With store of ladies, whose bright eyes

88. *Thestylis:* a slave girl in one of Theocritus' idylls; Corydon, Thyrsis, and Phillis are traditional pastoral characters from classical sources; their names appear frequently in English poetry.
91. *secure:* without care.
94. *rebecks:* three-stringed viols.
102. *eat:* ate.

Rain influence, and judge the prize,
Of wit, or arms, while both contend
To win her Grace, whom all commend,
There let Hymen oft appear   125
In saffron robe, with taper clear,
And pomp, and feast, and revelry,
With mask, and antique pageantry,
Such sights as youthful Poets dream
On summer eves by haunted stream.   130
Then to the well-trod stage anon,
If Jonson's learned sock be on,
Or sweetest Shakespeare, fancy's child,
Warble his native wood-notes wild,
And ever against eating cares,   135
Lap me in soft Lydian airs,
Married to immortal verse
Such as the meeting soul may pierce
In notes, with many a winding bout
Of linked sweetness long drawn out,   140
With wanton heed, and giddy cunning,
The melting voice through mazes running:
Untwisting all the chains that tie
The hidden soul of harmony.
That Orpheus' self may heave his head   145
From golden slumber on a bed
Of heap'd Elysian flow'rs, and hear
Such strains as would have won the ear
Of Pluto, to have quite set free
His half regain'd Eurydice.   150
These delights, if thou canst give,
Mirth, with thee I mean to live.

132. *sock*: the lightweight shoe worn by Greek comic actors.

IL PENSEROSO

Hence vain deluding joys,
        The brood of folly without father bred,
How little you bested,
        Or fill the fixed mind with all your toys;

3. *bested*: profit.

Dwell in some idle brain, 5
   And fancies fond with gaudy shapes possess,
As thick and numberless
   As the gay motes that people the Sunbeams,
Or likest hovering dreams,
   The fickle pensioners of Morpheus' train. 10
But hail thou Goddess, sage and holy,
Hail divinest Melancholy,
Whose saintly visage is too bright
To hit the sense of human sight;
And therefore to our weaker view, 15
O'er laid with black staid wisdom's hue.
Black, but such as in esteem,
Prince Memnon's sister might beseem,
Or that starr'd Ethiop Queen that strove
To set her beauty's praise above 20
The Sea Nymphs, and their powers offended,
Yet thou art higher far descended,
Thee bright-hair'd Vesta long of yore
To solitary Saturn bore;
His daughter she (in Saturn's reign 25
Such mixture was not held a stain)
Oft in glimmering Bow'rs, and glades
He met her, and in secret shades
Of woody Ida's inmost grove,
While yet there was no fear of Jove. 30
Come pensive Nun, devout and pure,
Sober, steadfast, and demure,
All in a robe of darkest grain,
Flowing with majestic train,
And sable stole of Cypress lawn, 35
Over thy decent shoulders drawn.
Come, but keep thy wonted state,
With ev'n step, and musing gait,
And looks commercing with the skies,
Thy rapt soul sitting in thine eyes: 40

18. *Prince Memnon's sister:* Hemera, devoted sister of the Ethiopian prince.
19. *starr'd Ethiop Queen:* because of her boasting, Cassiopeia was transformed into a constellation.
33. *grain:* color.
36. *decent:* beautiful.

There held in holy passion still,
Forget thy self to marble, till
With a sad leaden downward cast,
Thou fix them on the earth as fast.
And join with thee calm Peace, and Quiet,   45
Spare Fast, that oft with gods doth diet,
And hears the Muses in a ring,
Aye round about Jove's altar sing.
And add to these retired leisure,
That in trim gardens takes his pleasure;   50
But first, and chiefest, with thee bring,
Him that yon soars on golden wing,
Guiding the fiery-wheeled throne,
The cherub Contemplation,
And the mute Silence hist along,   55
'Less Philomel will deign a song,
In her sweetest, saddest plight,
Smoothing the rugged brow of night,
While Cynthia checks her dragon yoke,
Gently o'er th' accustom'd oak;   60
Sweet bird that shunn'st the noise of folly,
Most musical, most Melancholy!
Thee Chantress oft the woods among
I woo to hear thy evensong;
And missing thee, I walk unseen   65
On the dry smooth-shaven green,
To behold the wand'ring Moon,
Riding near her highest noon,
Like one that had been led astray
Through the heav'ns wide pathless way;   70
And oft, as if her head she bow'd,
Stooping through a fleecy cloud.
Oft on a plat of rising ground,
I hear the far-off curfew sound,
Over some wide-water'd shore,   75
Swinging slow with sullen roar;
Or if the air will not permit,
Some still removed place will fit,

55. *hist*: summon without noise.

Where glowing Embers through the room
Teach light to counterfeit a gloom,   80
Far from all resort of mirth,
Save the cricket on the hearth,
Or the bellman's drowsy charm,
To bless the doors from nightly harm:
Or let my lamp at midnight hour,   85
Be seen in some high lonely tow'r,
Where I may oft outwatch the Bear,
With thrice great Hermes, or unsphere
The spirit of Plato to unfold
What worlds, or what vast regions hold   90
The immortal mind that hath forsook
Her mansion in this fleshly nook:
And of those Demons that are found
In fire, air, flood, or under ground,
Whose power hath a true consent   95
With planet, or with element.
Sometime let gorgeous Tragedy
In scepter'd pall come sweeping by,
Presenting Thebes, or Pelops' line,
Or the tale of Troy divine.   100
Or what (though rare) of later age,
Ennobled hath the Buskin'd stage.
But, O sad Virgin, that thy power
Might raise Musæus from his bower,
Or bid the soul of Orpheus sing   105
Such notes as warbled to the string,
Drew iron tears down Pluto's cheek,
And made Hell grant what Love did seek.
Or call up him that left half told
The story of Cambuscan bold,   110
Of Camball, and of Algarsife,
And who had Canace to wife,
That own'd the virtuous ring and glass,

83. *bellman*: a night watchman who rang the hours; *charm*: song.
88. *thrice great Hermes*: great as king, priest, and philosopher.
104. *Musæus*: an ancient mythological hero mentioned in Vergil's *Æneid*.
110. *Cambuscan*: central character of a half-told story in Chaucer's Squire's Tale; Cambuscan had three children: Algarsyf, Cambalo, and Canacee; Canacee's lover presented her with a ring and mirror and he offered her father the brass horse.

And of the wondrous horse of brass,
On which the Tartar King did ride;   11
And if ought else great Bards beside
In sage and solemn tunes have sung,
Of tourneys and of trophies hung;
Of forests, and enchantments drear,
Where more is meant than meets the ear.   12
Thus night oft see me in thy pale career,
Till civil-suited Morn appear,
Not trick'd and frounc'd as she was wont,
With the Attic boy to hunt,
But kerchief't in a comely cloud,   12
While rocking winds are piping loud,
Or usher'd with a shower still,
When the gust hath blown his fill,
Ending on the rustling leaves,
With minute drops from off the eaves.   13
And when the Sun begins to fling
His flaring beams, me Goddess bring
To arched walks of twilight groves,
And shadows brown that Sylvan loves
Of pine, or monumental oak,   13
Where the rude ax with heaved stroke
Was never heard the Nymphs to daunt,
Or fright them from their hallow'd haunt.
There in close covert by some brook,
Where no profaner eye may look,   14
Hide me from Day's garish eye,
While the bee with honied thigh,
That at her flow'ry work doth sing,
And the waters murmuring
With such consort as they keep,   14
Entice the dewy-feather'd Sleep;
And let some strange mysterious dream,
Wave at his wings in airy stream,
Of lively portraiture display'd,
Softly on my eyelids laid.   15
And as I wake, sweet music breathe
Above, about, or underneath,
Sent by some spirit to mortals good,

Or th' unseen Genius of the wood.
But let my due feet never fail,   155
To walk the studious cloisters pale,
And love the high embowed roof,
With antick pillars massy proof,
And storied windows richly dight,
Casting a dim religious light.   160
There let the pealing organ blow,
To the full voic'd choir below,
In service high, and anthems clear,
As may with sweetness, through mine ear,
Dissolve me into ecstasies,   165
And bring all Heav'n before mine eyes.
And may at last my weary age
Find out the peaceful hermitage,
The hairy gown and mossy cell,
Where I may sit and rightly spell   170
Of every star that heav'n doth shew,
And every herb that sips the dew;
Till old experience do attain
To something like prophetic strain.
These pleasures Melancholy give,   175
And I with thee will choose to live.

158. *antick:* antique.
170. *spell:* make out by study, understand.

LYCIDAS

Yet once more, O ye Laurels, and once more
Ye Myrtles brown, with ivy never sere,
I come to pluck your berries harsh and crude,
And with forc'd fingers rude,
Shatter your leaves before the mellowing year.   5
Bitter constraint, and sad occasion dear,
Compels me to disturb your season due:
For Lycidas is dead, dead ere his prime,
Young Lycidas, and hath not left his peer:
Who would not sing for Lycidas? he knew   10

3. *crude:* unripe.

Himself to sing, and build the lofty rhyme.
He must not float upon his wat'ry bier
Unwept, and welter to the parching wind,
Without the meed of some melodious tear.
    Begin then, Sisters of the sacred well,   15
That from beneath the seat of Jove doth spring,
Begin, and somewhat loudly sweep the string.
Hence with denial vain, and coy excuse,
So may some gentle Muse
With lucky words favor my destin'd urn,   20
And as he passes turn,
And bid fair peace be to my sable shroud.
For we were nurs'd upon the self-same hill,
Fed the same flock, by fountain, shade, and rill.
    Together both, ere the high lawns appear'd   25
Under the opening eyelids of the morn,
We drove afield, and both together heard
What time the gray-fly winds her sultry horn,
Batt'ning our flocks with the fresh dews of night,
Oft till the star that rose, at ev'ning, bright,   30
Toward Heav'ns descent had slop'd his westering wheel,
Meanwhile the rural ditties were not mute,
Temper'd to th' oaten flute,
Rough Satyrs danc'd, and Fauns with clov'n heel,
From the glad sound would not be absent long,   35
And old Damætas lov'd to hear our song.
    But O the heavy change, now thou art gone,
Now thou art gone, and never must return!
Thee shepherd, thee the woods, and desert caves,
With wild thyme and the gadding vine o'ergrown,   40
And all their echoes mourn.
The willows, and the hazel copses green,
Shall now no more be seen,
Fanning their joyous leaves to thy soft lays.
As killing as the canker to the rose,   45
Or taint-worm to the weanling herds that graze,
Or frost to flowers, that their gay wardrop wear,
When first the white-thorn blows;

47. *wardrop:* wardrobe.

Such, Lycidas, thy loss to shepherd's ear.
    Where were ye Nymphs when the remorseless deep   50
Clos'd o'er the head of your lov'd Lycidas?
For neither were ye playing on the steep,
Where your old Bards, the famous Druids, lie,
Nor on the shaggy top of Mona high,
Nor yet where Deva spreads her wizard stream: 55
Ay me, I fondly dream!
Had ye been there—for what could that have done?
What could the Muse herself that Orpheus bore,
The Muse herself for her enchanting son
Whom universal nature did lament,   60
When by the rout that made the hideous roar,
His gory visage down the stream was sent,
Down the swift Hebrus to the Lesbian shore?
    Alas! What boots it with incessant care
To tend the homely slighted shepherd's trade,   65
And strictly meditate the thankless Muse?
Were it not better done as others use,
To sport with Amaryllis in the shade,
Or with the tangles of Neæra's hair?
Fame is the spur that the clear spirit doth raise   70
(That last infirmity of noble mind)
To scorn delights, and live laborious days;
But the fair guerdon when we hope to find,
And think to burst out into sudden blaze,
Comes the blind Fury with th' abhorred shears,   75
And slits the thin spun life. But not the praise,
Phœbus replied, and touch'd my trembling ears;
Fame is no plant that grows on mortal soil,
Nor in the glistering foil
Set off to th' world, nor in broad rumor lies,   80
But lives and spreads aloft by those pure eyes,
And perfect witness of all-judging Jove;
As he pronounces lastly on each deed,
Of so much fame in Heav'n expect thy meed.
    O Fountain Arethuse, and thou honor'd flood,   85

54. *Mona:* an island on which the Druids worshiped.
55. *Deva:* the prophetic river Dee which divides England and Wales.
69. *Neæra's:* a traditional name for a nymph, often spelled "Næra."

Smooth-sliding Mincius, crown'd with vocal reeds,
That strain I heard was of a higher mood:
But now my Oat proceeds,
And listens to the Herald of the Sea
That came in Neptune's plea,   9
He ask'd the Waves, and ask'd the felon Winds,
What hard mishap hath doom'd this gentle swain?
And question'd every gust of rugged wings
That blows from off each beaked promontory;
They knew not of his story,   9
And sage Hippotades their answer brings,
That not a blast was from his dungeon stray'd,
The Air was calm, and on the level brine
Sleek Panope with all her sisters play'd.
It was that fatal and perfidious Bark   10
Built in th' eclipse, and rigg'd with curses dark,
That sunk so low that sacred head of thine.

    Next Camus, reverend Sire, went footing slow,
His mantle hairy, and his bonnet sedge,
Inwrought with figures dim, and on the edge   105
Like to that sanguine flower inscrib'd with woe.
Ah; Who hath reft (quoth he) my dearest pledge?
Last came, and last did go,
The Pilot of the Galilean lake,
Two massy keys he bore of metals twain,   110
(The golden opens, the iron shuts amain).
He shook his mitred locks, and stern bespake,
How well could I have spar'd for thee, young swain,
Anow of such as for their bellies' sake,
Creep and intrude, and climb into the fold?   115
Of other care they little reck'ning make,
Than how to scramble at the shearers' feast,
And shove away the worthy bidden guest;

86. *Mincius:* a river in northern Italy.
96. *Hippotades:* another name for Æolus, god of the winds.
99. *Panope:* one of the Nereids, or sea nymphs.
103. *Camus:* ancient god of the river Cam.
106. *sanguine flower:* the hyacinth, created by Apollo in honor of the youth.
Hyacinth, whom he killed by accident.
109. *The Pilot:* St. Peter.
114. *Anow:* enough.

Blind mouths! that scarce themselves know how to hold
A sheep-hook, or have learn'd aught else the least   120
That to the faithful herdman's art belongs!
What recks it them? What need they? They are sped;
And when they list, their lean and flashy songs
Grate on their scrannel pipes of wretched straw,
The hungry Sheep look up, and are not fed,   125
But swol'n with wind, and the rank mist they draw,
Rot inwardly, and foul contagion spread:
Besides what the grim Wolf with privy paw
Daily devours apace, and nothing said;
But that two-handed engine at the door   130
Stands ready to smite once, and smite no more.
      Return Alpheus, the dread voice is past,
That shrunk thy streams; Return Sicilian Muse,
And call the Vales, and bid them hither cast
Their bells, and flowrets of a thousand hues.   135
Ye valleys low where the mild whispers use,
Of shades and wanton winds, and gushing brooks,
On whose fresh lap the swart star sparely looks,
Throw hither all your quaint enamel'd eyes,
That on the green turf suck the honied showers,   140
And purple all the ground with vernal flowers.
Bring the rathe primrose that forsaken dies,
The tufted crow-toe, and pale jessamine,
The white pink, and the pansy freak'd with jet,
The glowing violet.   145
The musk-rose, and the well attir'd woodbine,
With cowslips wan that hang the pensive head,
And every flower that sad embroidery wears:
Bid Amarantus all his beauty shed,
And daffadillies fill their cups with tears,   150
To strew the laureate hearse where Lycid lies.
For so to interpose a little ease,
Let our frail thoughts dally with false surmise.
Ay me! Whilst thee the shores, and sounding seas
Wash far away, where e'er thy bones are hurl'd,   155
Whether beyond the stormy Hebrides

142. *rathe*: early.

Where thou perhaps under the whelming tide
Visit'st the bottom of the monstrous world;
Or whether thou to our moist vows deny'd,
Sleep'st by the fable of Bellerus old,   16
Where the great vision of the guarded mount
Looks toward Namancos and Bayona's hold;
Look homeward Angel now, and melt with ruth;
And, O ye Dolphins, waft the hapless youth.

    Weep no more, woeful shepherds weep no more,   16
For Lycidas your sorrow is not dead,
Sunk though he be beneath the wat'ry floor.
So sinks the day star in the ocean bed,
And yet anon repairs his drooping head,
And tricks his beams, and with new spangled ore,   17
Flames in the forehead of the morning sky:
So Lycidas sunk low, but mounted high,
Through the dear might of him that walk'd the waves,
Where other groves, and other streams along,
With nectar pure his oozy locks he laves,   17
And hears the unexpressive nuptial song,
In the blest kingdoms meek of joy and love.
There entertain him all the Saints above,
In solemn troops, and sweet Societies
That sing, and singing in their glory move,   18
And wipe the tears forever from his eyes.
Now Lycidas the shepherds weep no more;
Henceforth thou art the genius of the shore,
In thy large recompense, and shalt be good
To all that wander in that perilous flood.   18
    Thus sang the uncouth Swain to th' oaks and rills,
While the still morn went out with sandals gray,
He touch'd the tender stops of various quills,
With eager thought warbling his *Doric* lay:
And now the Sun had stretch'd out all the hills,   19
And now was dropp'd into the western bay;

160. *Bellerus:* probably the name of a companion of the legendary Corineus for whom Cornwall was named; the precise fable is unknown.
162. *Namancos and Bayona:* Nemancos is a beautiful mountainous region in northwest Spain; Bayona is a coastal fortification nearby.

At last he rose, and twitch'd his mantle blue:
Tomorrow to fresh woods, and pastures new.

LADY, THAT IN THE PRIME
OF EARLIEST YOUTH

Lady, that in the prime of earliest youth
Wisely hast shunn'd the broad way and the green,
And with those few art eminently seen,
That labor up the hill of heav'nly truth,
The better part with Mary and with Ruth,   5
Chosen thou hast; and they that overween,
And at thy growing virtues fret their spleen,
No anger find in thee, but pity and ruth.
Thy care is fix'd and zealously attends
To fill thy odorous lamp with deeds of light,   10
And hope that reaps not shame. Therefore be sure
Thou, when the bridegroom with his feastful friends
Passes to bliss at the mid-hour of night,
Hast gain'd thy entrance, Virgin wise and pure.

WHEN FAITH AND LOVE WHICH
PARTED FROM THEE NEVER

When Faith and Love which parted from thee never,
Had ripen'd thy just soul to dwell with God,
Meekly thou didst resign this earthly load
Of Death, call'd Life; which us from Life doth sever.
Thy works and alms and all thy good endeavor   5
Stay'd not behind, nor in the grave were trod,
But as Faith pointed with her golden rod,
Follow'd thee up to joy and bliss for ever.
Love led them on, and Faith who knew them best
Thy handmaids, clad them o'er with purple beams   10
And azure wings, that up they flew so dress'd,
And speak the truth of thee in glorious themes
Before the Judge, who thenceforth bid thee rest
And drink thy fill of pure immortal streams.

WHEN I CONSIDER HOW MY LIGHT IS SPENT

When I consider how my light is spent,
Ere half my days, in this dark world and wide,
And that one talent which is death to hide,
Lodg'd with me useless, though my Soul more bent
To serve therewith my Maker, and present
My true account, lest he returning chide,
Doth God exact day-labor, light denied,
I fondly ask; But Patience to prevent
That murmur, soon replies, God doth not need
Either man's work or his own gifts, who best
Bear his mild yoke, they serve him best, his state
Is kingly. Thousands at his bidding speed
And post o'er land and ocean without rest:
They also serve who only stand and wait.

ON THE LATE MASSACRE IN PIEMONT*

Avenge, O Lord, thy slaughter'd Saints, whose bones
Lie scatter'd on the Alpine mountains cold,
Ev'n them who kept thy truth so pure of old
When all our Fathers worshipp'd stocks and stones,
Forget not: in thy book record their groans
Who were thy sheep and in their ancient fold
Slain by the bloody Piemontese that roll'd
Mother with infant down the rocks. Their moans
The Vales redoubl'd to the Hills, and they
To Heav'n. Their martyr'd blood and ashes sow
O'er all th' Italian fields where still doth sway
The triple Tyrant: that from these may grow
A hundred-fold, who having learnt thy way
Early may fly the Babylonian woe.

* In April, 1655, a group of Waldensian Protestants were cruelly massacred by soldiers whom they had received in friendship.
12. *The triple Tyrant:* the Pope, who wears a triple crown.
14. *Babylonian woe:* this expression picks up the Petrarchan concept of the Papal court as a modern Babylon.

TO MR. CYRIAC SKINNER

Cyriac, this three years' day, these eyes, though clear
To outward view of blemish or of spot,
Bereft of sight, their seeing have forgot:
Nor to their idle orbs doth day appear,
Or sun, or moon, or star, throughout the year,   5
Or man, or woman; yet I argue not
Against Heaven's hand, or will, nor bate one jot
Of heart or hope; but still bear up, and steer
Right onward. What supports me, dost thou ask?
The conscience, Friend, to have lost them overplied   10
In Liberty's defense, my noble task,
Of which all Europe rings from side to side.
This thought might lead me through this world's vain masque
Content, though blind, had I no other guide.

10. *conscience:* consciousness.

METHOUGHT I SAW MY LATE ESPOUSED SAINT

Methought I saw my late espoused Saint
Brought to me like Alcestis from the grave,
Whom Jove's great Son to her glad husband gave,
Rescu'd from death by force though pale and faint.
Mine as whom wash'd from spot of child-bed taint,   5
Purification in the old Law did save,
And such, as yet once more I trust to have
Full sight of her in heaven without restraint,
Came vested all in white, pure as her mind:
Her face was veil'd, yet to my fancied sight,   10
Love, sweetness, goodness, in her person shin'd
So clear, as in no face with more delight.
But O, as to embrace me she inclin'd,
I wak'd, she fled, and day brought back my night.

ℭ WILLIAM BLAKE was the son of a hosier who was prosperous enough to secure at least some education for his obviously gifted son. Young Blake's talent for drawing was manifest early, and he was sent to art school in the Strand. When he was only twelve he began to write original poetry.

William Blake

[1757-1827]

began to write original poetry. When he was fourteen he was apprenticed to an engraver. His master was kind and trained him in the trade which was to be the foundation for his art as well as his livelihood. After his apprenticeship he became a student at the Royal Academy, but his visionary bent and his taste in art led to inevitable conflicts with the academic artists. His support now mainly derived from his engraving work for booksellers.

Not long after his marriage in 1782 he opened his own printing shop. This venture failed. Blake and his wife then published his own *Songs of Innocence* (1789). Blake did all of the designing and execution of the elaborate drawings which surround each poem on the page; his wife assisted with the presswork and tinting. This volume and its companion *Songs of Experience* (1794) were the most successful union of his arts which he ever achieved. Yet neither was profitable as a publishing venture, and Blake's fortunes declined. He came to depend more and more on contracts for illustrating the books of others, but continued to publish works of his own. *The Book of Thel* (1789) and *The Marriage of Heaven and Hell* (1790), two earlier works, were followed by *Visions of the Daughters of Albion* (1793), *America* (1793), *Europe* (1794), *The Book of Urizen* (1794), *The Song of Los* (1795), *Jerusalem* (1804), and several others. Blake's mystical qualities intensified in his old age. His visions of a brighter world were coupled with prophetic insights into the corruption of his own environment. Blake died peacefully, but with his monumental work of illustrating the *Divina Commedia* only partially completed.

TO SPRING

O thou with dewy locks, who lookest down
Thro' the clear windows of the morning, turn
Thine angel eyes upon our western isle,
Which in full choir hails thy approach, O Spring!

The hills tell each other, and the list'ning   5
Valleys hear; all our longing eyes are turned
Up to thy bright pavilions: issue forth,
And let thy holy feet visit our clime.

Come o'er the eastern hills, and let our winds
Kiss thy perfumed garments; let us taste   10
Thy morn and evening breath; scatter thy pearls
Upon our love-sick land that mourns for thee.

O deck her forth with thy fair fingers; pour
Thy soft kisses on her bosom; and put
Thy golden crown upon her languish'd head,   15
Whose modest tresses were bound up for thee!

TO SUMMER

O thou, who passest thro' our valleys in
Thy strength, curb thy fierce steeds, allay the heat
That flames from their large nostrils! thou, O Summer,
Oft pitched'st here thy golden tent, and oft
Beneath our oaks hast slept, while we beheld   5
With joy thy ruddy limbs and flourishing hair.

Beneath our thickest shades we oft have heard
Thy voice, when noon upon his fervid car
Rode o'er the deep of heaven; beside our springs
Sit down, and in our mossy valleys, on   10
Some bank beside a river clear, throw thy
Silk draperies off, and rush into the stream:
Our valleys love the Summer in his pride.

Our bards are fam'd who strike the silver wire:
Our youth are bolder than the southern swains: 15

Our maidens fairer in the sprightly dance:
We lack not songs, nor instruments of joy,
Nor echoes sweet, nor waters clear as heaven,
Nor laurel wreaths against the sultry heat.

TO AUTUMN

O Autumn, laden with fruit, and stained
With the blood of the grape, pass not, but sit
Beneath my shady roof; there thou may'st rest,
And tune thy jolly voice to my fresh pipe;
And all the daughters of the year shall dance!
Sing now the lusty song of fruits and flowers.

"The narrow bud opens her beauties to
The sun, and love runs in her thrilling veins;
Blossoms hang round the brows of morning, and
Flourish down the bright cheek of modest eve,
Till clust'ring Summer breaks forth into singing,
And feather'd clouds strew flowers round her head.

"The spirits of the air live on the smells
Of fruit; and joy, with pinions light, roves round
The gardens, or sits singing in the trees."
Thus sang the jolly Autumn as he sat;
Then rose, girded himself, and o'er the bleak
Hills fled from our sight; but left his golden load.

TO WINTER

O Winter! bar thine adamantine doors:
The north is thine; there hast thou built thy dark
Deep-founded habitation. Shake not thy roofs,
Nor bend thy pillars with thine iron car.

He hears me not, but o'er the yawning deep
Rides heavy; his storms are unchain'd, sheathed
In ribbed steel; I dare not lift mine eyes,
For he hath rear'd his sceptre o'er the world.

Lo! now the direful monster, whose skin clings
To his strong bones, strides o'er the groaning rocks:

He withers all in silence, and his hand
Unclothes the earth, and freezes up frail life.

He takes his seat upon the cliffs; the mariner
Cries in vain. Poor little wretch! that deal'st
With storms, till heaven smiles, and the monster   15
Is driv'n yelling to his caves beneath mount Hecla.

TO THE EVENING STAR

Thou fair-hair'd angel of the evening,
Now, whilst the sun rests on the mountains, light
Thy bright torch of love; thy radiant crown
Put on, and smile upon our evening bed!
Smile on our loves, and, while thou drawest the   5
Blue curtains of the sky, scatter thy silver dew
On every flower that shuts its sweet eyes
In timely sleep. Let thy west wind sleep on
The lake; speak silence with thy glimmering eyes,
And wash the dusk with silver. Soon, full soon,   10
Dost thou withdraw; then the wolf rages wide,
And the lion glares thro' the dun forest:
The fleeces of our flocks are cover'd with
Thy sacred dew: protect them with thine influence.

TO MORNING

O holy virgin! clad in purest white,
Unlock heav'n's golden gates, and issue forth;
Awake the dawn that sleeps in heaven; let light
Rise from the chambers of the east, and bring
The honied dew that cometh on waking day.   5
O radiant morning, salute the sun,
Rous'd like a huntsman to the chase, and, with
Thy buskin'd feet, appear upon our hills.

FAIR ELENOR

The bell struck one, and shook the silent tower;
The graves give up their dead: fair Elenor

Walk'd by the castle gate, and looked in.
A hollow groan ran thro' the dreary vaults.

She shriek'd aloud, and sunk upon the steps
On the cold stone her pale cheeks. Sickly smells
Of death issue as from a sepulchre,
And all is silent but the sighing vaults.

Chill death withdraws his hand, and she revives;
Amaz'd, she finds herself upon her feet,
And, like a ghost, thro' narrow passages
Walking, feeling the cold walls with her hands.

Fancy returns, and now she thinks of bones,
And grinning skulls, and corruptible death,
Wrap'd in his shroud; and now fancies she hears
Deep sighs, and sees pale sickly ghosts gliding.

At length, no fancy, but reality
Distracts her. A rushing sound, and the feet
Of one that fled, approaches—Ellen stood,
Like a dumb statue, froze to stone with fear.

The wretch approaches, crying, "The deed is done;
Take this, and send it by whom thou wilt send;
It is my life—send it to Elenor:—
He's dead, and howling after me for blood!

"Take this," he cry'd; and thrust into her arms
A wet napkin, wrap'd about; then rush'd
Past, howling: she receiv'd into her arms
Pale death, and follow'd on the wings of fear.

They pass'd swift thro' the outer gate; the wretch,
Howling, leap'd o'er the wall into the moat,
Stifling in mud. Fair Ellen pass'd the bridge,
And heard a gloomy voice cry, "Is it done?"

As the deer wounded, Ellen flew over
The pathless plain; as the arrows that fly
By night, destruction flies, and strikes in darkness.
She fled from fear, till at her house arriv'd.

Her maids await her; on her bed she falls,
That bed of joy, where erst her lord hath press'd:
"Ah, woman's-fear!" she cry'd; "Ah, cursed duke!
Ah, my dear lord! ah, wretched Elenor! 40

"My lord was like a flower upon the brows
Of lusty May! Ah, life as frail as flower!
O ghastly death! withdraw thy cruel hand,
Seek'st thou that flow'r to deck thy horrid temples?

"My lord was like a star, in highest heav'n 45
Drawn down to earth by spells and wickedness;
My lord was like the opening eyes of day,
When western winds creep softly o'er the flowers:

"But he is darken'd; like the summer's noon,
Clouded; fall'n like the stately tree, cut down; 50
The breath of heaven dwelt among his leaves.
O Elenor, weak woman, fill'd with woe!"

Thus having spoke, she raised up her head,
And saw the bloody napkin by her side,
Which in her arms she brought; and now, tenfold 55
More terrified, saw it unfold itself.

Her eyes were fix'd; the bloody cloth unfolds,
Disclosing to her sight the murder'd head
Of her dear lord, all ghastly pale, clotted
With gory blood; it groan'd, and thus it spake: 60

"O Elenor, I am thy husband's head,
Who, sleeping on the stones of yonder tower,
Was 'reft of life by the accursed duke!
A hired villain turn'd my sleep to death!

"O Elenor, beware the cursed duke; 65
O give not him thy hand now I am dead;
He seeks thy love, who, coward, in the night,
Hired a villain to bereave my life."

She sat with dead cold limbs, stiffen'd to stone;
She took the gory head up in her arms; 70
She kiss'd the pale lips; she had no tears to shed;
She hugg'd it to her breast, and groan'd her last.

SONG

How Sweet I Roam'd from Field to Field

How sweet I roam'd from field to field,
    And tasted all the summer's pride,
'Til I the prince of love beheld,
    Who in the sunny beams did glide!

He shew'd me lilies for my hair,
    And blushing roses for my brow;
He led me through his gardens fair,
    Where all his golden pleasures grow.

With sweet May dews my wings were wet,
    And Phœbus fir'd my vocal rage;
He caught me in his silken net,
    And shut me in his golden cage.

He loves to sit and hear me sing,
    Then, laughing, sports and plays with me;
Then stretches out my golden wing,
    And mocks my loss of liberty.

SONG

My Silks and Fine Array

My silks and fine array,
    My smiles and languish'd air,
By love are driv'n away;
    And mournful lean Despair
Brings me yew to deck my grave:
Such end true lovers have.

His face is fair as heav'n,
    When springing buds unfold;
O why to him was't giv'n,
    Whose heart is wintry cold?
His breast is love's all worship'd tomb,
Where all love's pilgrims come.

Bring me an axe and spade,
  Bring me a winding sheet;
When I my grave have made,
  Let winds and tempests beat:
Then down I'll lie, as cold as clay.
True love doth pass away!

15

SONG

Fresh from the Dewy Hill, the Merry Year

Fresh from the dewy hill, the merry year
Smiles on my head, and mounts his flaming car;
Round my young brows the laurel wreathes a shade,
And rising glories beam around my head.

My feet are wing'd, while o'er the dewy lawn
I meet my maiden, risen like the morn:
Oh bless those holy feet, like angels' feet;
Oh bless those limbs, beaming with heav'nly light!

5

Like as an angel glitt'ring in the sky
In times of innocence and holy joy;
The joyful shepherd stops his grateful song
To hear the music of an angel's tongue.

10

So when she speaks, the voice of Heaven I hear:
So when we walk, nothing impure comes near;
Each field seems Eden, and each calm retreat;
Each village seems the haunt of holy feet.

15

But that sweet village, where my black-ey'd maid
Closes her eyes in sleep beneath night's shade,
Whene'er I enter, more than mortal fire
Burns in my soul, and does my song inspire.

20

SONG

When Early Morn Walks Forth in Sober Gray

When early morn walks forth in sober gray,
Then to my black ey'd maid I haste away;

When evening sits beneath her dusky bow'r,
And gently sighs away the silent hour,
The village bell alarms, away I go,
And the vale darkens at my pensive woe.

To that sweet village, where my black ey'd maid
Doth drop a tear beneath the silent shade,
I turn my eyes; and, pensive as I go,
Curse my black stars, and bless my pleasing woe.

Oft when the summer sleeps among the trees,
Whisp'ring faint murmurs to the scanty breeze,
I walk the village round; if at her side
A youth doth walk in stolen joy and pride,
I curse my stars in bitter grief and woe,
That made my love so high, and me so low.

O should she e'er prove false, his limbs I'd tear,
And throw all pity on the burning air;
I'd curse bright fortune for my mixed lot,
And then I'd die in peace, and be forgot.

MOTTO TO THE SONGS OF INNOCENCE AND OF EXPERIENCE

The Good are attracted by Men's perceptions,
And think not for themselves;
Till Experience teaches them to catch
And to cage the Fairies and Elves.

And then the Knave begins to snarl
And the Hypocrite to howl;
And all his good Friends shew their private ends,
And the Eagle is known from the Owl.

FROM *SONGS OF INNOCENCE*

The Lamb

Little Lamb, who made thee?
Dost thou know who made thee?
Gave thee life, and bid thee feed

By the stream and o'er the mead;
Gave thee clothing of delight,   5
Softest clothing, wooly, bright;
Gave thee such a tender voice,
Making all the vales rejoice?
    Little Lamb, who made thee?
    Dost thou know who made thee?   10

    Little Lamb, I'll tell thee,
    Little Lamb, I'll tell thee:
He is called by thy name,
For he calls himself a Lamb.
He is meek, and he is mild;   15
He became a little child.
I a child, and thou a lamb,
We are called by his name.
    Little Lamb, God bless thee!
    Little Lamb, God bless thee!   20

The Blossom

Merry, Merry Sparrow!
Under leaves so green
A happy Blossom
Sees you swift as arrow
Seek your cradle narrow   5
Near my Bosom.

Pretty, Pretty Robin!
Under leaves so green
A happy Blossom
Hears you sobbing, sobbing,   10
Pretty, Pretty Robin,
Near my Bosom.

The Chimney Sweeper

When my mother died I was very young,
And my father sold me while yet my tongue
Could scarcely cry "'weep! 'weep! 'weep! 'weep!"
So your chimneys I sweep, and in soot I sleep.

There's little Tom Dacre, who cried when his head,
That curl'd like a lamb's back, was shav'd: so I said
"Hush, Tom! never mind it, for when your head's bare
You know that the soot cannot spoil your white hair."

And so he was quiet, and that very night,
As Tom was a-sleeping, he had such a sight!
That thousands of sweepers, Dick, Joe, Ned, and Jack,
Were all of them lock'd up in coffins of black.

And by came an Angel who had a bright key,
And he open'd the coffins and set them all free;
Then down a green plain leaping, laughing, they run,
And wash in a river, and shine in the Sun.

Then naked and white, all their bags left behind,
They rise upon clouds and sport in the wind;
And the Angel told Tom, if he'd be a good boy,
He'd have God for his father, and never want joy.

And so Tom awoke; and we rose in the dark,
And got with our bags and our brushes to work.
Tho' the morning was cold, Tom was happy and warm;
So if all do their duty they need not fear harm.

Nurse's Song

When the voices of children are heard on the green
And laughing is heard on the hill,
My heart is at rest within my breast
        And everything else is still.

"Then come home, my children, the sun is gone down
And the dews of night arise;
Come, come, leave off play, and let us away
Till the morning appears in the skies."

"No, no, let us play, for it is yet day
And we cannot go to sleep;
Besides, in the sky the little birds fly
And the hills are all cover'd with sheep."

"Well, well, go and play till the light fades away
And then go home to bed."

The little ones leaped and shouted and laugh'd   15
  And all the hills echoed.

Infant Joy

"I have no name:
I am but two days old."
What shall I call thee?
"I happy am,
Joy is my name."   5
Sweet joy befall thee!

Pretty joy!
Sweet joy but two days old,
Sweet joy I call thee:
  Thou dost smile,   10
I sing the while,
Sweet joy befall thee!

Holy Thursday

'Twas on a Holy Thursday, their innocent faces clean,
The children walking two and two, in red and blue and green,
Gray-headed beadles walk'd before, with wands as white as snow,
Till into the high dome of Paul's they like Thames' waters flow.

O what a multitude they seem'd, these flowers of London town!   5
Seated in companies they sit with radiance all their own.
The hum of multitudes was there, but multitudes of lambs,
Thousands of little boys and girls raising their innocent hands.

Now like a mighty wind they raise to heaven the voice of song,
Or like harmonious thunderings the seats of Heaven among.   10
Beneath them sit the aged men, wise guardians of the poor;
Then cherish pity, lest you drive an angel from your door.

  4. *Paul's:* St. Paul's Cathedral in London.

The Little Black Boy

My mother bore me in the southern wild,
And I am black, but O! my soul is white;

White as an angel is the English child,
But I am black, as if bereav'd of light.

My mother taught me underneath a tree,
And sitting down before the heat of day,
She took me on her lap and kissed me,
And pointing to the east, began to say:

"Look on the rising sun: there God does live,
And gives his light, and gives his heat away;
And flowers and trees and beasts and men receive
Comfort in morning, joy in the noonday.

"And we are put on earth a little space,
That we may learn to bear the beams of love;
And these black bodies and this sunburnt face
Is but a cloud, and like a shady grove.

"For when our souls have learn'd the heat to bear,
The cloud will vanish; we shall hear his voice,
Saying: 'Come out from the grove, my love and care,
And round my golden tent like lambs rejoice.' "

Thus did my mother say, and kissed me;
And thus I say to little English boy:
When I from black and he from white cloud free,
And round the tent of God like lambs we joy,

I'll shade him from the heat, till he can bear
To lean in joy upon our father's knee;
And then I'll stand and stroke his silver hair,
And be like him, and he will then love me.

FROM *SONGS OF EXPERIENCE*

The Tyger

Tyger! Tyger! burning bright
In the forests of the night,
What immortal hand or eye
Could frame thy fearful symmetry?

In what distant deeps or skies   5
Burnt the fire of thine eyes?
On what wings dare he aspire?
What the hand dare seize the fire?

And what shoulder, and what art,
Could twist the sinews of thy heart?   10
And when thy heart began to beat,
What dread hand? and what dread feet?

What the hammer? what the chain?
In what furnace was thy brain?
What the anvil? what dread grasp   15
Dare its deadly terrors clasp?

When the stars threw down their spears,
And water'd heaven with their tears,
Did he smile his work to see?
Did he who made the Lamb make thee?   20

Tyger! Tyger! burning bright
In the forests of the night,
What immortal hand or eye,
Dare frame thy fearful symmetry?

The Sick Rose

O rose, thou art sick!
The invisible worm
That flies in the night,
In the howling storm,

Has found out thy bed   5
Of crimson joy,
And his dark secret love
Does thy life destroy.

The Chimney Sweeper

A little black thing among the snow,
Crying " 'weep! 'weep!" in notes of woe!

"Where are thy father and mother? say?"
"They are both gone up to the church to pray.

"Because I was happy upon the heath,
And smil'd among the winter's snow,
They clothed me in the clothes of death,
And taught me to sing the notes of woe.

"And because I am happy and dance and sing,
They think they have done me no injury,
And are gone to praise God and his Priest and King,
Who make up a heaven of our misery."

Nurse's Song

When the voices of children are heard on the green
And whisp'rings are in the dale,
The days of my youth rise fresh in my mind,
My face turns green and pale.

Then come home, my children, the sun is gone down,
And the dews of night arise;
Your spring and your day are wasted in play,
And your winter and night in disguise.

Infant Sorrow

My mother groan'd! my father wept.
Into the dangerous world I leapt:
Helpless, naked, piping loud:
Like a fiend hid in a cloud.

Struggling in my father's hands,
Striving against my swadling bands,
Bound and weary I thought best
To sulk upon my mother's breast.

London

I wander thro' each charter'd street,
Near where the charter'd Thames does flow,

And mark in every face I meet
Marks of weakness, marks of woe.

In every cry of every Man,   5
In every Infant's cry of fear,
In every voice, in every ban,
The mind-forg'd manacles I hear.

How the Chimney-sweeper's cry
Every black'ning Church appalls;   10
And the hapless Soldier's sigh
Runs in blood down Palace walls.

But most thro' midnight streets I hear
How the youthful Harlot's curse
Blasts the new born Infant's tear,   15
And blights with plagues the Marriage hearse.

My Pretty Rose-tree

A flower was offer'd to me,
Such a flower as May never bore;
But I said "I've a Pretty Rose-tree,"
And I passed the sweet flower o'er.

Then I went to my Pretty Rose-tree,   5
To tend her by day and by night;
But my Rose turn'd away with jealousy,
And her thorns were my only delight.

Ah! Sun-flower

Ah, Sun-flower! weary of time,
Who countest the steps of the Sun,
Seeking after that sweet golden clime
Where the traveller's journey is done:

Where the Youth pined away with desire,   5
And the pale Virgin shrouded in snow
Arise from their graves, and aspire
Where my Sun-flower wishes to go.

The Lilly

The modest Rose puts forth a thorn,
The humble Sheep a threat'ning horn;
While the Lilly white shall in Love delight,
Nor a thorn, nor a threat, stain her beauty bright.

The Garden of Love

I went to the Garden of Love,
And saw what I never had seen:
A Chapel was built in the midst,
Where I used to play on the green.

And the gates of this Chapel were shut,
And "Thou shalt not" writ over the door;
So I turn'd to the Garden of Love
That so many sweet flowers bore;

And I saw it was filled with graves,
And tomb-stones where flowers should be;
And Priests in black gowns were walking their rounds,
And binding with briars my joys and desires.

A Poison Tree

I was angry with my friend:
I told my wrath, my wrath did end.
I was angry with my foe:
I told it not, my wrath did grow.

And I water'd it in fears,
Night and morning with my tears;
And I sunned it with smiles,
And with soft deceitful wiles.

And it grew both day and night,
Till it bore an apple bright;
And my foe beheld it shine,
And he knew that it was mine,

And into my garden stole
When the night had veil'd the pole:
In the morning glad I see   15
My foe outstretch'd beneath the tree.

THE BOOK OF THEL

Thel's Motto

Does the Eagle know what is in the pit?
Or wilt thou go ask the Mole?
Can Wisdom be put in a silver rod?
Or Love in a golden bowl?

1

The daughters of the Seraphim led round their sunny flocks,
All but the youngest: she in paleness sought the secret air,
To fade away like morning beauty from her mortal day:
Down by the river of Adona her soft voice is heard,
And thus her gentle lamentation falls like morning dew: 5

"O life of this our spring! why fades the lotus of the water,
Why fade these children of the spring, born but to smile and fall?
Ah! Thel is like a wat'ry bow, and like a parting cloud;
Like a reflection in a glass; like shadows in the water;
Like dreams of infants, like a smile upon an infant's face;   10
Like the dove's voice; like transient day; like music in the air.
Ah! gentle may I lay me down, and gentle rest my head,
And gentle sleep the sleep of death, and gentle hear the voice
Of him that walketh in the garden in the evening time."

The Lilly of the valley, breathing in the humble grass,   15
Answer'd the lovely maid and said: "I am a wat'ry weed,
And I am very small and love to dwell in lowly vales;
So weak, the gilded butterfly scarce perches on my head.
Yet I am visited from heaven, and he that smiles on all
Walks in the valley and each morn over me spreads his hand,   20
Saying, 'Rejoice, thou humble grass, thou new-born lilly flower,
Thou gentle maid of silent valleys and of modest brooks;
For thou shalt be clothed in light, and fed with morning manna,

Till summer's heat melts thee beside the fountains and the springs
To flourish in eternal vales.' Then why should Thel complain?
Why should the mistress of the vales of Har utter a sigh?''

She ceas'd and smil'd in tears, then sat down in her silver shrine.

Thel answer'd: "O thou little virgin of the peaceful valley,
Giving to those that cannot crave, the voiceless, the o'ertired;
Thy breath doth nourish the innocent lamb, he smells thy milky
        garments,
He crops thy flowers while thou sittest smiling in his face,
Wiping his mild and meekin mouth from all contagious taints.
Thy wine doth purify the golden honey; thy perfume,
Which thou dost scatter on every little blade of grass that springs,
Revives the milked cow, and tames the fire-breathing steed.
But Thel is like a faint cloud kindled at the rising sun:
I vanish from my pearly throne, and who shall find my place?''

"Queen of the vales," the Lilly answer'd, "ask the tender cloud,
And it shall tell thee why it glitters in the morning sky,
And why it scatters its bright beauty thro' the humid air.
Descend, O little Cloud, and hover before the eyes of Thel.''

The Cloud descended, and the Lilly bow'd her modest head
And went to mind her numerous charge among the verdant grass.

2

"O little Cloud," the virgin said, "I charge thee tell to me
Why thou complainest not when in one hour thou fade away:
Then we shall seek thee, but not find. Ah! Thel is like to thee:
I pass away: yet I complain, and no one hears my voice.''

The Cloud then shew'd his golden head and his bright form
        emerg'd,
Hovering and glittering on the air before the face of Thel.

"O virgin, know'st thou not our steeds drink of the golden
        springs
Where Luvah doth renew his horses? Look'st thou on my youth,
And fearest thou, because I vanish and am seen no more,
Nothing remains? O maid, I tell thee, when I pass away

32. *meekin*: humble.

It is to tenfold life, to love, to peace and raptures holy:
Unseen descending, weigh my light wings upon balmy flowers,   55
And court the fair-eyed dew to take me to her shining tent:
The weeping virgin, trembling kneels before the risen sun,
Till we arise link'd in a golden band and never part,
But walk united, bearing food to all our tender flowers."

"Dost thou, O little Cloud? I fear that I am not like thee,   60
For I walk thro' the vales of Har, and smell the sweetest flowers,
But I feed not the little flowers; I hear the warbling birds,
But I feed not the warbling birds; they fly and seek their food:
But Thel delights in these no more, because I fade away;
And all shall say, 'Without a use this shining woman liv'd,   65
Or did she only live to be at death the food of worms?' "

The Cloud reclin'd upon his airy throne and answer'd thus:

"Then if thou art the food of worms, O virgin of the skies,
How great thy use, how great thy blessing! Every thing that lives
Lives not alone nor for itself. Fear not, and I will call   70
The weak worm from its lowly bed, and thou shalt hear its voice.
Come forth, worm of the silent valley, to thy pensive queen."

The helpless worm arose, and sat upon the Lilly's leaf,
And the bright Cloud sail'd on, to find his partner in the vale.

3

Then Thel astonish'd view'd the Worm upon its dewy bed.   75

"Art thou a Worm? Image of weakness, art thou but a Worm?
I see thee like an infant wrapped in the Lilly's leaf.
Ah! weep not, little voice, thou canst not speak, but thou canst
    weep.
Is this a Worm? I see thee lay helpless and naked, weeping,
And none to answer, none to cherish thee with mother's smiles."   80

The Clod of Clay heard the Worm's voice and rais'd her pitying
    head:
She bow'd over the weeping infant, and her life exhal'd
In milky fondness: then on Thel she fix'd her humble eyes.

"O beauty of the vales of Har! we live not for ourselves.
Thou seest me the meanest thing, and so I am indeed.   85

My bosom of itself is cold, and of itself is dark;
But he, that loves the lowly, pours his oil upon my head,
And kisses me, and binds his nuptial bands around my breast,
And says: 'Thou mother of my children, I have loved thee
And I have given thee a crown that none can take away.'   9
But how this is, sweet maid, I know not, and I cannot know;
I ponder, and I cannot ponder; yet I live and love."

The daughter of beauty wip'd her pitying tears with her white
        veil,
And said: "Alas! I knew not this, and therefore did I weep.
That God would love a Worm I knew, and punish the evil foot   9
That willful bruis'd its helpless form; but that he cherish'd it
With milk and oil I never knew, and therefore did I weep;
And I complain'd in the mild air, because I fade away,
And lay me down in thy cold bed, and leave my shining lot."

"Queen of the vales," the matron Clay answer'd, "I heard thy sighs, 100
And all thy moans flew o'er my roof, but I have call'd them down.
Wilt thou, O Queen, enter my house? 'Tis given thee to enter
And to return: fear nothing, enter with thy virgin feet."

                                4

The eternal gates' terrific porter lifted the northern bar:
Thel enter'd in and saw the secrets of the land unknown.   105
She saw the couches of the dead, and where the fibrous roots
Of every heart on earth infixes deep its restless twists:
A land of sorrows and of tears where never smile was seen.

She wander'd in the land of clouds thro' valleys dark, list'ning
Dolors and lamentations; waiting oft beside a dewy grave   110
She stood in silence, list'ning to the voices of the ground,
Till to her own grave plot she came, and there she sat down,
And heard this voice of sorrow breathed from the hollow pit.

"Why cannot the Ear be closed to its own destruction?
Or the glist'ning Eye to the poison of a smile?   115
Why are Eyelids stor'd with arrows ready drawn,
Where a thousand fighting men in ambush lie?
Or an Eye of gifts and graces show'ring fruits and coined gold?
Why a Tongue impress'd with honey from every wind?

Why an Ear, a whirlpool fierce to draw creations in?   120
Why a Nostril wide inhaling terror, trembling, and affright?
Why a tender curb upon the youthful burning boy?
Why a little curtain of flesh on the bed of our desire?"

The Virgin started from her seat, and with a shriek
Fled back unhinder'd till she came into the vales of Har.   125

℘ WILLIAM WORDSWORTH was strikingly influenced in his intellectual development by the beauties of the Lake District in the west of England. He was born in Cumberland and was sent to grammar school at Hawkshead. There he gave little time to systematic study, preferring to read what struck his fancy and to take long walks around the countryside. Wordsworth's indifference to the academic life continued during his career at St. John's College, Cambridge. Before and after his graduation (without honors) he left England for trips through

William Wordsworth

[1770-1850]

France. Revolutionary ideas absorbed him and he became deeply committed to political reform. In the late 1790's, most of these energies were channeled into his devotion to the reform of poetic conventions. In 1798, with the collaboration of his friend Samuel Taylor Coleridge, he published *Lyrical Ballads*. In the preface which he added to the second edition of 1800, Wordsworth explained his concern with the lives of ordinary people and his conviction that the language of poetry should be modeled after the normal talk of the folk.

When his precarious financial circumstances and health permitted, Wordsworth traveled throughout Britain and also made a trip to Germany, but home was always in his familiar Lake Country. Only in the late 1830's did Wordsworth achieve any particular fame. Previous volumes, *Poems in Two Volumes* (1807), *The Excursion* (1814), *The White Doe of Rylstone* (1815), and *Peter Bell* (1819), now recognized as important, rarely met expenses when first published. By 1843, however, Wordsworth's early radicalism had mellowed sufficiently and his fame had increased so much that he was the logical choice for poet laureate on the death of Southey. His public poems were few indeed, but in 1850, after his death, Wordsworth's great work, *The Prelude*, was published. He had completed the first version of this long autobiographical poem as early as 1805. It was originally intended as a beginning to his ultimate masterpiece, *The Recluse*, which was never completed; *The Prelude*, much revised, was printed only when the grand scheme was forever foiled by his death.

MY HEART LEAPS UP WHEN I BEHOLD

My heart leaps up when I behold
   A rainbow in the sky:
So was it when my life began;
So is it now I am a man;
So be it when I shall grow old,   5
   Or let me die!
The Child is father of the Man;
And I could wish my days to be
Bound each to each by natural piety.

LUCY GRAY

Or, Solitude

Oft I had heard of Lucy Gray:
And, when I crossed the wild,
I chanced to see at break of day
The solitary child.

No mate, no comrade Lucy knew;   5
She dwelt on a wide moor,
—The sweetest thing that ever grew
Beside a human door!

You yet may spy the fawn at play,
The hare upon the green;   10
But the sweet face of Lucy Gray
Will never more be seen.

"To-night will be a stormy night—
You to the town must go;
And take a lantern, Child, to light   15
Your mother through the snow."

"That, Father! will I gladly do:
'Tis scarcely afternoon—
The minster-clock has just struck two,
And yonder is the moon!"   20

At this the Father raised his hook,
And snapped a faggot-band;
He plied his work;—and Lucy took
The lantern in her hand.

Not blither is the mountain roe: 25
With many a wanton stroke
Her feet disperse the powdery snow,
That rises up like smoke.

The storm came on before its time:
She wandered up and down;   30
And many a hill did Lucy climb:
But never reached the town.

The wretched parents all that night
Went shouting far and wide;
But there was neither sound nor sight   35
To serve them for a guide.

At day-break on a hill they stood
That overlooked the moor;
And thence they saw the bridge of wood,
A furlong from their door.   40

They wept—and, turning homeward, cried,
"In heaven we all shall meet";
—When in the snow the mother spied
The print of Lucy's feet.

Then downwards from the steep hill's edge   45
They tracked the footmarks small;
And through the broken hawthorn hedge,
And by the long stone-wall;

And then an open field they crossed:
The marks were still the same;   50
They tracked them on, nor ever lost;
And to the bridge they came.

They followed from the snowy bank
Those footmarks, one by one,

Into the middle of the plank;   55
And further there were none!

—Yet some maintain that to this day
She is a living child;
That you may see sweet Lucy Gray
Upon the lonesome wild.   60

O'er rough and smooth she trips along,
And never looks behind;
And sings a solitary song
That whistles in the wind.

THERE WAS A BOY *

There was a Boy; ye knew him well, ye cliffs
And islands of Winander!—many a time,
At evening, when the earliest stars began
To move along the edges of the hills,
Rising or setting, would he stand alone,   5
Beneath the trees, or by the glimmering lake;
And there, with fingers interwoven, both hands
Pressed closely palm to palm and to his mouth
Uplifted, he, as through an instrument,
Blew mimic hootings to the silent owls,   10
That they might answer him.—And they would shout
Across the watery vale, and shout again,
Responsive to his call,—with quivering peals,
And long halloos, and screams, and echoes loud
Redoubled and redoubled; concourse wild   15
Of jocund din! And, when there came a pause
Of silence such as baffled his best skill:
Then sometimes, in that silence, while he hung
Listening, a gentle shock of mild surprise
Has carried far into his heart the voice   20
Of mountain-torrents; or the visible scene
Would enter unawares into his mind

* These lines subsequently appeared as part of *The Prelude*, Book V,
ll. 364–397.

With all its solemn imagery, its rocks,
Its woods, and that uncertain heaven received
Into the bosom of the steady lake.   25

    This boy was taken from his mates, and died
In childhood, ere he was full twelve years old.
Pre-eminent in beauty is the vale
Where he was born and bred: the churchyard hangs
Upon a slope above the village-school;   30
And through that churchyard when my way has led
On summer-evenings, I believe that there
A long half-hour together I have stood
Mute—looking at the grave in which he lies!

A NIGHT-PIECE

        ——The sky is overcast
With a continuous cloud of texture close,
Heavy and wan, all whitened by the Moon,
Which through that veil is indistinctly seen,
A dull, contracted circle, yielding light   5
So feebly spread that not a shadow falls,
Chequering the ground—from rock, plant, tree, or tower.
At length a pleasant instantaneous gleam
Startles the pensive traveller while he treads
His lonesome path, with unobserving eye   10
Bent earthwards; he looks up—the clouds are split
Asunder,—and above his head he sees
The clear Moon, and the glory of the heavens.
There in a black-blue vault she sails along,
Followed by multitudes of stars, that, small   15
And sharp, and bright, along the dark abyss
Drive as she drives: how fast they wheel away,
Yet vanish not!—the wind is in the tree,
But they are silent;—still they roll along
Immeasurably distant; and the vault,   20
Built round by those white clouds, enormous clouds,
Still deepens its unfathomable depth.
At length the vision closes; and the mind,

Not undisturbed by the delight it feels,
Which slowly settles into peaceful calm,   25
Is left to muse upon the solemn scene.

YEW-TREES

There is a yew-tree, pride of Lorton Vale,
Which to this day stands single, in the midst
Of its own darkness, as it stood of yore:
Not loth to furnish weapons for the bands
Of Umfraville or Percy ere they marched   5
To Scotland's heaths; or those that crossed the sea
And drew their sounding bows at Azincour,
Perhaps at earlier Crecy, or Poictiers.
Of vast circumference and gloom profound
This solitary tree! a living thing   10
Produced too slowly ever to decay;
Of form and aspect too magnificent
To be destroyed. But worthier still of note
Are those fraternal four of Borrowdale,
Joined in one solemn and capacious grove;   15
Huge trunks! and each particular trunk a growth
Of intertwisted fibres serpentine
Up-coiling, and inveterately convolved;
Nor uninformed with phantasy, and looks
That threaten the profane; a pillared shade,   20
Upon whose grassless floor of red-brown hue,
By sheddings from the pining umbrage tinged
Perennially—beneath whose sable roof
Of boughs, as if for festal purpose decked
With unrejoicing berries—ghostly shapes   25
May meet at noontide; fear and trembling hope,
Silence and foresight; Death the Skeleton
And Time the Shadow;—there to celebrate,
As in a natural temple scattered o'er
With altars undisturbed of mossy stone,   30
United worship; or in mute repose
To lie, and listen to the mountain flood
Murmuring from Glaramara's inmost caves.

SHE WAS A PHANTOM OF DELIGHT

She was a phantom of delight
When first she gleamed upon my sight;
A lovely apparition, sent
To be a moment's ornament;
Her eyes as stars of twilight fair;   5
Like twilight's, too, her dusky hair;
But all things else about her drawn
From May-time and the cheerful dawn;
A dancing shape, an image gay,
To haunt, to startle, and way-lay.   10

I saw her upon nearer view,
A spirit, yet a woman too!
Her household motions light and free,
And steps of virgin-liberty;
A countenance in which did meet   15
Sweet records, promises as sweet;
A creature not too bright or good
For human nature's daily food;
For transient sorrows, simple wiles,
Praise, blame, love, kisses, tears, and smiles.   20

And now I see with eye serene
The very pulse of the machine;
A being breathing thoughtful breath,
A traveller between life and death;
The reason firm, the temperate will,   25
Endurance, foresight, strength, and skill;
A perfect woman, nobly planned,
To warn, to comfort, and command;
And yet a spirit still, and bright
With something of angelic light.   30

A SLUMBER DID MY SPIRIT SEAL

A slumber did my spirit seal;
    I had no human fears:
She seemed a thing that could not feel
    The touch of earthly years.

No motion has she now, no force;   5
　　She neither hears nor sees;
Rolled round in earth's diurnal course,
　　With rocks, and stones, and trees.

I WANDERED LONELY AS A CLOUD

I wandered lonely as a cloud
That floats on high o'er vales and hills,
When all at once I saw a crowd,
A host, of golden daffodils;
Beside the lake, beneath the trees,   5
Fluttering and dancing in the breeze.

Continuous as the stars that shine
And twinkle on the milky way,
They stretched in never-ending line
Along the margin of a bay: 10
Ten thousand saw I at a glance,
Tossing their heads in sprightly dance.

The waves beside them danced; but they
Out-did the sparkling waves in glee:
A poet could not but be gay,   15
In such a jocund company:
I gazed—and gazed—but little thought
What wealth the show to me had brought:

For oft, when on my couch I lie
In vacant or in pensive mood,   20
They flash upon that inward eye
Which is the bliss of solitude;
And then my heart with pleasure fills,
And dances with the daffodils.

LINES

*Composed a Few Miles Above Tintern Abbey, on Revisiting
the Banks of the Wye During a Tour. July 13, 1798*

Five years have past; five summers, with the length
Of five long winters! and again I hear

These waters, rolling from their mountain-springs
With a soft inland murmur.——Once again
Do I behold these steep and lofty cliffs,   5
That on a wild secluded scene impress
Thoughts of more deep seclusion; and connect
The landscape with the quiet of the sky.
The day is come when I again repose
Here, under this dark sycamore, and view   10
These plots of cottage-ground, these orchard-tufts,
Which at this season, with their unripe fruits,
Are clad in one green hue, and lose themselves
'Mid groves and copses. Once again I see
These hedge-rows, hardly hedge-rows, little lines   15
Of sportive wood run wild: these pastoral farms,
Green to the very door; and wreaths of smoke
Sent up, in silence, from among the trees!
With some uncertain notice, as might seem
Of vagrant dwellers in the houseless woods,   20
Or of some hermit's cave, where by his fire
The hermit sits alone.

                   These beauteous forms,
Through a long absence, have not been to me
As is a landscape to a blind man's eye:
But oft, in lonely rooms, and 'mid the din   25
Of towns and cities, I have owed to them,
In hours of weariness, sensations sweet,
Felt in the blood, and felt along the heart;
And passing even into my purer mind,
With tranquil restoration:——feelings too   30
Of unremembered pleasure: such, perhaps,
As have no slight or trivial influence
On that best portion of a good man's life,
His little, nameless, unremembered, acts
Of kindness and of love. Nor less, I trust,   35
To them I may have owed another gift,
Of aspect more sublime; that blessed mood,
In which the burthen of the mystery,
In which the heavy and the weary weight
Of all this unintelligible world,   40
Is lightened:——that serene and blessed mood,

In which the affections gently lead us on,—
Until, the breath of this corporeal frame
And even the motion of our human blood
Almost suspended, we are laid asleep   45
In body, and become a living soul:
While with an eye made quiet by the power
Of harmony, and the deep power of joy,
We see into the life of things.

                               If this
Be but a vain belief, yet, oh! how oft—   50
In darkness and amid the many shapes
Of joyless daylight; when the fretful stir
Unprofitable, and the fever of the world,
Have hung upon the beatings of my heart—
How oft, in spirit, have I turned to thee,   55
O sylvan Wye! thou wanderer thro' the woods,
How often has my spirit turned to thee!
    And now, with gleams of half-extinguished thought,
With many recognitions dim and faint,
And somewhat of a sad perplexity,   60
The picture of the mind revives again:
While here I stand, not only with the sense
Of present pleasure, but with pleasing thoughts
That in this moment there is life and food
For future years. And so I dare to hope,   65
Though changed, no doubt, from what I was when first
I came among these hills; when like a roe
I bounded o'er the mountains, by the sides
Of the deep rivers, and the lonely streams,
Wherever nature led: more like a man   70
Flying from something that he dreads than one
Who sought the thing he loved. For nature then
(The coarser pleasures of my boyish days,
And their glad animal movements all gone by)
To me was all in all.—I cannot paint   75
What then I was. The sounding cataract
Haunted me like a passion: the tall rock,
The mountain, and the deep and gloomy wood,
Their colors and their forms, were then to me
An appetite; a feeling and a love,   80

That had no need of a remoter charm,
By thought supplied, nor any interest
Unborrowed from the eye.—That time is past,
And all its aching joys are now no more,
And all its dizzy raptures. Not for this   85
Faint I, nor mourn nor murmur; other gifts
Have followed; for such loss, I would believe,
Abundant recompense. For I have learned
To look on nature, not as in the hour
Of thoughtless youth; but hearing often-times   90
The still, sad music of humanity,
Nor harsh nor grating, though of ample power
To chasten and subdue. And I have felt
A presence that disturbs me with the joy
Of elevated thoughts; a sense sublime   95
Of something far more deeply interfused,
Whose dwelling is the light of setting suns,
And the round ocean and the living air,
And the blue sky, and in the mind of man:
A motion and a spirit, that impels   100
All thinking things, all objects of all thought,
And rolls through all things. Therefore am I still
A lover of the meadows and the woods,
And mountains; and of all that we behold
From this green earth; of all the mighty world   105
Of eye, and ear,—both what they half create,
And what perceive; well pleased to recognize
In nature and the language of the sense
The anchor of my purest thoughts, the nurse,
The guide, the guardian of my heart, and soul   110
Of all my moral being.
                        Nor perchance,
If I were not thus taught, should I the more
Suffer my genial spirits to decay:
For thou art with me here upon the banks
Of this fair river; thou my dearest Friend,   115
My dear, dear Friend; and in thy voice I catch
The language of my former heart, and read
My former pleasures in the shooting lights
Of thy wild eyes. Oh! yet a little while

May I behold in thee what I was once,   120
My dear, dear Sister! and this prayer I make,
Knowing that Nature never did betray
The heart that loved her; 'tis her privilege,
Through all the years of this our life, to lead
From joy to joy: for she can so inform   125
The mind that is within us, so impress
With quietness and beauty, and so feed
With lofty thoughts, that neither evil tongues,
Rash judgments, nor the sneers of selfish men,
Nor greetings where no kindness is, nor all   130
The dreary intercourse of daily life,
Shall e'er prevail against us, or disturb
Our cheerful faith, that all which we behold
Is full of blessings. Therefore let the moon
Shine on thee in thy solitary walk;   135
And let the misty mountain-winds be free
To blow against thee: and, in after years,
When these wild ecstasies shall be matured
Into a sober pleasure; when thy mind
Shall be a mansion for all lovely forms,   140
Thy memory be as a dwelling-place
For all sweet sounds and harmonies; oh! then,
If solitude, or fear, or pain, or grief,
Should be thy portion, with what healing thoughts
Of tender joy wilt thou remember me,   145
And these my exhortations! Nor, perchance—
If I should be where I no more can hear
Thy voice, nor catch from thy wild eyes these gleams
Of past existence—wilt thou then forget
That on the banks of this delightful stream   150
We stood together; and that I, so long
A worshipper of Nature, hither came
Unwearied in that service: rather say
With warmer love—oh! with far deeper zeal
Of holier love. Nor wilt thou then forget   155
That after many wanderings, many years
Of absence, these steep woods and lofty cliffs,
And this green pastoral landscape, were to me
More dear, both for themselves and for thy sake!

SURPRISED BY JOY

Surprised by joy—impatient as the wind
I turned to share the transport—Oh! with whom
But Thee, deep buried in the silent tomb,
That spot which no vicissitude can find?
Love, faithful love, recalled thee to my mind—
But how could I forget thee? Through what power,
Even for the least division of an hour,
Have I been so beguiled as to be blind
To my most grievous loss!—That thought's return
Was the worst pang that sorrow ever bore,
Save one, one only, when I stood forlorn,
Knowing my heart's best treasure was no more;
That neither present time, nor years unborn
Could to my sight that heavenly face restore.

IT IS A BEAUTEOUS EVENING, CALM AND FREE

It is a beauteous evening, calm and free,
The holy time is quiet as a nun
Breathless with adoration; the broad sun
Is sinking down in its tranquillity;
The gentleness of heaven broods o'er the sea:
Listen! the mighty being is awake,
And doth with his eternal motion make
A sound like thunder—everlastingly.
Dear Child! dear Girl! that walkest with me here,
If thou appear untouched by solemn thought,
Thy nature is not therefore less divine:
Thou liest in Abraham's bosom all the year;
And worshipp'st at the temple's inner shrine,
God being with thee when we know it not.

THE WORLD IS TOO MUCH WITH US

The world is too much with us; late and soon,
Getting and spending, we lay waste our powers:

Little we see in Nature that is ours;
We have given our hearts away, a sordid boon!
This Sea that bares her bosom to the moon;   5
The winds that will be howling at all hours,
And are up-gathered now like sleeping flowers;
For this, for everything, we are out of tune;
It moves us not.—Great God! I'd rather be
A pagan suckled in a creed outworn;   10
So might I, standing on this pleasant lea,
Have glimpses that would make me less forlorn;
Have sight of Proteus rising from the sea;
Or hear old Triton blow his wreathèd horn.

SEPTEMBER, 1815

While not a leaf seems faded; while the fields,
With ripening harvest prodigally fair,
In brightest sunshine bask; this nipping air,
Sent from some distant clime where Winter wields
His icy scimitar, a foretaste yields   5
Of bitter change, and bids the flowers beware;
And whispers to the silent birds, "Prepare
Against the threatening foe your trustiest shields."
For me, who under kindlier laws belong
To Nature's tuneful quire, this rustling dry   10
Through leaves yet green, and yon crystalline sky,
Announce a season potent to renew,
'Mid frost and snow, the instinctive joys of song,
And nobler cares than listless summer knew.

COMPOSED UPON WESTMINSTER BRIDGE, SEPTEMBER 3, 1802

Earth has not anything to show more fair:
Dull would he be of soul who could pass by
A sight so touching in its majesty:
This city now doth, like a garment, wear
The beauty of the morning; silent, bare,   5
Ships, towers, domes, theatres, and temples lie

Open unto the fields, and to the sky;
All bright and glittering in the smokeless air.
Never did sun more beautifully steep
In his first splendor, valley, rock, or hill;   10
Ne'er saw I, never felt, a calm so deep!
The river glideth at his own sweet will:
Dear God! the very houses seem asleep;
And all that mighty heart is lying still!

THE SOLITARY REAPER

Behold her, single in the field,
Yon solitary Highland Lass!
Reaping and singing by herself;
Stop here, or gently pass!
Alone she cuts and binds the grain,   5
And sings a melancholy strain;
O listen! for the vale profound
Is overflowing with the sound.

No nightingale did ever chaunt
More welcome notes to weary bands   10
Of travellers in some shady haunt,
Among Arabian sands:
A voice so thrilling ne'er was heard
In spring-time from the cuckoo-bird,
Breaking the silence of the seas   15
Among the farthest Hebrides.

Will no one tell me what she sings?—
Perhaps the plaintive numbers flow
For old, unhappy, far-off things,
And battles long ago: 20
Or is it some more humble lay,
Familiar matter of to-day?
Some natural sorrow, loss, or pain,
That has been, and may be again?

Whate'er the theme, the maiden sang   25
As if her song could have no ending;
I saw her singing at her work,

And o'er the sickle bending;——
I listened, motionless and still;
And, as I mounted up the hill,   30
The music in my heart I bore,
Long after it was heard no more.

LONDON, 1802

Milton! thou shouldst be living at this hour:
England hath need of thee: she is a fen
Of stagnant waters: altar, sword, and pen,
Fireside, the heroic wealth of hall and bower,
Have forfeited their ancient English dower   5
Of inward happiness. We are selfish men;
Oh! raise us up, return to us again;
And give us manners, virtue, freedom, power.
Thy soul was like a star, and dwelt apart;
Thou hadst a voice whose sound was like the sea: 10
Pure as the naked heavens, majestic, free,
So didst thou travel on life's common way,
In cheerful godliness; and yet thy heart
The lowliest duties on herself did lay.

MUTABILITY

From low to high doth dissolution climb,
And sink from high to low, along a scale
Of awful notes, whose concord shall not fail;
A musical but melancholy chime,
Which they can hear who meddle not with crime,   5
Nor avarice, nor over-anxious care.
Truth fails not; but her outward forms that bear
The longest date do melt like frosty rime,
That in the morning whitened hill and plain
And is no more; drop like the tower sublime   10
Of yesterday, which royally did wear
His crown of weeds, but could not even sustain
Some casual shout that broke the silent air,
Or the unimaginable touch of Time.

THE SMALL CELANDINE

There is a flower, the lesser Celandine,
That shrinks, like many more, from cold and rain;
And, the first moment that the sun may shine,
Bright as the sun himself, 'tis out again!

When hailstones have been falling, swarm on swarm,   5
Or blasts the green field and the trees distrest,
Oft have I seen it muffled up from harm,
In close self-shelter, like a thing at rest.

But lately, one rough day, this flower I passed
And recognised it, though an altered form,   10
Now standing forth an offering to the blast,
And buffeted at will by rain and storm.

I stopped, and said with inly-muttered voice,
"It doth not love the shower, nor seek the cold:
This neither is its courage nor its choice,   15
But its necessity in being old.

"The sunshine may not cheer it, nor the dew;
It cannot help itself in its decay;
Stiff in its members, withered, changed of hue."
And, in my spleen, I smiled that it was gray.   20

To be a prodigal's favorite—then, worse truth,
A miser's pensioner—behold our lot!
O Man, that from thy fair and shining youth
Age might but take the things Youth needed not!

ODE

Intimations of Immortality from Recollections of Early Childhood

> *The Child is father of the Man;*
> *And I could wish my days to be*
> *Bound each to each by natural piety.*

1

There was a time when meadow, grove, and stream,
The earth, and every common sight,
        To me did seem

  Apparelled in celestial light,
The glory and the freshness of a dream.   5
It is not now as it hath been of yore;—
   Turn wheresoe'er I may,
    By night or day,
The things which I have seen I now can see no more.

     2

  The rainbow comes and goes,   10
  And lovely is the rose,
  The moon doth with delight
Look round her when the heavens are bare,
  Waters on a starry night
  Are beautiful and fair;   15
  The sunshine is a glorious birth;
 But yet I know, where'er I go,
That there hath past away a glory from the earth.

     3

Now, while the birds thus sing a joyous song,
  And while the young lambs bound   20
   As to the tabor's sound,
To me alone there came a thought of grief:
A timely utterance gave that thought relief,
   And I again am strong:
The cataracts blow their trumpets from the steep; 25
No more shall grief of mine the season wrong;
I hear the echoes through the mountains throng,
The winds come to me from the fields of sleep,
   And all the earth is gay;
    Land and sea   30
  Give themselves up to jollity,
   And with the heart of May
  Doth every beast keep holiday;—
   Thou child of joy,
Shout round me, let me hear thy shouts, thou happy shepherd-boy! 35

     4

Ye blessèd creatures, I have heard the call
  Ye to each other make; I see

The heavens laugh with you in your jubilee;
　My heart is at your festival,
　　My head hath its coronal,　　　　　　　　　　40
The fulness of your bliss, I feel—I feel it all.
　　Oh evil day! if I were sullen
　　While Earth herself is adorning,
　　　This sweet May-morning,
　　And the children are culling　　　　　　　　45
　　　On every side,
　In a thousand valleys far and wide,
　Fresh flowers; while the sun shines warm,
And the Babe leaps up on his Mother's arm:—
　I hear, I hear, with joy I hear!　　　　　　　50
　—But there's a tree, of many, one,
A single field which I have looked upon,
Both of them speak of something that is gone:
　　The pansy at my feet
　　Doth the same tale repeat:　　　　　　　55
Whither is fled the visionary gleam?
Where is it now, the glory and the dream?

5

Our birth is but a sleep and a forgetting:
The Soul that rises with us, our life's star,
　　Hath had elsewhere its setting,　　　　　　60
　　　And cometh from afar:
　　Not in entire forgetfulness,
　　And not in utter nakedness,
But trailing clouds of glory do we come
　　From God, who is our home:　　　　　　65
Heaven lies about us in our infancy!
Shades of the prison-house begin to close
　　Upon the growing Boy
But he beholds the light, and whence it flows,
　　He sees it in his joy;　　　　　　　　70
The Youth, who daily farther from the east
　　Must travel, still is Nature's priest,
　　And by the vision splendid
　　Is on his way attended;

At length the Man perceives it die away,   75
And fade into the light of common day.

6

Earth fills her lap with pleasures of her own;
Yearnings she hath in her own natural kind,
And, even with something of a Mother's mind,
    And no unworthy aim,   80
    The homely nurse doth all she can
To make her foster-child, her inmate Man,
    Forget the glories he hath known,
And that imperial palace whence he came.

7

Behold the Child among his new-born blisses,   85
A six years' darling of a pigmy size!
See, where 'mid work of his own hand he lies,
Fretted by sallies of his mother's kisses,
With light upon him from his father's eyes!
See, at his feet, some little plan or chart,   90
Some fragment from his dream of human life,
Shaped by himself with newly-learned art;
    A wedding or a festival,
    A mourning or a funeral;
    And this hath now his heart,   95
    And unto this he frames his song:
    Then will he fit his tongue
To dialogues of business, love, or strife;
    But it will not be long
    Ere this be thrown aside,   100
    And with new joy and pride
The little Actor cons another part;
Filling from time to time his "humorous stage"
With all the persons, down to palsied age,
That Life brings with her in her equipage;   105
    As if his whole vocation
    Were endless imitation.

8

Thou, whose exterior semblance doth belie
    Thy Soul's immensity;
Thou best philosopher, who yet dost keep   110
Thy heritage, thou eye among the blind,
That, deaf and silent, read'st the eternal deep,
Haunted for ever by the eternal mind,—
    Mighty Prophet! Seer blest!
    On whom those truths do rest,   115
Which we are toiling all our lives to find,
In darkness lost, the darkness of the grave;
Thou, over whom thy immortality
Broods like the day, a master o'er a slave,
A presence which is not to be put by;   120
    [To whom the grave
Is but a lonely bed without the sense or sight
    Of day or the warm light,
A place of thought where we in waiting lie;]
Thou little Child, yet glorious in the might   125
Of heaven-born freedom on thy being's height,
Why with such earnest pains dost thou provoke
The years to bring the inevitable yoke,
Thus blindly with thy blessedness at strife?
Full soon thy Soul shall have her earthly freight,   130
And custom lie upon thee with a weight,
Heavy as frost, and deep almost as life!

9

    O joy! that in our embers
    Is something that doth live,
    That nature yet remembers   135
    What was so fugitive!
The thought of our past years in me doth breed
Perpetual benediction: not indeed
For that which is most worthy to be blest;
Delight and liberty, the simple creed   140
Of childhood, whether busy or at rest,

121–124. These lines were omitted from Wordsworth's editions after 1820
because of adverse criticism by Coleridge.

With new-fledged hope still fluttering in his breast:—
    Not for these I raise
    The song of thanks and praise;
  But for those obstinate questionings   145
Of sense and outward things,
Fallings from us, vanishings;
  Blank misgivings of a creature
Moving about in worlds not realized,
High instincts before which our mortal Nature   150
Did tremble like a guilty thing surprised:
    But for those first affections,
    Those shadowy recollections,
  Which, be they what they may,
Are yet the fountain-light of all our day,   155
Are yet a master-light of all our seeing;
  Uphold us, cherish, and have power to make
Our noisy years seem moments in the being
Of the eternal silence: truths that wake,
    To perish never: 160
Which neither listlessness, nor mad endeavor,
    Nor Man nor Boy,
Nor all that is at enmity with joy,
Can utterly abolish or destroy!
  Hence in a season of calm weather   165
    Though inland far we be,
Our Souls have sight of that immortal sea
    Which brought us hither,
  Can in a moment travel thither,
And see the children sport upon the shore,   170
And hear the mighty waters rolling evermore.

10

Then sing, ye Birds, sing, sing a joyous song!
    And let the young lambs bound
    As to the tabor's sound!
We in thought will join your throng,   175
    Ye that pipe and ye that play,
    Ye that through your hearts today
    Feel the gladness of the May!
What though the radiance which was once so bright

Be now for ever taken from my sight,   180
    Though nothing can bring back the hour
Of splendor in the grass, of glory in the flower;
        We will grieve not, rather find
        Strength in what remains behind;
        In the primal sympathy   185
        Which having been must ever be;
        In the soothing thoughts that spring
        Out of human suffering;
        In the faith that looks through death,
In years that bring the philosophic mind.   190

11

And O, ye Fountains, Meadows, Hills, and Groves,
Forebode not any severing of our loves!
Yet in my heart of hearts I feel your might;
I only have relinquished one delight
To live beneath your more habitual sway.   195
I love the brooks which down their channels fret,
Even more than when I tripped lightly as they;
The innocent brightness of a new-born day
        Is lovely yet;
The clouds that gather round the setting sun   200
Do take a sober coloring from an eye
That hath kept watch o'er man's mortality;
Another race hath been, and other palms are won.
Thanks to the human heart by which we live,
Thanks to its tenderness, its joys, and fears,   205
To me the meanest flower that blows can give
Thoughts that do often lie too deep for tears.

℃ JOHN KEATS was recognized even in childhood as an exceptional person. His first friends recorded that he was remarkably vivacious, high-minded, and generous when but a schoolboy. Although he was born in London, the death of his father and subsequent family difficulties resulted in a move to Edmonton, then a small village near London. Before the boy was fourteen he became passionately devoted to his books, but his mother's untimely death resulted in his being apprenticed to a surgeon. The medical studies were not pursued with

John Keats

[1795-1821]

enthusiasm, for more and more he found his true vocation in poetry. An acquaintance with Leigh Hunt developed in the fall of 1816, and led to the publication of some of Keats' sonnets in *The Examiner*. In March, 1817, his first volume, *Poems by John Keats*, was published. Although many poems were imperfect, the promising volume received some applause from a few friends; generally, however, the reception was poor.

Not discouraged, Keats set to work on a long poem, *Endymion*. When it first appeared in 1818 it received several harsh notices but, again, Keats was at work almost immediately. In midsummer, 1820, he brought out *Lamia, Isabella, The Eve of Saint Agnes, and Other Poems*. This volume contained Keats' most mature work, the great odes. In 1819 and 1820 the poet's health began to fail. His spirits remained undepressed in spite of the poor reception of his poems and his obvious physical decline. His sweetheart, Fanny Brawne, and good friends, particularly Charles Brown and the Hunts, cared for Keats diligently. Only a month after some critical acclaim belatedly came to his work, Keats set off for Italy in a desperate attempt to improve his health. Less than three months after his arrival in Rome, he died of multiple hemorrhages. He is buried near the poet Shelley in the Protestant Cemetery at Rome.

ON FIRST LOOKING INTO
CHAPMAN'S HOMER

Much have I travell'd in the realms of gold,
    And many goodly states and kingdoms seen;
    Round many western islands have I been
Which bards in fealty to Apollo hold.
Oft of one wide expanse had I been told   5
    That deep-brow'd Homer ruled as his demesne;
    Yet did I never breathe its pure serene
Till I heard Chapman speak out loud and bold:
Then felt I like some watcher of the skies
    When a new planet swims into his ken;   10
Or like stout Cortez when with eagle eyes
    He star'd at the Pacific—and all his men
Look'd at each other with a wild surmise—
    Silent, upon a peak in Darien.

ON THE GRASSHOPPER AND CRICKET

The poetry of earth is never dead:
    When all the birds are faint with the hot sun,
    And hide in cooling trees, a voice will run
From hedge to hedge about the new-mown mead;
That is the Grasshopper's—he takes the lead   5
    In summer luxury,—he has never done
    With his delights; for when tired out with fun
He rests at ease beneath some pleasant weed.
The poetry of earth is ceasing never:
    On a lone winter evening, when the frost   10
    Has wrought a silence, from the stove there shrills
The Cricket's song, in warmth increasing ever,
    And seems to one in drowsiness half lost,
    The Grasshopper's among some grassy hills.

DEDICATION

To Leigh Hunt, Esq.

Glory and loveliness have passed away;
　　For if we wander out in early morn,
　　No wreathed incense do we see upborne
Into the east, to meet the smiling day:
No crowd of nymphs soft voic'd and young, and gay,　　5
　　In woven baskets bringing ears of corn,
　　Roses, and pinks, and violets, to adorn
The shrine of Flora in her early May.
But there are left delights as high as these,
　　And I shall ever bless my destiny,　　10
That in a time, when under pleasant trees
　　Pan is no longer sought, I feel a free,
A leafy luxury, seeing I could please
　　With these poor offerings, a man like thee.

ON SEEING THE ELGIN MARBLES *

My spirit is too weak; mortality
　　Weighs heavily on me like unwilling sleep,
　　And each imagined pinnacle and steep
Of godlike hardship tells me I must die
Like a sick eagle looking at the sky.　　5
　　Yet 'tis a gentle luxury to weep,
　　That I have not the cloudy winds to keep
Fresh for the opening of the morning's eye.
Such dim-conceived glories of the brain
　　Bring round the heart an indescribable feud;　　10
So do these wonders a most dizzy pain,
　　That mingles Grecian grandeur with the rude
Wasting of old Time—with a billowy main,
　　A sun, a shadow of a magnitude.

* A collection of Greek sculpture, including most of the elaborate decoration of the Parthenon, which was brought from Athens to London in the early nineteenth century. The British government purchased the collection from Lord Elgin in 1816.

ON THE SEA

It keeps eternal whisperings around
　　Desolate shores, and with its mighty swell
　　Gluts twice ten thousand caverns, till the spell
Of Hecate leaves them their old shadowy sound.
Often 'tis in such gentle temper found,　　　　　　　　　　5
　　That scarcely will the very smallest shell
　　Be moved for days from where it sometime fell,
When last the winds of heaven were unbound.
Oh ye! who have your eye-balls vexed and tired,
　　Feast them upon the wideness of the Sea;　　　　　　　10
　　　　Oh ye! whose ears are dinn'd with uproar rude,
　　Or fed too much with cloying melody—
　　　　Sit ye near some old cavern's mouth, and brood
Until ye start, as if the sea-nymphs quired!

ON SITTING DOWN TO READ
KING LEAR ONCE AGAIN

O golden-tongued Romance with serene lute!
　　Fair plumed Syren! Queen of far away!
　　Leave melodizing on this wintry day,
Shut up thine olden pages, and be mute:
Adieu! for once again the fierce dispute　　　　　　　　5
　　Betwixt damnation and impassion'd clay
　　Must I burn through; once more humbly assay
The bitter-sweet of this Shakespearian fruit.
Chief Poet! and ye clouds of Albion,
　　Begetters of our deep eternal theme,　　　　　　　　10
When through the old oak forest I am gone,
　　Let me not wander in a barren dream,
But when I am consumed in the fire,
Give me new Phœnix wings to fly at my desire.

WHEN I HAVE FEARS THAT I MAY CEASE TO BE

When I have fears that I may cease to be
   Before my pen has glean'd my teeming brain,
Before high-piled books, in charact'ry,
   Hold like rich garners the full-ripen'd grain;
When I behold, upon the night's starr'd face,   5
   Huge cloudy symbols of a high romance,
And think that I may never live to trace
   Their shadows, with the magic hand of chance;
And when I feel, fair creature of an hour!
   That I shall never look upon thee more,   10
Never have relish in the faery power
   Of unreflecting love!—then on the shore
Of the wide world I stand alone, and think
Till Love and Fame to nothingness do sink.

THE EVE OF ST. AGNES

1

St. Agnes' Eve—Ah, bitter chill it was!
The owl, for all his feathers, was a-cold;
The hare limp'd trembling through the frozen grass,
And silent was the flock in woolly fold:
Numb were the Beadsman's fingers, while he told   5
His rosary, and while his frosted breath,
Like pious incense from a censer old,
Seem'd taking flight for heaven, without a death,
Past the sweet Virgin's picture, while his prayer he saith.

2

His prayer he saith, this patient, holy man;   10
Then takes his lamp, and riseth from his knees,

And back returneth, meagre, barefoot, wan,
Along the chapel aisle by slow degrees:
The sculptur'd dead, on each side, seem to freeze,
Emprison'd in black, purgatorial rails: 15
Knights, ladies, praying in dumb orat'ries,
He passeth by; and his weak spirit fails
To think how they may ache in icy hoods and mails.

                                    3

Northward he turneth through a little door,
And scarce three steps, ere Music's golden tongue   20
Flatter'd to tears this aged man and poor;
But no—already had his deathbell rung:
The joys of all his life were said and sung:
His was harsh penance on St. Agnes' Eve:
Another way he went, and soon among   25
Rough ashes sat he for his soul's reprieve,
And all night kept awake, for sinners' sake to grieve.

                                    4

That ancient Beadsman heard the prelude soft;
And so it chanc'd, for many a door was wide,
From hurry to and fro. Soon, up aloft,   30
The silver, snarling trumpets 'gan to chide:
The level chambers, ready with their pride,
Were glowing to receive a thousand guests:
The carved angels, ever eager-eyed,
Star'd, where upon their heads the cornice rests,   35
With hair blown back, and wings put cross-wise on their breasts.

                                    5

At length burst in the argent revelry,
With plume, tiara, and all rich array,
Numerous as shadows haunting fairily
The brain, new stuff'd, in youth, with triumphs gay   40
Of old romance. These let us wish away,
And turn, sole-thoughted, to one Lady there,

Whose heart had brooded, all that wintry day,
On love, and wing'd St. Agnes' saintly care,
As she had heard old dames full many times declare. 45

6

They told her how, upon St. Agnes' Eve,
Young virgins might have visions of delight,
And soft adorings from their loves receive
Upon the honey'd middle of the night,
If ceremonies due they did aright; 50
As, supperless to bed they must retire,
And couch supine their beauties, lily white;
Nor look behind, nor sideways, but require
Of Heaven with upward eyes for all that they desire.

7

Full of this whim was thoughtful Madeline: 55
The music, yearning like a God in pain,
She scarcely heard: her maiden eyes divine,
Fix'd on the floor, saw many a sweeping train
Pass by—she heeded not at all: in vain
Came many a tiptoe, amorous cavalier, 60
And back retir'd; not cool'd by high disdain,
But she saw not: her heart was otherwhere:
She sigh'd for Agnes' dreams, the sweetest of the year.

8

She danc'd along with vague, regardless eyes,
Anxious her lips, her breathing quick and short: 65
The hallow'd hour was near at hand: she sighs
Amid the timbrels, and the throng'd resort
Of whisperers in anger, or in sport;
'Mid looks of love, defiance, hate, and scorn,
Hoodwink'd with faery fancy; all amort, 70
Save to St. Agnes and her lambs unshorn,
And all the bliss to be before tomorrow morn.

9

So, purposing each moment to retire,
She linger'd still. Meantime, across the moors,
Had come young Porphyro, with heart on fire   75
For Madeline. Beside the portal doors,
Buttress'd from moonlight, stands he, and implores
All saints to give him sight of Madeline,
But for one moment in the tedious hours,
That he might gaze and worship all unseen;   80
Perchance speak, kneel, touch, kiss—in sooth such things have been.

10

He ventures in: let no buzz'd whisper tell:
All eyes be muffled, or a hundred swords
Will storm his heart, Love's fev'rous citadel:
For him, those chambers held barbarian hordes,   85
Hyena foemen, and hot-blooded lords,
Whose very dogs would execrations howl
Against his lineage: not one breast affords
Him any mercy, in that mansion foul,
Save one old beldame, weak in body and in soul.   90

11

Ah, happy chance! the aged creature came,
Shuffling along with ivory-headed wand,
To where he stood, hid from the torch's flame,
Behind a broad hall-pillar, far beyond
The sound of merriment and chorus bland: 95
He startled her; but soon she knew his face,
And grasp'd his fingers in her palsied hand,
Saying, "Mercy, Porphyro! hie thee from this place;
They are all here tonight, the whole blood-thirsty race!

12

"Get hence! get hence! there's dwarfish Hildebrand;   100
He had a fever late, and in the fit

He cursed thee and thine, both house and land:
Then there's that old Lord Maurice, not a whit
More tame for his gray hairs—Alas me! flit!
Flit like a ghost away."—"Ah, Gossip dear,   105
We're safe enough; here in this arm-chair sit,
And tell me how"—"Good Saints! not here, not here;
Follow me, child, or else these stones will be thy bier."

13

He follow'd through a lowly arched way,
Brushing the cobwebs with his lofty plume,   110
And as she mutter'd "Well-a—well-a-day!"
He found him in a little moonlight room,
Pale, lattic'd, chill, and silent as a tomb.
"Now tell me where is Madeline," said he,
"O tell me, Angela, by the holy loom   115
Which none but secret sisterhood may see,
When they St. Agnes' wool are weaving piously."

14

"St. Agnes! Ah! it is St. Agnes' Eve—
Yet men will murder upon holy days:
Thou must hold water in a witch's sieve,   120
And be liege-lord of all the Elves and Fays,
To venture so: it fills me with amaze
To see thee, Porphyro!—St. Agnes' Eve!
God's help! my lady fair the conjuror plays
This very night: good angels her deceive!   125
But let me laugh awhile, I've mickle time to grieve."

15

Feebly she laugheth in the languid moon,
While Porphyro upon her face doth look,
Like puzzled urchin on an aged crone
Who keepeth clos'd a wond'rous riddle-book,   130
As spectacled she sits in chimney nook.
But soon his eyes grew brilliant, when she told

His lady's purpose; and he scarce could brook
Tears, at the thought of those enchantments cold
And Madeline asleep in lap of legends old.

16

Sudden a thought came like a full-blown rose,
Flushing his brow, and in his pained heart
Made purple riot: then doth he propose
A stratagem, that makes the beldame start:
"A cruel man and impious thou art:
Sweet lady, let her pray, and sleep, and dream
Alone with her good angels, far apart
From wicked men like thee. Go, go!—I deem
Thou canst not surely be the same that thou didst seem."

17

"I will not harm her, by all saints I swear,"
Quoth Porphyro: "O may I ne'er find grace
When my weak voice shall whisper its last prayer,
If one of her soft ringlets I displace,
Or look with ruffian passion in her face:
Good Angela, believe me by these tears;
Or I will, even in a moment's space,
Awake, with horrid shout, my foemen's ears,
And beard them, though they be more fang'd than wolves and bears."

18

"Ah! why wilt thou affright a feeble soul?
A poor, weak, palsy-stricken, churchyard thing,
Whose passing-bell may ere the midnight toll;
Whose prayers for thee, each morn and evening,
Were never miss'd."—Thus plaining, doth she bring
A gentler speech from burning Porphyro;
So woful, and of such deep sorrowing,
That Angela gives promise she will do
Whatever he shall wish, betide her weal or woe.

19

Which was, to lead him, in close secrecy,
Even to Madeline's chamber, and there hide
Him in a closet, of such privacy   165
That he might see her beauty unespied,
And win perhaps that night a peerless bride,
While legion'd fairies pac'd the coverlet,
And pale enchantment held her sleepy-eyed.
Never on such a night have lovers met,   170
Since Merlin paid his Demon all the monstrous debt.

20

"It shall be as thou wishest," said the Dame:
"All cates and dainties shall be stored there
Quickly on this feast-night: by the tambour frame
Her own lute thou wilt see: no time to spare,   175
For I am slow and feeble, and scarce dare
On such a catering trust my dizzy head.
Wait here, my child, with patience; kneel in prayer
The while: Ah! thou must needs the lady wed,
Or may I never leave my grave among the dead."   180

21

So saying, she hobbled off with busy fear.
The lover's endless minutes slowly pass'd:
The dame return'd, and whisper'd in his ear
To follow her; with aged eyes aghast
From fright of dim espial. Safe at last,   185
Through many a dusky gallery, they gain
The maiden's chamber, silken, hush'd, and chaste;
Where Porphyro took covert, pleas'd amain.
His poor guide hurried back with agues in her brain.

22

Her falt'ring hand upon the balustrade,   190
Old Angela was feeling for the stair,

When Madeline, St. Agnes' charmed maid,
Rose, like a mission'd spirit, unaware:
With silver taper's light, and pious care,
She turn'd, and down the aged gossip led   19
To a safe level matting. Now prepare,
Young Porphyro, for gazing on that bed;
She comes, she comes again, like ring-dove fray'd and fled.

23

Out went the taper as she hurried in;
Its little smoke, in pallid moonshine, died: 20
She clos'd the door, she panted, all akin
To spirits of the air, and visions wide:
No uttered syllable, or, woe betide!
But to her heart, her heart was voluble,
Paining with eloquence her balmy side;   205
As though a tongueless nightingale should swell
Her throat in vain, and die, heart-stifled, in her dell.

24

A casement high and triple-arch'd there was,
All garlanded with carven imag'ries
Of fruits, and flowers, and bunches of knot-grass,   210
And diamonded with panes of quaint device,
Innumerable of stains and splendid dyes,
As are the tiger-moth's deep-damask'd wings;
And in the midst, 'mong thousand heraldries,
And twilight saints, and dim emblazonings,   215
A shielded scutcheon blush'd with blood of queens and kings.

25

Full on this casement shone the wintry moon,
And threw warm gules on Madeline's fair breast,
As down she knelt for heaven's grace and boon;
Rose-bloom fell on her hands, together prest,   220
And on her silver cross soft amethyst,

And on her hair a glory, like a saint:
  She seem'd a splendid angel, newly drest,
  Save wings, for heaven:——Porphyro grew faint:
She knelt, so pure a thing, so free from mortal taint.   225

26

Anon his heart revives: her vespers done,
  Of all its wreathed pearls her hair she frees;
  Unclasps her warmed jewels one by one;
  Loosens her fragrant boddice; by degrees
  Her rich attire creeps rustling to her knees: 230
  Half-hidden, like a mermaid in sea-weed,
  Pensive awhile she dreams awake, and sees,
  In fancy, fair St. Agnes in her bed,
But dares not look behind, or all the charm is fled.

27

Soon, trembling in her soft and chilly nest,   235
  In sort of wakeful swoon, perplex'd she lay,
  Until the poppied warmth of sleep oppress'd
  Her soothed limbs, and soul fatigued away;
  Flown, like a thought, until the morrow-day;
  Blissfully haven'd both from joy and pain;   240
  Clasp'd like a missal where swart Paynims pray;
  Blinded alike from sunshine and from rain,
As though a rose should shut, and be a bud again.

28

Stol'n to this paradise, and so entranced,
  Porphyro gazed upon her empty dress,   245
  And listen'd to her breathing, if it chanced
  To wake into a slumberous tenderness;
  Which when he heard, that minute did he bless,
  And breath'd himself: then from the closet crept,
  Noiseless as fear in a wide wilderness,   250
  And over the hush'd carpet, silent, stept,
And 'tween the curtains peep'd, where, lo!——how fast she slept.

29

Then by the bed-side, where the faded moon
Made a dim, silver twilight, soft he set
A table, and, half anguish'd, threw thereon   2
A cloth of woven crimson, gold, and jet:——
O for some drowsy Morphean amulet!
The boisterous, midnight, festive clarion,
The kettle-drum, and far-heard clarinet,
Affray his ears, though but in dying tone:——   2
The hall door shuts again, and all the noise is gone.

30

And still she slept an azure-lidded sleep,
In blanched linen, smooth, and lavender'd,
While he from forth the closet brought a heap
Of candied apple, quince, and plum, and gourd;   2
With jellies soother than the creamy curd,
And lucent syrops, tinct with cinnamon;
Manna and dates, in argosy transferr'd
From Fez; and spiced dainties, every one,
From silken Samarcand to cedar'd Lebanon.   2

31

These delicates he heap'd with glowing hand
On golden dishes and in baskets bright
Of wreathed silver: sumptuous they stand
In the retired quiet of the night,
Filling the chilly room with perfume light.——   27
"And now, my love, my seraph fair, awake!
Thou art my heaven, and I thine eremite:
Open thine eyes, for meek St. Agnes' sake,
Or I shall drowse beside thee, so my soul doth ache."

32

Thus whispering, his warm, unnerved arm
Sank in her pillow, Shaded was her dream   28

By the dusk curtains:——'twas a midnight charm
Impossible to melt as iced stream:
The lustrous salvers in the moonlight gleam;
Broad golden fringe upon the carpet lies: 285
It seem'd he never, never could redeem
From such a stedfast spell his lady's eyes;
So mus'd awhile, entoil'd in woofed phantasies.

33

Awakening up, he took her hollow lute,——
Tumultuous,——and, in chords that tenderest be,   290
He play'd an ancient ditty, long since mute,
In Provence call'd, "La belle dame sans mercy":
Close to her ear touching the melody;——
Wherewith disturb'd, she utter'd a soft moan:
He ceased—she panted quick—and suddenly   295
Her blue affrayed eyes wide open shone:
Upon his knees he sank, pale as smooth-sculptured stone.

34

Her eyes were open, but she still beheld,
Now wide awake, the vision of her sleep:
There was a painful change, that nigh expell'd   300
The blisses of her dream so pure and deep,
At which fair Madeline began to weep,
And moan forth witless words with many a sigh;
While still her gaze on Porphyro would keep;
Who knelt, with joined hands and piteous eye,   305
Fearing to move or speak, she look'd so dreamingly.

35

"Ah, Porphyro!" said she, "but even now
Thy voice was at sweet tremble in mine ear,
Made tuneable with every sweetest vow;
And those sad eyes were spiritual and clear: 310
How chang'd thou art! how pallid, chill, and drear!

292. *La belle dame sans mercy:* the beautiful lady without mercy.

Give me that voice again, my Porphyro,
Those looks immortal, those complainings dear!
Oh leave me not in this eternal woe,
For if thou diest, my Love, I know not where to go."   31

36

Beyond a mortal man impassion'd far
At these voluptuous accents, he arose,
Ethereal, flush'd, and like a throbbing star
Seen mid the sapphire heaven's deep repose;
Into her dream he melted, as the rose   32
Blendeth its odor with the violet,—
Solution sweet: meantime the frost-wind blows
Like Love's alarum pattering the sharp sleet
Against the window-panes; St. Agnes' moon hath set.

37

'Tis dark: quick pattereth the flaw-blown sleet: 32
"This is no dream, my bride, my Madeline!"
'Tis dark: the iced gusts still rave and beat:
"No dream, alas! alas! and woe is mine!
Porphyro will leave me here to fade and pine.—
Cruel! what traitor could thee hither bring?   33
I curse not, for my heart is lost in thine,
Though thou forsakest a deceived thing;—
A dove forlorn and lost with sick unpruned wing."

38

"My Madeline! sweet dreamer! lovely bride!
Say, may I be for aye thy vassal blest?   33
Thy beauty's shield, heart-shap'd and vermeil dyed?
Ah, silver shrine, here will I take my rest
After so many hours of toil and quest,
A famish'd pilgrim,—saved by miracle.
Though I have found, I will not rob thy nest   34
Saving of thy sweet self; if thou think'st well
To trust, fair Madeline, to no rude infidel.

39

"Hark! 'tis an elfin-storm from faery land,
Of haggard seeming, but a boon indeed:
Arise—arise! the morning is at hand;—   345
The bloated wassaillers will never heed:—
Let us away, my love, with happy speed;
There are no ears to hear, or eyes to see,—
Drown'd all in Rhenish and the sleepy mead:
Awake! arise! my love, and fearless be,   350
For o'er the southern moors I have a home for thee."

40

She hurried at his words, beset with fears,
For there were sleeping dragons all around,
At glaring watch, perhaps, with ready spears—
Down the wide stairs a darkling way they found.—   355
In all the house was heard no human sound.
A chain-droop'd lamp was flickering by each door;
The arras, rich with horseman, hawk, and hound,
Flutter'd in the besieging wind's uproar;
And the long carpets rose along the gusty floor.   360

41

They glide, like phantoms, into the wide hall;
Like phantoms, to the iron porch, they glide;
Where lay the Porter, in uneasy sprawl,
With a huge empty flaggon by his side:
The wakeful bloodhound rose, and shook his hide,   365
But his sagacious eye an inmate owns:
By one, and one, the bolts full easy slide:—
The chains lie silent on the footworn stones;—
The key turns, and the door upon its hinges groans.

42

And they are gone: ay, ages long ago   370
These lovers fled away into the storm.

That night the Baron dreamt of many a woe,
And all his warrior-guests, with shade and form
Of witch, and demon, and large coffin-worm,
Were long be-nightmar'd. Angela the old
Died palsy-twitch'd, with meagre face deform;
The Beadsman, after thousand aves told,
For aye unsought for slept among his ashes cold.

BRIGHT STAR, WOULD I WERE STEADFAST AS THOU ART

Bright star, would I were steadfast as thou art—
    Not in lone splendor hung aloft the night
And watching, with eternal lids apart,
    Like nature's patient, sleepless Eremite,
The moving waters at their priestlike task
    Of pure ablution round earth's human shores,
Or gazing on the new soft fallen mask
    Of snow upon the mountains and the moors—
No—yet still steadfast, still unchangeable,
    Pillow'd upon my fair love's ripening breast,
To feel for ever its soft fall and swell,
    Awake for ever in a sweet unrest,
Still, still to hear her tender-taken breath,
And so live ever—or else swoon to death.

LA BELLE DAME SANS MERCI*

Ah, what can ail thee, wretched wight,
    Alone and palely loitering;
The sedge is wither'd from the lake,
    And no birds sing.

Ah, what can ail thee, wretched wight,
    So haggard and so woe-begone?
The squirrel's granary is full,
    And the harvest's done.

* The revised version is printed here. As previously noted, the title means "the
beautiful lady without mercy."

I see a lily on thy brow,
    With anguish moist and fever dew;   10
And on thy cheek a fading rose
    Fast withereth too.

I met a lady in the meads
    Full beautiful, a fairy's child;
Her hair was long, her foot was light,   15
    And her eyes were wild.

I set her on my pacing steed,
    And nothing else saw all day long;
For sideways would she lean, and sing
    A fairy's song.   20

I made a garland for her head,
    And bracelets too, and fragrant zone:
She look'd at me as she did love,
    And made sweet moan.

She found me roots of relish sweet,   25
    And honey wild, and manna dew;
And sure in language strange she said,
    "I love thee true."

She took me to her elfin grot,
    And there she gaz'd and sighed deep,   30
And there I shut her wild sad eyes—
    So kiss'd to sleep.

And there we slumber'd on the moss,
    And there I dream'd, ah woe betide,
The latest dream I ever dream'd   35
    On the cold hill side.

I saw pale kings, and princes too,
    Pale warriors, death-pale were they all;
Who cry'd—"La belle Dame sans mercy
    Hath thee in thrall!"   40

I saw their starv'd lips in the gloom
    With horrid warning gaped wide,
And I awoke, and found me here
    On the cold hill side.

And this is why I sojourn here   4
   Alone and palely loitering,
Though the sedge is wither'd from the lake,
   And no birds sing.

T O   S L E E P

O soft embalmer of the still midnight,
   Shutting, with careful fingers and benign,
Our gloom-pleased eyes, embower'd from the light,
   Enshaded in forgetfulness divine;
O soothest Sleep! if so it please thee, close,
   In midst of this thine hymn, my willing eyes,
Or wait the amen, ere thy poppy throws
   Around my bed its lulling charities;
Then save me, or the passed day will shine
Upon my pillow, breeding many woes;   1
   Save me from curious conscience, that still lords
Its strength for darkness, burrowing like a mole;
   Turn the key deftly in the oiled wards,
And seal the hushed casket of my soul.

ODE   TO   A   NIGHTINGALE

1

My heart aches, and a drowsy numbness pains
   My sense, as though of hemlock I had drunk,
Or emptied some dull opiate to the drains
   One minute past, and Lethe-wards had sunk:
'Tis not through envy of thy happy lot,
   But being too happy in thine happiness,—
      That thou, light-winged Dryad of the trees,
      In some melodious plot
Of beechen green, and shadows numberless,
   Singest of summer in full-throated ease.   1

2

O, for a draught of vintage! that hath been
  Cool'd a long age in the deep-delved earth,
Tasting of Flora and the country green,
  Dance, and Provençal song, and sunburnt mirth!
O for a beaker full of the warm South,   15
  Full of the true, the blushful Hippocrene,
    With beaded bubbles winking at the brim,
      And purple-stained mouth;
  That I might drink, and leave the world unseen,
    And with thee fade away into the forest dim: 20

3

Fade far away, dissolve, and quite forget
  What thou among the leaves hast never known,
The weariness, the fever, and the fret
  Here, where men sit and hear each other groan;
Where palsy shakes a few, sad, last gray hairs,   25
  Where youth grows pale, and spectre-thin, and dies;
    Where but to think is to be full of sorrow
      And leaden-eyed despairs,
  Where Beauty cannot keep her lustrous eyes,
    Or new Love pine at them beyond tomorrow.   30

4

Away! away! for I will fly to thee,
  Not charioted by Bacchus and his pards,
But on the viewless wings of Poesy,
  Though the dull brain perplexes and retards:
Already with thee! tender is the night,   35
  And haply the Queen-Moon is on her throne,
    Cluster'd around by all her starry Fays;
      But here there is no light,
  Save what from heaven is with the breezes blown
    Through verdurous glooms and winding mossy ways.   40

5

I cannot see what flowers are at my feet,
   Nor what soft incense hangs upon the boughs,
But, in embalmed darkness, guess each sweet
   Wherewith the seasonable month endows
The grass, the thicket, and the fruit-tree wild;
   White hawthorn, and the pastoral eglantine;
     Fast fading violets cover'd up in leaves;
      And mid-May's eldest child,
   The coming musk-rose, full of dewy wine,
     The murmurous haunt of flies on summer eves.

6

Darkling I listen; and, for many a time
   I have been half in love with easeful Death,
Call'd him soft names in many a mused rhyme,
   To take into the air my quiet breath;
Now more than ever seems it rich to die,
   To cease upon the midnight with no pain,
     While thou art pouring forth thy soul abroad
      In such an ecstasy!
   Still wouldst thou sing, and I have ears in vain—
   To thy high requiem become a sod.

7

Thou wast not born for death, immortal Bird!
   No hungry generations tread thee down;
The voice I hear this passing night was heard
   In ancient days by emperor and clown:
Perhaps the self-same song that found a path
   Through the sad heart of Ruth, when, sick for home,
     She stood in tears amid the alien corn;
      The same that oft-times hath
   Charm'd magic casements, opening on the foam
   Of perilous seas, in faery lands forlorn.

8

Forlorn! the very word is like a bell
    To toll me back from thee to my sole self!
Adieu! the fancy cannot cheat so well
    As she is fam'd to do, deceiving elf.
Adieu! adieu! thy plaintive anthem fades   75
    Past the near meadows, over the still stream,
        Up the hill-side; and now 'tis buried deep
            In the next valley-glades:
    Was it a vision, or a waking dream?
        Fled is that music:——Do I wake or sleep?   80

ODE ON A GRECIAN URN

1

Thou still unravish'd bride of quietness,
    Thou foster-child of silence and slow time,
Sylvan historian, who canst thus express
    A flowery tale more sweetly than our rhyme:
What leaf-fring'd legend haunts about thy shape   5
    Of deities or mortals, or of both,
        In Tempe or the dales of Arcady?
    What men or gods are these? What maidens loth?
What mad pursuit? What struggle to escape?
    What pipes and timbrels? What wild ecstasy?   10

2

Heard melodies are sweet, but those unheard
    Are sweeter; therefore, ye soft pipes, play on;
Not to the sensual ear, but, more endear'd,
    Pipe to the spirit ditties of no tone:
Fair youth, beneath the trees, thou canst not leave   15
    Thy song, nor ever can those trees be bare;
        Bold Lover, never, never canst thou kiss,

Though winning near the goal—yet, do not grieve;
  She cannot fade, though thou hast not thy bliss,
  For ever wilt thou love, and she be fair!   2

3

Ah, happy, happy boughs! that cannot shed
  Your leaves, nor ever bid the Spring adieu;
And, happy melodist, unwearied,
  For ever piping songs for ever new;
More happy love! more happy, happy love!   2
  For ever warm and still to be enjoy'd,
    For ever panting, and for ever young;
All breathing human passion far above,
  That leaves a heart high-sorrowful and cloy'd,
    A burning forehead, and a parching tongue.   3

4

Who are these coming to the sacrifice?
  To what green altar, O mysterious priest,
Lead'st thou that heifer lowing at the skies,
  And all her silken flanks with garlands drest?
What little town by river or sea shore,   3
  Or mountain-built with peaceful citadel,
    Is emptied of this folk, this pious morn?
And, little town, thy streets for evermore
  Will silent be; and not a soul to tell
    Why thou art desolate, can e'er return.   4

5

O Attic shape! Fair attitude! with brede
  Of marble men and maidens overwrought,
With forest branches and the trodden weed;
  Thou, silent form, dost tease us out of thought
As doth eternity: Cold Pastoral!   4
  When old age shall this generation waste,
    Thou shalt remain, in midst of other woe

Than ours, a friend to man, to whom thou say'st,
　"Beauty is truth, truth beauty,—that is all
　　Ye know on earth, and all ye need to know."   50

ODE ON MELANCHOLY

1

No, no, go not to Lethe, neither twist
　Wolf's-bane, tight-rooted, for its poisonous wine;
Nor suffer thy pale forehead to be kiss'd
　By nightshade, ruby grape of Proserpine;
Make not your rosary of yew-berries,   5
　　Nor let the beetle, nor the death-moth be
　　　Your mournful Psyche, nor the downy owl
A partner in your sorrow's mysteries;
　For shade to shade will come too drowsily,
　　And drown the wakeful anguish of the soul.   10

2

But when the melancholy fit shall fall
　Sudden from heaven like a weeping cloud,
That fosters the droop-headed flowers all,
　And hides the green hill in an April shroud;
Then glut thy sorrow on a morning rose,   15
　　Or on the rainbow of the salt sand-wave,
　　　Or on the wealth of globed peonies;
Or if thy mistress some rich anger shows,
　Emprison her soft hand, and let her rave,
　　And feed deep, deep upon her peerless eyes.   20

3

She dwells with Beauty—Beauty that must die;
　And Joy, whose hand is ever at his lips
Bidding adieu; and aching Pleasure nigh,
　Turning to poison while the bee-mouth sips:

Ay, in the very temple of Delight
  Veil'd Melancholy has her sovran shrine,
    Though seen of none save him whose strenuous tongue
Can burst Joy's grape against his palate fine;
  His soul shall taste the sadness of her might,
    And be among her cloudy trophies hung.

TO AUTUMN

1

Season of mists and mellow fruitfulness,
  Close bosom-friend of the maturing sun;
Conspiring with him how to load and bless
  With fruit the vines that round the thatch-eves run;
To bend with apples the moss'd cottage-trees,
  And fill all fruit with ripeness to the core;
    To swell the gourd, and plump the hazel shells
With a sweet kernel; to set budding more,
  And still more, later flowers for the bees,
  Until they think warm days will never cease,
    For Summer has o'er-brimm'd their clammy cells.

2

Who hath not seen thee oft amid thy store?
  Sometimes whoever seeks abroad may find
Thee sitting careless on a granary floor,
  Thy hair soft-lifted by the winnowing wind;
Or on a half-reap'd furrow sound asleep,
  Drows'd with the fume of poppies, while thy hook
    Spares the next swath and all its twined flowers:
And sometimes like a gleaner thou dost keep
  Steady thy laden head across a brook;
  Or by a cyder-press, with patient look,
    Thou watchest the last oozings hours by hours.

3

Where are the songs of Spring? Ay, where are they?
   Think not of them, thou hast thy music too,—
While barred clouds bloom the soft-dying day,   25
   And touch the stubble-plains with rosy hue;
Then in a wailful choir the small gnats mourn
    Among the river sallows, borne aloft
      Or sinking as the light wind lives or dies;
And full-grown lambs loud bleat from hilly bourn;   30
    Hedge-crickets sing; and now with treble soft
    The red-breast whistles from a garden-croft;
      And gathering swallows twitter in the skies.

❡ ALFRED TENNYSON grew to young manhood in the place where he was born—the rectory at Somersby, a remote hamlet in the Lincolnshire wolds. His strong-minded intellectual father cultivated his son's love for the classics, while a rural environment led the young Tennyson to an intense love of the natural world. His formal education included grammar school at Louth and a few years at Trinity College, Cambridge, which he left without taking a degree. Certainly by the age of thirteen, Tennyson was able to write acceptable poetry. His first venture into print was in 1827 with *Poems by Two Brothers,* a volume which he shared with his

Alfred, Lord Tennyson

[1809-1892]

brother Charles (and also with their elder brother Frederick). His poem "Timbuctoo" received honors at Cambridge in 1829. Encouraged by friends in college, Tennyson published *Poems, Chiefly Lyrical* (1830) and *Poems* (1832). These volumes were recognized as exciting contributions by a promising young poet; the limited enthusiasm of the critics and his own desire for technical perfection, however, led Tennyson to devote the next ten years of his life to a careful revision of his work. The result, *Poems* (two volumes, 1842), was a success, and in 1847 *The Princess* marked his secure arrival in the ranks of prominent poets. Three years later Tennyson published *In Memoriam,* married his sweetheart of many years, and was made poet laureate.

After 1850 Tennyson was constantly in the public eye and his reputation soared. *Maud* (1855) preceded publication of the major portion of his great work, *Idylls of the King,* in 1859. To the original idylls were added four more in *The Holy Grail* (1870) and two more in *Gareth and Lynette* (1872). The final division and ordering was published later in 1872. In subsequent years Tennyson published six more volumes of poetry, as well as several dramas. When Victoria's laureate died in 1892 he had been elevated to the peerage and was easily among the half-dozen most famous people in the Western world.

THE KRAKEN

Below the thunders of the upper deep,
Far, far beneath in the abysmal sea,
His ancient, dreamless, uninvaded sleep
The Kraken sleepeth: faintest sunlights flee
About his shadowy sides; above him swell   5
Huge sponges of millennial growth and height;
And far away into the sickly light,
From many a wondrous grot and secret cell
Unnumber'd and enormous polypi
Winnow with giant arms the slumbering green.   10
There hath he lain for ages, and will lie
Battening upon huge sea-worms in his sleep,
Until the latter fire shall heat the deep;
Then once by man and angels to be seen,
In roaring he shall rise and on the surface die.   15

THE LOTOS-EATERS

"Courage!" he said, and pointed toward the land,
"This mounting wave will roll us shoreward soon."
In the afternoon they came unto a land
In which it seemed always afternoon.
All round the coast the languid air did swoon,   5
Breathing like one that hath a weary dream.
Full-faced above the valley stood the moon;
And, like a downward smoke, the slender stream
Along the cliff to fall and pause and fall did seem.

A land of streams! some, like a downward smoke,   10
Slow-dropping veils of thinnest lawn, did go;
And some thro' wavering lights and shadows broke,
Rolling a slumbrous sheet of foam below.
They saw the gleaming river seaward flow
From the inner land; far off, three mountain-tops,   15
Three silent pinnacles of aged snow,
Stood sunset-flush'd; and, dew'd with showery drops,
Up-clomb the shadowy pine above the woven copse.

The charmed sunset linger'd low adown
In the red West; thro' mountain clefts the dale   2
Was seen far inland, and the yellow down
Border'd with palm, and many a winding vale
And meadow, set with slender galingale;
A land where all things always seem'd the same!
And round about the keel with faces pale,   2
Dark faces pale against that rosy flame,
The mild-eyed melancholy Lotos-eaters came.

Branches they bore of that enchanted stem,
Laden with flower and fruit, whereof they gave
To each, but whoso did receive of them   3
And taste, to him the gushing of the wave
Far far away did seem to mourn and rave
On alien shores; and if his fellow spake,
His voice was thin, as voices from the grave;
And deep-asleep he seem'd, yet all awake,   3
And music in his ears his beating heart did make.

They sat them down upon the yellow sand,
Between the sun and moon upon the shore;
And sweet it was to dream of Fatherland,
Of child, and wife, and slave; but evermore   4
Most weary seem'd the sea, weary the oar,
Weary the wandering fields of barren foam.
Then some one said, "We will return no more";
And all at once they sang, "Our island home
Is far beyond the wave; we will no longer roam."   4

Choric Song

1

There is sweet music here that softer falls
Than petals from blown roses on the grass,
Or night-dews on still waters between walls
Of shadowy granite, in a gleaming pass;
Music that gentler on the spirit lies,   5
Than tired eyelids upon tired eyes;
Music that brings sweet sleep down from the blissful skies.
Here are cool mosses deep,

And thro' the moss the ivies creep,
And in the stream the long-leaved flowers weep,   10
And from the craggy ledge the poppy hangs in sleep.

2

Why are we weigh'd upon with heaviness,
And utterly consumed with sharp distress,
While all things else have rest from weariness?
All things have rest: why should we toil alone,   15
We only toil, who are the first of things,
And make perpetual moan,
Still from one sorrow to another thrown;
Nor ever fold our wings,
And cease from wanderings,   20
Nor steep our brows in slumber's holy balm;
Nor harken what the inner spirit sings,
"There is no joy but calm!"—
Why should we only toil, the roof and crown of things?

3

Lo! in the middle of the wood,   25
The folded leaf is woo'd from out the bud
With winds upon the branch, and there
Grows green and broad, and takes no care,
Sun-steep'd at noon, and in the moon
Nightly dew-fed; and turning yellow   30
Falls, and floats adown the air.
Lo! sweeten'd with the summer light,
The full-juiced apple, waxing over-mellow,
Drops in a silent autumn night.
All its allotted length of days   35
The flower ripens in its place,
Ripens and fades, and falls, and hath no toil,
Fast-rooted in the fruitful soil.

4

Hateful is the dark-blue sky,
Vaulted o'er the dark-blue sea.   40

Death is the end of life; ah, why
Should life all labor be?
Let us alone. Time driveth onward fast,
And in a little while our lips are dumb.
Let us alone. What is it that will last?   4
All things are taken from us, and become
Portions and parcels of the dreadful past.
Let us alone. What pleasure can we have
To war with evil? Is there any peace
In ever climbing up the climbing wave?   5
All things have rest, and ripen toward the grave
In silence—ripen, fall, and cease:
Give us long rest or death, dark death, or dreamful ease.

5

How sweet it were, hearing the downward stream,
With half-shut eyes ever to seem   5
Falling asleep in a half-dream!
To dream and dream, like yonder amber light,
Which will not leave the myrrh-bush on the height;
To hear each other's whisper'd speech;
Eating the Lotos day by day,   6
To watch the crisping ripples on the beach,
And tender curving lines of creamy spray;
To lend our hearts and spirits wholly
To the influence of mild-minded melancholy;
To muse and brood and live again in memory,   6
With those old faces of our infancy
Heap'd over with a mound of grass,
Two handfuls of white dust, shut in an urn of brass!

6

Dear is the memory of our wedded lives,
And dear the last embraces of our wives   7
And their warm tears; but all hath suffer'd change;
For surely now our household hearths are cold,
Our sons inherit us, our looks are strange,
And we should come like ghosts to trouble joy.
Or else the island princes over-bold

Have eat our substance, and the minstrel sings
Before them of the ten years' war in Troy,
And our great deeds, as half-forgotten things.
Is there confusion in the little isle?
Let what is broken so remain.   80
The Gods are hard to reconcile;
'T is hard to settle order once again.
There *is* confusion worse than death,
Trouble on trouble, pain on pain,
Long labor unto aged breath,   85
Sore task to hearts worn out by many wars
And eyes grown dim with gazing on the pilot-stars.

7

But, propt on beds of amaranth and moly,
How sweet—while warm airs lull us, blowing lowly—
With half-dropt eyelid still,   90
Beneath a heaven dark and holy,
To watch the long bright river drawing slowly
His waters from the purple hill—
To hear the dewy echoes calling
From cave to cave thro' the thick-twined vine—   95
To watch the emerald-color'd water falling
Thro' many a woven acanthus-wreath divine!
Only to hear and see the far-off sparkling brine,
Only to hear were sweet, stretch'd out beneath the pine.

8

The Lotos blooms below the barren peak,   100
The Lotos blows by every winding creek;
All day the wind breathes low with mellower tone;
Thro' every hollow cave and alley lone
Round and round the spicy downs the yellow Lotos-dust is blown.
We have had enough of action, and of motion we,   105
Roll'd to starboard, roll'd to larboard, when the surge was seething
    free,
Where the wallowing monster spouted his foam-fountains in the
    sea.
Let us swear an oath, and keep it with an equal mind,

In the hollow Lotos-land to live and lie reclined
On the hills like Gods together, careless of mankind.   11
For they lie beside their nectar, and the bolts are hurl'd
Far below them in the valleys, and the clouds are lightly curl'd
Round their golden houses, girdled with the gleaming world;
Where they smile in secret, looking over wasted lands,
Blight and famine, plague and earthquake, roaring deeps and fiery
          sands,   11
Clanging fights, and flaming towns, and sinking ships, and praying
          hands.
But they smile, they find a music centred in a doleful song
Steaming up, a lamentation and an ancient tale of wrong,
Like a tale of little meaning tho' the words are strong;
Chanted from an ill-used race of men that cleave the soil,   12
Sow the seed, and reap the harvest with enduring toil,
Storing yearly little dues of wheat, and wine and oil;
Till they perish and they suffer—some, 't is whisper'd—down in
          hell
Suffer endless anguish, others in Elysian valleys dwell,
Resting weary limbs at last on beds of asphodel.   12
Surely, surely, slumber is more sweet than toil, the shore
Than labor in the deep mid-ocean, wind and wave and oar;
O, rest ye, brother mariners, we will not wander more.

ULYSSES

It little profits that an idle king,
By this still hearth, among these barren crags,
Match'd with an aged wife, I mete and dole
Unequal laws unto a savage race,
That hoard, and sleep, and feed, and know not me.   5
I cannot rest from travel; I will drink
Life to the lees. All times I have enjoy'd
Greatly, have suffer'd greatly, both with those
That loved me, and alone; on shore, and when
Thro' scudding drifts the rainy Hyades   10
Vext the dim sea. I am become a name;
For always roaming with a hungry heart
Much have I seen and known,—cities of men

And manners, climates, councils, governments,
Myself not least, but honor'd of them all,—   15
And drunk delight of battle with my peers,
Far on the ringing plains of windy Troy.
I am a part of all that I have met;
Yet all experience is an arch wherethro'
Gleams that untravell'd world whose margin fades   20
For ever and for ever when I move.
How dull it is to pause, to make an end,
To rust unburnish'd, not to shine in use!
As tho' to breathe were life! Life piled on life
Were all too little, and of one to me   25
Little remains; but every hour is saved
From that eternal silence, something more,
A bringer of new things; and vile it were
For some three suns to store and hoard myself,
And this gray spirit yearning in desire   30
To follow knowledge like a sinking star,
Beyond the utmost bound of human thought.
    This is my son, mine own Telemachus,
To whom I leave the sceptre and the isle,—
Well-loved of me, discerning to fulfil   35
This labor, by slow prudence to make mild
A rugged people, and thro' soft degrees
Subdue them to the useful and the good.
Most blameless is he, centred in the sphere
Of common duties, decent not to fail   40
In offices of tenderness, and pay
Meet adoration to my household gods,
When I am gone. He works his work, I mine.
    There lies the port; the vessel puffs her sail;
There gloom the dark, broad seas. My mariners,   45
Souls that have toil'd, and wrought, and thought with me,—
That ever with a frolic welcome took
The thunder and the sunshine, and opposed
Free hearts, free foreheads,—you and I are old;
Old age hath yet his honor and his toil.   50
Death closes all; but something ere the end,
Some work of noble note, may yet be done,
Not unbecoming men that strove with Gods.

The lights begin to twinkle from the rocks;
The long day wanes; the slow moon climbs; the deep   55
Moans round with many voices. Come, my friends.
'T is not too late to seek a newer world.
Push off, and sitting well in order smite
The sounding furrows; for my purpose holds
To sail beyond the sunset, and the baths   60
Of all the western stars, until I die.
It may be that the gulfs will wash us down;
It may be we shall touch the Happy Isles,
And see the great Achilles, whom we knew.
Tho' much is taken, much abides; and tho'   65
We are not now that strength which in old days
Moved earth and heaven, that which we are, we are,—
One equal temper of heroic hearts,
Made weak by time and fate, but strong in will
To strive, to seek, to find, and not to yield.   70

TITHONUS

The woods decay, the woods decay and fall,
The vapors weep their burthen to the ground,
Man comes and tills the field and lies beneath,
And after many a summer dies the swan.
Me only cruel immortality   5
Consumes; I wither slowly in thine arms,
Here at the quiet limit of the world,
A white-hair'd shadow roaming like a dream
The ever-silent spaces of the East,
Far-folded mists, and gleaming halls of morn.   10
    Alas! for this gray shadow, once a man—
So glorious in his beauty and thy choice,
Who madest him thy chosen, that he seem'd
To his great heart none other than a God!
I ask'd thee, "Give me immortality."   15
Then didst thou grant mine asking with a smile,
Like wealthy men who care not how they give.
But thy strong Hours indignant work'd their wills,
And beat me down and marr'd and wasted me,

And tho' they could not end me, left me maim'd   20
To dwell in presence of immortal youth,
Immortal age beside immortal youth,
And all I was in ashes. Can thy love,
Thy beauty, make amends, tho' even now,
Close over us, the silver star, thy guide,   25
Shines in those tremulous eyes that fill with tears
To hear me? Let me go; take back thy gift.
Why should a man desire in any way
To vary from the kindly race of men,
Or pass beyond the goal of ordinance   30
Where all should pause, as is most meet for all?
    A soft air fans the cloud apart; there comes
A glimpse of that dark world where I was born.
Once more the old mysterious glimmer steals
From thy pure brows, and from thy shoulders pure,   35
And bosom beating with a heart renew'd.
Thy cheek begins to redden thro' the gloom,
Thy sweet eyes brighten slowly close to mine.
Ere yet they blind the stars, and the wild team
Which love thee, yearning for thy yoke, arise,   40
And shake the darkness from their loosen'd manes,
And beat the twilight into flakes of fire.
    Lo! ever thus thou growest beautiful
In silence, then before thine answer given
Departest, and thy tears are on my cheek.   45
    Why wilt thou ever scare me with thy tears,
And make me tremble lest a saying learnt,
In days far-off, on that dark earth, be true?
"The Gods themselves cannot recall their gifts."
    Ay me! ay me! with what another heart   50
In days far-off, and with what other eyes
I used to watch—if I be he that watch'd—
The lucid outline forming round thee; saw
The dim curls kindle into sunny rings;
Changed with thy mystic change, and felt my blood   55
Glow with the glow that slowly crimson'd all
Thy presence and thy portals, while I lay,
Mouth, forehead, eyelids, growing dewy-warm
With kisses balmier than half-opening buds

Of April, and could hear the lips that kiss'd   6(
Whispering I knew not what of wild and sweet,
Like that strange song I heard Apollo sing,
While Ilion like a mist rose into towers.
     Yet hold me not for ever in thine East;
How can my nature longer mix with thine?   6[
Coldly thy rosy shadows bathe me, cold
Are all thy lights, and cold my wrinkled feet
Upon thy glimmering thresholds, when the steam
Floats up from those fields about the homes
Of happy men that have the power to die,   7(
And grassy barrows of the happier dead.
Release me, and restore me to the ground.
Thou seest all things, thou wilt see my grave;
Thou wilt renew thy beauty morn by morn,
I earth in earth forget these empty courts,   75
And thee returning on thy silver wheels.

BREAK, BREAK, BREAK

Break, break, break,
     On thy cold gray stones, O Sea!
And I would that my tongue could utter
     The thoughts that arise in me.

O, well for the fisherman's boy,   5
     That he shouts with his sister at play!
O, well for the sailor lad,
     That he sings in his boat on the bay!

And the stately ships go on
     To their haven under the hill;   10
But O for the touch of a vanish'd hand,
     And the sound of a voice that is still!

Break, break, break,
     At the foot of thy crags, O Sea!
But the tender grace of a day that is dead   15
     Will never come back to me.

SONGS FROM *THE PRINCESS*

As Thro' the Land at Eve We Went

As thro' the land at eve we went,
    And pluck'd the ripen'd ears,
We fell out, my wife and I,
O, we fell out, I know not why,
    And kiss'd again with tears.   5
And blessings on the falling out
    That all the more endears,
When we fall out with those we love
    And kiss again with tears!
For when we came where lies the child   10
    We lost in other years,
There above the little grave,
O, there above the little grave,
    We kiss'd again with tears.

Sweet and Low

Sweet and low, sweet and low,
    Wind of the western sea,
Low, low, breathe and blow,
    Wind of the western sea!
Over the rolling waters go,   5
Come from the dying moon, and blow,
    Blow him again to me;
While my little one, while my pretty one sleeps.

Sleep and rest, sleep and rest,
    Father will come to thee soon;   10
Rest, rest, on mother's breast,
    Father will come to thee soon;
Father will come to his babe in the nest,
Silver sails all out of the west
    Under the silver moon;   15
Sleep, my little one, sleep, my pretty one, sleep.

The Splendor Falls on Castle Walls

The splendor falls on castle walls
    And snowy summits old in story;
The long light shakes across the lakes,
    And the wild cataract leaps in glory.
Blow, bugle, blow, set the wild echoes flying,   5
Blow, bugle; answer, echoes, dying, dying, dying.

    O, hark, O, hear! how thin and clear,
        And thinner, clearer, farther going!
    O, sweet and far from cliff and scar
        The horns of Elfland faintly blowing!   10
Blow, let us hear the purple glens replying,
Blow, bugle; answer, echoes, dying, dying, dying.

    O love, they die in yon rich sky,
        They faint on hill or field or river;
    Our echoes roll from soul to soul,   15
        And grow for ever and for ever.
Blow, bugle, blow, set the wild echoes flying,
And answer, echoes, answer, dying, dying, dying.

Tears, Idle Tears

Tears, idle tears, I know not what they mean,
Tears from the depth of some divine despair
Rise in the heart, and gather to the eyes,
In looking on the happy autumn-fields,
And thinking of the days that are no more.   5

Fresh as the first beam glittering on a sail,
That brings our friends up from the underworld,
Sad as the last which reddens over one
That sinks with all we love below the verge;
So sad, so fresh, the days that are no more.   10

Ah, sad and strange as in dark summer dawns
The earliest pipe of half-awaken'd birds
To dying ears, when unto dying eyes
The casement slowly grows a glimmering square;
So sad, so strange, the days that are no more.   15

Dear as remember'd kisses after death,
And sweet as those by hopeless fancy feign'd
On lips that are for others; deep as love,
Deep as first love, and wild with all regret;
O Death in Life, the days that are no more!   20

Home They Brought Her Warrior Dead

Home they brought her warrior dead;
    She nor swoon'd nor utter'd cry.
All her maidens, watching, said,
    "She must weep or she will die."

Then they praised him, soft and low,   5
    Call'd him worthy to be loved,
Truest friend and noblest foe;
    Yet she neither spoke nor moved.

Stole a maiden from her place,
    Lightly to the warrior stept,   10
Took the face-cloth from the face;
    Yet she neither moved nor wept.

Rose a nurse of ninety years,
    Set his child upon her knee—
Like summer tempest came her tears—   15
    "Sweet my child, I live for thee."

Ask Me No More

Ask me no more: the moon may draw the sea;
    The cloud may stoop from heaven and take the shape,
    With fold to fold, of mountain or of cape;
But O too fond, when have I answer'd thee?
        Ask me no more.   5

Ask me no more: what answer should I give?
    I love not hollow cheek or faded eye:
    Yet, O my friend, I will not have thee die!
Ask me no more, lest I should bid thee live;
        Ask me no more.   10

Ask me no more: thy fate and mine are seal'd;
   I strove against the stream and all in vain;
   Let the great river take me to the main.
No more, dear love, for at a touch I yield;
              Ask me no more.   15

Come Down, O Maid

Come down, O maid, from yonder mountain height.
What pleasure lives in height (the shepherd sang),
In height and cold, the splendor of the hills?
But cease to move so near the heavens, and cease
To glide a sunbeam by the blasted pine,   5
To sit a star upon the sparkling spire;
And come, for Love is of the valley, come,
For Love is of the valley, come thou down
And find him; by the happy threshold, he,
Or hand in hand with Plenty in the maize,   10
Or red with spirited purple of the vats,
Or foxlike in the vine; nor cares to walk
With Death and Morning on the Silver Horns,
Nor wilt thou snare him in the white ravine,
Nor find him dropt upon the firths of ice,   15
That huddling slant in furrow-cloven falls
To roll the torrent out of dusky doors.
But follow; let the torrent dance thee down
To find him in the valley; let the wild
Lean-headed eagles yelp alone, and leave   20
The monstrous ledges there to slope, and spill
Their thousand wreaths of dangling water-smoke,
That like a broken purpose waste in air.
So waste not thou, but come; for all the vales
Await thee; azure pillars of the hearth   25
Arise to thee; the children call, and I
Thy shepherd pipe, and sweet is every sound,
Sweeter thy voice, but every sound is sweet;
Myriads of rivulets hurrying thro' the lawn,
The moan of doves in immemorial elms,   30
And murmuring of innumerable bees.

FROM *IN MEMORIAM*

1. *I Held It Truth, with Him Who Sings*

I held it truth, with him who sings
    To one clear harp in divers tones,
    That men may rise on stepping-stones
Of their dead selves to higher things.

But who shall so forecast the years   5
    And find in loss a gain to match?
    Or reach a hand thro' time to catch
The far-off interest of tears?

Let Love clasp Grief lest both be drown'd,
    Let darkness keep her raven gloss.   10
    Ah, sweeter to be drunk with loss,
To dance with Death, to beat the ground,

Than that the victor Hours should scorn
    The long result of love, and boast,
    "Behold the man that loved and lost,   15
But all he was is overworn."

2. *Old Yew, Which Graspest at the Stones*

Old yew, which graspest at the stones
    That name the underlying dead,
    Thy fibres net the dreamless head,
Thy roots are wrapt about the bones.

The seasons bring the flower again,   5
    And bring the firstling to the flock;
    And in the dusk of thee the clock
Beats out the little lives of men.

O, not for thee the glow, the bloom,
    Who changest not in any gale,   10
    Nor branding summer suns avail
To touch thy thousand years of gloom;

And gazing on thee, sullen tree,
   Sick for thy stubborn hardihood,
   I seem to fail from out my blood   1
And grow incorporate into thee.

7. Dark House, by Which Once More I Stand

Dark house, by which once more I stand
   Here in the long unlovely street,
   Doors, where my heart was used to beat
So quickly, waiting for a hand,

A hand that can be clasp'd no more—
   Behold me, for I cannot sleep,
   And like a guilty thing I creep
At earliest morning to the door.

He is not here; but far away
   The noise of life begins again,   10
   And ghastly thro' the drizzling rain
On the bald street breaks the blank day.

11. Calm Is the Morn Without a Sound

Calm is the morn without a sound,
   Calm as to suit a calmer grief,
   And only thro' the faded leaf
The chestnut pattering to the ground;

Calm and deep peace on this high wold,   5
   And on these dews that drench the furze,
   And all the silvery gossamers
That twinkle into green and gold;

Calm and still light on yon great plain
   That sweeps with all its autumn bowers,   10
   And crowded farms and lessening towers,
To mingle with the bounding main;

Calm and deep peace in this wide air,
   These leaves that redden to the fall,
   And in my heart, if calm at all,   15
If any calm, a calm despair;

Calm on the seas, and silver sleep,
   And waves that sway themselves in rest,
   And dead calm in that noble breast
Which heaves but with the heaving deep.   20

19. *The Danube to the Severn Gave* *

The Danube to the Severn gave
   The darken'd heart that beat no more;
   They laid him by the pleasant shore,
And in the hearing of the wave.

There twice a day the Severn fills;   5
   The salt sea-water passes by,
   And hushes half the babbling Wye,
And makes a silence in the hills.

The Wye is hush'd nor moved along,
   And hush'd my deepest grief of all,   10
   When fill'd with tears that cannot fall,
I brim with sorrow drowning song.

The tide flows down, the wave again
   Is vocal in its wooded walls;
   My deeper anguish also falls,   15
And I can speak a little then.

28. *The Time Draws Near the Birth of Christ*

The time draws near the birth of Christ.
   The moon is hid, the night is still;
   The Christmas bells from hill to hill
Answer each other in the mist.

Four voices of four hamlets round,   5
   From far and near, on mead and moor,
   Swell out and fail, as if a door
Were shut between me and the sound;

* Arthur Hallam, in whose honor *In Memoriam* was written, died in Vienna, on the Danube, and was buried at Clevedon, on the river Severn, of which the Wye is a tributary.

Each voice four changes on the wind,
   That now dilate, and now decrease,   10
   Peace and goodwill, goodwill and peace,
Peace and goodwill, to all mankind.

This year I slept and woke with pain,
   I almost wish'd no more to wake,
   And that my hold on life would break   15
Before I heard those bells again;

But they my troubled spirit rule,
   For they controll'd me when a boy;
   They bring me sorrow touch'd with joy,
The merry, merry bells of Yule.   20

39. Old Warder of These Buried Bones

Old warder of these buried bones,
   And answering now my random stroke
   With fruitful cloud and living smoke,
Dark yew, that graspest at the stones

And dippest toward the dreamless head,   5
   To thee too comes the golden hour
   When flower is feeling after flower;
But Sorrow,—fixt upon the dead,

And darkening the dark graves of men,—
   What whisper'd from her lying lips?   10
   Thy gloom is kindled at the tips,
And passes into gloom again.

43. If Sleep and Death Be Truly One

If Sleep and Death be truly one,
   And every spirit's folded bloom
   Thro' all its intervital gloom
In some long trance should slumber on;

Unconscious of the sliding hour,   5
   Bare of the body, might it last,
   And silent traces of the past
Be all the color of the flower:

So then were nothing lost to man;
   So that still garden of the souls   10
   In many a figured leaf enrolls
The total world since life began;

And love will last as pure and whole
   As when he loved me here in Time,
   And at the spiritual prime   15
Rewaken with the dawning soul.

50. *Be Near Me When My Light Is Low*

Be near me when my light is low,
   When the blood creeps, and the nerves prick
   And tingle; and the heart is sick,
And all the wheels of being slow.

Be near me when the sensuous frame   5
   Is rack'd with pangs that conquer trust;
   And Time, a maniac scattering dust,
And Life, a Fury slinging flame.

Be near me when my faith is dry,
   And men the flies of latter spring,   10
   That lay their eggs, and sting and sing
And weave their petty cells and die.

Be near me when I fade away,
   To point the term of human strife,
   And on the low dark verge of life   15
The twilight of eternal day.

96. *You Say, but with No Touch of Scorn*

You say, but with no touch of scorn,
   Sweet-hearted, you, whose light-blue eyes
   Are tender over drowning flies,
You tell me, doubt is Devil-born.

I know not: one indeed I knew   5
   In many a subtle question versed,
   Who touch'd a jarring lyre at first,
But ever strove to make it true;

Perplext in faith, but pure in deeds,
　　At last he beat his music out.　　　　　　　　　　10
　　There lives more faith in honest doubt,
Believe me, than in half the creeds.

He fought his doubts and gather'd strength,
　　He would not make his judgment blind,
　　He faced the spectres of the mind　　　　　　　15
And laid them; thus he came at length

To find a stronger faith his own,
　　And Power was with him in the night,
　　Which makes the darkness and the light,
And dwells not in the light alone,　　　　　　　20

But in the darkness and the cloud,
　　As over Sinaï's peaks of old,
　　While Israel made their gods of gold,
Altho' the trumpet blew so loud.

100. I Climb the Hill: From End to End

I climb the hill: from end to end
　　Of all the landscape underneath,
　　I find no place that does not breathe
Some gracious memory of my friend;

No gray old grange, or lonely fold,　　　　　　　5
　　Or low morass and whispering reed,
　　Or simple stile from mead to mead,
Or sheepwalk up the windy wold;

Nor hoary knoll of ash and haw
　　That hears the latest linnet trill,　　　　　　　10
　　Nor quarry trench'd along the hill
And haunted by the wrangling daw;

Nor runlet tinkling from the rock;
　　Nor pastoral rivulet that swerves
　　To left and right thro' meadowy curves,　　　　15
That feed the mothers of the flock;

But each has pleased a kindred eye,
　　And each reflects a kindlier day;

And, leaving these, to pass away,
I think once more he seems to die.   20

104. *The Time Draws Near the Birth of Christ*

The time draws near the birth of Christ;
   The moon is hid, the night is still;
   A single church below the hill
Is pealing, folded in the mist.

A single peal of bells below,   5
   That wakens at this hour of rest
   A single murmur in the breast,
That these are not the bells I know.

Like strangers' voices here they sound,
   In lands where not a memory strays,   10
   Nor landmark breathes of other days,
But all is new unhallow'd ground.

106. *Ring Out, Wild Bells, to the Wild Sky*

Ring out, wild bells, to the wild sky,
   The flying cloud, the frosty light:
   The year is dying in the night;
Ring out, wild bells, and let him die.

Ring out the old, ring in the new,   5
   Ring, happy bells, across the snow:
   The year is going, let him go;
Ring out the false, ring in the true.

Ring out the grief that saps the mind,
   For those that here we see no more;   10
   Ring out the feud of rich and poor,
Ring in redress to all mankind.

Ring out a slowly dying cause,
   And ancient forms of party strife;
   Ring in the nobler modes of life,   15
With sweeter manners, purer laws.

Ring out the want, the care, the sin,
   The faithless coldness of the times;

Ring out, ring out my mournful rhymes,
But ring the fuller minstrel in. 20

Ring out false pride in place and blood,
The civic slander and the spite;
Ring in the love of truth and right,
Ring in the common love of good.

Ring out old shapes of foul disease; 25
Ring out the narrowing lust of gold;
Ring out the thousand wars of old,
Ring in the thousand years of peace.

Ring in the valiant man and free,
The larger heart, the kindlier hand; 30
Ring out the darkness of the land,
Ring in the Christ that is to be.

116. Is It, Then, Regret for Buried Time

Is it, then, regret for buried time
That keenlier in sweet April wakes,
And meets the year, and gives and takes
The colors of the crescent prime?

Not all: the songs, the stirring air, 5
The life re-orient out of dust,
Cry thro' the sense to hearten trust
In that which made the world so fair.

Not all regret: the face will shine
Upon me, while I muse alone, 10
And that dear voice, I once have known,
Still speak to me of me and mine.

Yet less of sorrow lives in me
For days of happy commune dead,
Less yearning for the friendship fled 15
Than some strong bond which is to be.

123. There Rolls the Deep Where Grew the Tree

There rolls the deep where grew the tree.
O earth, what changes hast thou seen!

There where the long street roars hath been
The stillness of the central sea.

The hills are shadows, and they flow 5
  From form to form, and nothing stands;
  They melt like mist, the solid lands,
Like clouds they shape themselves and go.

But in my spirit will I dwell,
  And dream my dream, and hold it true; 10
  For tho' my lips may breathe adieu,
I cannot think the thing farewell.

131. *O Living Will That Shalt Endure*

O living will that shalt endure
  When all that seems shall suffer shock,
  Rise in the spiritual rock,
Flow thro' our deeds and make them pure,

That we may lift from out of dust 5
  A voice as unto him that hears,
  A cry above the conquer'd years
To one that with us works, and trust,

With faith that comes of self-control,
  The truths that never can be proved 10
  Until we close with all we loved,
And all we flow from, soul in soul.

THE REVENGE

A Ballad of the Fleet

1

At Flores in the Azores Sir Richard Grenville lay,
And a pinnace, like a flutter'd bird, came flying from far away:
"Spanish ships of war at sea! we have sighted fifty-three!"
Then sware Lord Thomas Howard: " 'Fore God I am no coward;
But I cannot meet them here, for my ships are out of gear, 5

And the half my men are sick. I must fly, but follow quick.
We are six ships of the line; can we fight with fifty-three?"

2

Then spake Sir Richard Grenville: "I know you are no coward;
You fly them for a moment to fight with them again.
But I 've ninety men and more that are lying sick ashore.   1
I should count myself the coward if I left them, my Lord Howard,
To these Inquisition dogs and the devildoms of Spain."

3

So Lord Howard past away with five ships of war that day,
Till he melted like a cloud in the silent summer heaven;
But Sir Richard bore in hand all his sick men from the land   1
Very carefully and slow,
Men of Bideford in Devon,
And we laid them on the ballast down below;
For we brought them all aboard,
And they blest him in their pain, that they were not left to Spain, 2
To the thumb-screw and the stake, for the glory of the Lord.

4

He had only a hundred seamen to work the ship and to fight.
And he sailed away from Flores till the Spaniard came in sight,
With his huge sea-castles heaving upon the weather bow.
"Shall we fight or shall we fly?   25
Good Sir Richard, tell us now,
For to fight is but to die!
There 'll be little of us left by the time this sun be set."
And Sir Richard said again: "We be all good English men.
Let us bang these dogs of Seville, the children of the devil,   30
For I never turn'd my back upon Don or devil yet."

5

Sir Richard spoke and he laugh'd and we roar'd a hurrah, and so
The little Revenge ran on sheer into the heart of the foe,

With her hundred fighters on deck, and her ninety sick below;
For half of their fleet to the right and half to the left were seen,   35
And the little Revenge ran on thro' the long sea-lane between.

6

Thousands of their soldiers look'd down from their decks and
  laugh'd,
Thousands of their seamen made mock at the mad little craft
Running on and on, till delay'd
By their mountain-like San Philip that, of fifteen hundred tons,   40
And up-shadowing high above us with her yawning tiers of guns,
Took the breath from our sails, and we stay'd.

7

And while now the great San Philip hung above us like a cloud
Whence the thunderbolt will fall
Long and loud,   45
Four galleons drew away
From the Spanish fleet that day,
And two upon the larboard and two upon the starboard lay,
And the battle-thunder broke from them all.

8

But anon the great San Philip, she bethought herself and went,   50
Having that within her womb that had left her ill content;
And the rest they came aboard us, and they fought us hand to hand,
For a dozen times they came with their pikes and musqueteers,
And a dozen times we shook 'em off as a dog that shakes his ears
When he leaps from the water to the land.   55

9

And the sun went down, and the stars came out far over the summer
  sea,
But never a moment ceased the fight of the one and the fifty-three.
Ship after ship, the whole night long, their high-built galleons
  came,

Ship after ship, the whole night long, with her battle-thunder and
  flame;
Ship after ship, the whole night long, drew back with her dead and
  her shame.   6(
For some were sunk and many were shatter'd, and so could fight us
  no more—
God of battles, was ever a battle like this in the world before?

10

For he said, "Fight on! fight on!"
Tho' his vessel was all but a wreck;
And it chanced that, when half of the short summer night was
  gone,   65
With a grisly wound to be drest he had left the deck,
But a bullet struck him that was dressing it suddenly dead,
And himself he was wounded again in the side and the head,
And he said, "Fight on! fight on!"

11

And the night went down, and the sun smiled out far over the
  summer sea,   7(
And the Spanish fleet with broken sides lay round us all in a ring;
But they dared not touch us again, for they fear'd that we still could
  sting,
So they watch'd what the end would be.
And we had not fought them in vain,
But in perilous plight were we.   75
Seeing forty of our poor hundred were slain,
And half of the rest of us maim'd for life
In the crash of the cannonades and the desperate strife;
And the sick men down in the hold were most of them stark and
  cold,
And the pikes were all broken or bent, and the powder was all of it
  spent;   8(
And the masts and the rigging were lying over the side:
But Sir Richard cried in his English pride:
"We have fought such a fight for a day and a night
As may never be fought again!

We have won great glory, my men!   85
And a day less or more
At sea or ashore,
We die—does it matter when?
Sink me the ship, Master Gunner—sink her, split her in twain.
Fall into the hands of God, not into the hands of Spain!"   90

12

And the gunner said, "Ay, ay," but the seamen made reply:
"We have children, we have wives,
And the Lord hath spared our lives.
We will make the Spaniard promise, if we yield, to let us go;
We shall live to fight again and to strike another blow."   95
And the lion there lay dying, and they yielded to the foe.

13

And the stately Spanish men to their flagship bore him then,
Where they laid him by the mast, old Sir Richard caught at last,
And they praised him to his face with their courtly foreign grace;
But he rose upon their decks, and he cried: 100
"I have fought for Queen and Faith like a valiant man and true;
I have only done my duty as a man is bound to do.
With a joyful spirit I Sir Richard Grenville die!"
And he fell upon their decks, and he died.

14

And they stared at the dead that had been so valiant and true,   105
And had holden the power and glory of Spain so cheap
That he dared her with one little ship and his English few;
Was he devil or man? He was devil for aught they knew,
But they sank his body with honor down into the deep,
And they mann'd the Revenge with a swarthier alien crew,   110
And away she sail'd with her loss and long'd for her own;
When a wind from the lands they had ruin'd awoke from sleep,
And the water began to heave and the weather to moan,
And or ever that evening ended a great gale blew,
And a wave like the wave that is raised by an earthquake grew,   115

Till it smote on their hulls and their sails and their masts and their
    flags,
And the whole sea plunged and fell on the shot-shatter'd navy of
    Spain,
And the little Revenge herself went down by the island crags
To be lost evermore in the main.

CROSSING THE BAR

    Sunset and evening star,
        And one clear call for me!
    And may there be no moaning of the bar,
        When I put out to sea,

    But such a tide as moving seems asleep,
        Too full for sound and foam,
    When that which drew from out the boundless deep
        Turns again home.

    Twilight and evening bell,
        And after that the dark!   10
    And may there be no sadness of farewell,
        When I embark;

    For tho' from out our bourne of Time and Place
        The flood may bear me far,
    I hope to see my Pilot face to face   15
        When I have crost the bar.

MERLIN AND THE GLEAM

1

    O young Mariner,
    You from the haven
    Under the sea-cliff,
    You that are watching
    The gray Magician   5
    With eyes of wonder,

I am Merlin,
And *I* am dying,
I am Merlin
Who follow the Gleam. 10

2

Mighty the Wizard
Who found me at sunrise
Sleeping, and woke me
And learn'd me Magic!
Great the Master, 15
And sweet the Magic,
When over the valley,
In early summers,
Over the mountain,
On human faces, 20
And all around me,
Moving to melody,
Floated the Gleam.

3

Once at the croak of a Raven who crost it
A barbarous people, 25
Blind to the magic
And deaf to the melody,
Snarl'd at and cursed me,
A demon vext me,
The light retreated, 30
The landskip darken'd,
The melody deaden'd,
The Master whisper'd,
"Follow the Gleam."

4

Then to the melody, 35
Over a wilderness
Gliding, and glancing at

Elf of the woodland,
Gnome of the cavern,
Griffin and Giant,
And dancing of Fairies
In desolate hollows,
And wraiths of the mountain,
And rolling of dragons
By warble of water,
Or cataract music
Of falling torrents,
Flitted the Gleam.

5

Down from the mountain
And over the level,
And streaming and shining on
Silent river,
Silvery willow,
Pasture and plowland,
Innocent maidens,
Garrulous children,
Homestead and harvest,
Reaper and gleaner,
And rough-ruddy faces
Of lowly labor,
Slided the Gleam—

6

Then, with a melody
Stronger and statelier,
Led me at length
To the city and palace
Of Arthur the King;
Touch'd at the golden
Cross of the churches,
Flash'd on the tournament,
Flicker'd and bicker'd

From helmet to helmet,
And last on the forehead
Of Arthur the blameless
Rested the Gleam.

7

Clouds and darkness   75
Closed upon Camelot;
Arthur had vanish'd
I knew not whither,
The king who loved me,
And cannot die;   80
For out of the darkness
Silent and slowly
The Gleam, that had waned to a wintry glimmer
On icy fallow
And faded forest,   85
Drew to the valley
Named of the shadow,
And slowly brightening
Out of the glimmer,
And slowly moving again to a melody   90
Yearningly tender,
Fell on the shadow,
No longer a shadow,
But clothed with the Gleam.

8

And broader and brighter   95
The Gleam flying onward,
Wed to the melody,
Sang thro' the world;
And slower and fainter,
Old and weary,   100
But eager to follow,
I saw, whenever
In passing it glanced upon

Hamlet or city,
That under the Crosses   10
The dead man's garden,
The mortal hillock,
Would break into blossom;
And so to the land's
Last limit I came—   11
And can no longer,
But die rejoicing,
For thro' the Magic
Of Him the Mighty,
Who taught me in childhood,   11
There on the border
Of boundless Ocean,
And all but in Heaven
Hovers the Gleam.

9

Not of the sunlight,   12
Not of the moonlight,
Not of the starlight!
O young Mariner,
Down to the haven,
Call your companions,   12
Launch your vessel
And crowd your canvas,
And, ere it vanishes
Over the margin,
After it, follow it,   13
Follow the Gleam.

"FRATER AVE ATQUE VALE" *

Row us out from Desenzano, to your Sirmione row!
So they row'd, and there we landed—"O venusta Sirmio!"

---

* The last words of a song by Gaius Valerius Catullus (84?–54? B.C.),
"Hail, brother, and farewell."

2. *O venusta Sirmio:* "O beautiful Sirmio"; Sirmio, a peninsula in Lake
Garda, was the site of Catullus' villa.

There to me thro' all the groves of olive in the summer glow,
There beneath the Roman ruin where the purple flowers grow,
Came that "Ave atque Vale" of the Poet's hopeless woe,   5
Tenderest of Roman poets nineteen hundred years ago,
"Frater Ave atque Vale"—as we wander'd to and fro
Gazing at the Lydian laughter of the Garda Lake below
Sweet Catullus's all-but-island, olive-silvery Sirmio!

❲ WALT WHITMAN was a young child when his family moved from his birthplace in Huntington, Long Island, to Brooklyn. In subsequent summers he went back to the country and remained close to the farm and seashore. The young Whitman had little formal schooling and went to work as an office boy at the age of eleven. Later he was a printer's devil, schoolteacher, newspaper reporter, and editor. Although he was connected with many newspapers in New York, Brooklyn, and New Orleans, his contributions did not include poems. Whitman's first

Walt Whitman

[1819-1892]

published book, *Franklin Evans, or The Inebriate* (1842), was a temperance novel. His first volume of poetry, *Leaves of Grass,* was published in 1855; it was immediately labeled shocking and lewd. *Leaves of Grass* was revised and supplemented in many subsequent editions. Its reputation grew but very gradually in America; Rossetti, Swinburne, Stevenson, and Symonds, however, recognized Whitman as a great poet rather early, and, in the nineteenth century, his fame was always greater in Europe than in his homeland.

The Civil War had a deep and lasting effect on Whitman. At the end of 1862 he went south to look for his injured brother. After he found his brother not seriously wounded, he stayed to serve as a nurse in the army hospitals in Washington. In 1865 he published *Drum Taps,* to which he appended "When Lilacs Last in the Dooryard Bloom'd," one of his memorials to President Lincoln. That same year he received an appointment to a minor post in the Department of Interior. Six months later he was discharged because of the reputation of his poems for immorality. This setback did not long deter him from publishing his work. In 1871 he issued *Democratic Vistas,* a volume of prose, and the highly successful "Passage to India." In succeeding years he brought out *As a Strong Bird on Pinions Free* (1872), *Two Rivulets* (1876), *Specimen Days and Collect* (1882–1883), *November Boughs* (1888), and *Good-Bye, My Fancy* (1891); Whitman's final revision of *Leaves of Grass* was published in 1892, and several other volumes were issued posthumously. In 1873 Whitman suffered a stroke which left him partially paralyzed. Until the end of his life he was cared for by his brother in Camden, New Jersey.

I HEAR AMERICA SINGING

I hear America singing, the varied carols I hear,
Those of mechanics, each one singing his as it should be blithe and
    strong,
The carpenter singing his as he measures his plank or beam,
The mason singing his as he makes ready for work, or leaves off
    work,
The boatman singing what belongs to him in his boat, the deck-
    hand singing on the steamboat deck,   5
The shoemaker singing as he sits on his bench, the hatter singing as
    he stands,
The wood-cutter's song, the ploughboy's on his way in the morn-
    ing, or at noon intermission or at sundown,
The delicious singing of the mother, or of the young wife at work,
    or of the girl sewing or washing,
Each singing what belongs to him or her and to none else,
The day what belongs to the day—at night the party of young
    fellows, robust, friendly,   10
Singing with open mouths their strong melodious songs.

OUT OF THE ROLLING OCEAN
THE CROWD

Out of the rolling ocean the crowd came a drop gently to me,
Whispering *I love you, before long I die,*
I have travel'd a long way merely to look on you to touch you,
For I could not die till I once look'd on you,
For I fear'd I might afterward lose you.   5

Now we have met, we have look'd, we are safe,
Return in peace to the ocean my love,
I too am part of that ocean my love, we are not so much separated,
Behold the great rondure, the cohesion of all, how perfect!
But as for me, for you, the irresistible sea is to separate us,   10
As for an hour carrying us diverse, yet cannot carry us diverse
    forever;

Be not impatient—a little space—know you I salute the air, the
    ocean and the land,
Every day at sundown for your dear sake my love.

ONCE I PASS'D THROUGH A
POPULOUS CITY

Once I pass'd through a populous city imprinting my brain for
    future use with its shows, architecture, customs, traditions,
Yet now of all that city I remember only a woman I casually met
    there who detain'd me for love of me,
Day by day and night by night we were together—all else has long
    been forgotten by me,
I remember I say only that woman who passionately clung to me,
Again we wander, we love, we separate again,   5
Again she holds me by the hand, I must not go,
I see her close beside me with silent lips sad and tremulous.

I SAW IN LOUISIANA A
LIVE-OAK GROWING

I saw in Louisiana a live-oak growing,
All alone stood it and the moss hung down from the branches,
Without any companion it grew there uttering joyous leaves of
    dark green,
And its look, rude, unbending, lusty, made me think of myself,
But I wonder'd how it could utter joyous leaves standing alone
    there without its friend near, for I knew I could not,   5
And I broke off a twig with a certain number of leaves upon it, and
    twined around it a little moss,
And brought it away, and I have placed it in sight in my room,
It is not needed to remind me as of my own dear friends,
(For I believe lately I think of little else than of them,)
Yet it remains to me a curious token, it makes me think of manly
    love;   10
For all that, and though the live-oak glistens there in Louisiana
    solitary in a wide flat space,
Uttering joyous leaves all its life without a friend a lover near,
I know very well I could not.

O YOU WHOM I OFTEN AND
SILENTLY COME

O you whom I often and silently come where you are that I may be
with you,

As I walk by your side or sit near, or remain in the same room with
you,

Little you know the subtle electric fire that for your sake is playing
within me.

OUT OF THE CRADLE
ENDLESSLY ROCKING

Out of the cradle endlessly rocking,

Out of the mocking-bird's throat, the musical shuttle,

Out of the Ninth-month midnight,

Over the sterile sands and the fields beyond, where the child leaving
his bed wander'd alone, bareheaded, barefoot,

Down from the shower'd halo,   5

Up from the mystic play of shadows twining and twisting as if
they were alive,

Out from the patches of briers and blackberries,

From the memories of the bird that chanted to me,

From your memories sad brother, from the fitful risings and fallings
I heard,

From under that yellow half-moon late-risen and swollen as if
with tears,   10

From those beginning notes of yearning and love there in the mist,

From the thousand responses of my heart never to cease,

From the myriad thence-arous'd words,

From the word stronger and more delicious than any,

From such as now they start the scene revisiting,   15

As a flock, twittering, rising, or overhead passing,

Borne hither, ere all eludes me, hurriedly,

A man, yet by these tears a little boy again,

Throwing myself on the sand, confronting the waves,

I, chanter of pains and joys, uniter of here and hereafter,   20

Taking all hints to use them, but swiftly leaping beyond them,

A reminiscence sing.

Once Paumanok,
When the lilac-scent was in the air and Fifth-month grass was
    growing,
Up this seashore in some briers,
Two feather'd guests from Alabama, two together,
And their nest, and four light-green eggs spotted with brown,
And every day the he-bird to and fro near at hand,
And every day the she-bird crouch'd on her nest, silent, with bright
    eyes,
And every day I, a curious boy, never too close, never disturbing
    them,
Cautiously peering, absorbing, translating.

Shine! shine! shine!
Pour down your warmth, great sun!
While we bask, we two together.
Two together!
Winds blow south, or winds blow north,
Day come white, or night come black,
Home, or rivers and mountains from home,
Singing all time, minding no time,
While we two keep together.

Till of a sudden,
May-be kill'd, unknown to her mate,
One forenoon the she-bird crouch'd not on the nest,
Nor return'd that afternoon, nor the next,
Nor ever appear'd again.

And thenceforward all summer in the sound of the sea,
And at night under the full of the moon in calmer weather,
Over the hoarse surging of the sea,
Or flitting from brier to brier by day,
I saw, I heard at intervals the remaining one, the he-bird,
The solitary guest from Alabama.

Blow! blow! blow!
Blow up sea-winds along Paumanok's shore;
I wait and I wait till you blow my mate to me.

Yes, when the stars glisten'd,
All night long on the prong of a moss-scallop'd stake,

23. *Paumanok:* an American Indian name for Long Island.

Down almost amid the slapping waves,
Sat the lone singer wonderful causing tears.

He call'd on his mate,
He pour'd forth the meanings which I of all men know. 60

Yes my brother I know,
The rest might not, but I have treasur'd every note,
For more than once dimly down to the beach gliding,
Silent, avoiding the moonbeams, blending myself with the shadows,
Recalling now the obscure shapes, the echoes, the sounds and sights
    after their sorts, 65
The white arms out in the breakers tirelessly tossing,
I, with bare feet, a child, the wind wafting my hair,
Listen'd long and long.

Listen'd to keep, to sing, now translating the notes,
Following you my brother. 70

Soothe! soothe! soothe!
Close on its wave soothes the wave behind,
And again another behind embracing and lapping, every one close,
But my love soothes not me, not me.

Low hangs the moon, it rose late, 75
It is lagging—O I think it is heavy with love, with love.

O madly the sea pushes upon the land,
With love, with love.

O night! do I not see my love fluttering out among the breakers?
What is that little black thing I see there in the white? 80

Loud! loud! loud!
Loud I call to you, my love!
High and clear I shoot my voice over the waves,
Surely you must know who is here, is here,
You must know who I am, my love. 85

Low-hanging moon!
What is that dusky spot in your brown yellow?
O it is the shape, the shape of my mate!
O moon do not keep her from me any longer.

Land! land! O land!   9(

Whichever way I turn, O I think you could give me my mate back
    again if you only would,
For I am almost sure I see her dimly whichever way I look.

O rising stars!
Perhaps the one I want so much will rise, will rise with some of
    you.

O throat! O trembling throat!   9!
Sound clearer through the atmosphere!
Pierce the woods, the earth,
Somewhere listening to catch you must be the one I want.

Shake out carols!
Solitary here, the night's carols!   10(
Carols of lonesome love! death's carols!
Carols under that lagging, yellow, waning moon!
O under that moon where she droops almost down into the sea!
O reckless despairing carols.

But soft! sink low!   10;
Soft! let me just murmur,
And do you wait a moment you husky-nois'd sea,
For somewhere I believe I heard my mate responding to me,
So faint, I must be still, be still to listen,
But not altogether still, for then she might not come immediately
    to me.   11(

Hither my love!
Here I am! here!

With this just-sustain'd note I announce myself to you,
This gentle call is for you my love, for you.

Do not be decoy'd elsewhere,   11!
That is the whistle of the wind, it is not my voice,
That is the fluttering, the fluttering of the spray,
Those are the shadows of leaves.

O darkness! O in vain!
O I am very sick and sorrowful.   12(

O brown halo in the sky near the moon, drooping upon the sea!
O troubled reflection in the sea!

O throat! O throbbing heart!
And I singing uselessly, uselessly all the night.

O past! O happy life! O songs of joy! 125
In the air, in the woods, over fields,
Loved! loved! loved! loved! loved!
But my mate no more, no more with me!
We two together no more.

The aria sinking, 130
All else continuing, the stars shining,
The winds blowing, the notes of the bird continuous echoing,
With angry moans the fierce old mother incessantly moaning,
On the sands of Paumanok's shore gray and rustling,
The yellow half-moon enlarged, sagging down, drooping, the face
    of the sea almost touching, 135
The boy ecstatic, with his bare feet the waves, with his hair the
    atmosphere dallying,
The love in the heart long pent, now loose, now at last tumul-
    tuously bursting,
The aria's meaning, the ears, the soul, swiftly depositing,
The strange tears down the cheeks coursing,
The colloquy there, the trio, each uttering, 140
The undertone, the savage old mother incessantly crying,
To the boy's soul's questions sullenly timing, some drown'd secret
    hissing,
To the outsetting bard.

Demon or bird! (said the boy's soul,)
Is it indeed toward your mate you sing? or is it really to me? 145
For I, that was a child, my tongue's use sleeping, now I have heard
    you,
Now in a moment I know what I am for, I awake,
And already a thousand singers, a thousand songs, clearer, louder
    and more sorrowful than yours,
A thousand warbling echoes have started to life within me, never to
    die.

O you singer solitary, singing by yourself, projecting me, 150
O solitary me listening, never more shall I cease perpetuating you,
Never more shall I escape, never more the reverberations,
Never more the cries of unsatisfied love be absent from me,

Never again leave me to be the peaceful child I was before what
    there in the night,
By the sea under the yellow and sagging moon,   155
The messenger there arous'd, the fire, the sweet hell within,
The unknown want, the destiny of me.

O give me the clew! (it lurks in the night here somewhere,)
O if I am to have so much, let me have more!

A word then, (for I will conquer it,)   160
The word final, superior to all,
Subtle, sent up—what is it?—I listen;
Are you whispering it, and have been all the time, you sea waves?
Is that it from your liquid rims and wet sands?

Whereto answering, the sea,   165
Delaying not, hurrying not,
Whisper'd me through the night, and very plainly before daybreak,
Lisp'd to me the low and delicious word death,
And again death, death, death, death,
Hissing melodious, neither like the bird nor like my arous'd child's
    heart,   170
But edging near as privately for me rustling at my feet,
Creeping thence steadily up to my ears and laving me softly all over
Death, death, death, death, death.

Which I do not forget,
But fuse the song of my dusky demon and brother,   175
That he sang to me in the moonlight on Paumanok's gray beach,
With the thousand responsive songs at random,
My own songs awaked from that hour,
And with them the key, the word up from the waves,
The word of the sweetest song and all songs,   180
That strong and delicious word which, creeping to my feet,
(Or like some old crone rocking the cradle, swathed in sweet gar-
    ments, bending aside,)
The sea whisper'd me.

BEAT! BEAT! DRUMS!

Beat! beat! drums!—blow! bugles! blow!
Through the windows—through doors—burst like a ruthless
    force,

Into the solemn church, and scatter the congregation,
Into the school where the scholar is studying;
Leave not the bridegroom quiet—no happiness must he have now
    with his bride,   5
Nor the peaceful farmer any peace, ploughing his field or gathering
    his grain,
So fierce you whirr and pound you drums—so shrill you bugles
    blow.

Beat! beat! drums!—blow! bugles! blow
Over the traffic of cities—over the rumble of wheels in the streets;
Are beds procured for sleepers at night in the houses? no sleepers
    must sleep in those beds,   10
No bargainers' bargains by day—no brokers or speculators—would
    they continue?
Would the talkers be talking? would the singer attempt to sing?
Would the lawyer rise in the court to state his case before the judge?
Then rattle quicker, heavier drums—you bugles wilder blow.

Beat! beat! drums!—blow! bugles! blow!   15
Make no parley—stop for no expostulation,
Mind not the timid—mind not the weeper or prayer,
Mind not the old man beseeching the young man,
Let not the child's voice be heard, nor the mother's entreaties,
Make even the trestles to shake the dead where they lie awaiting the
    hearses,   20
So strong you thump O terrible drums—so loud you bugles blow.

VIGIL STRANGE I KEPT ON THE
FIELD ONE NIGHT

Vigil strange I kept on the field one night;
When you my son and my comrade dropt at my side that day,
One look I but gave which your dear eyes return'd with a look I
    shall never forget,
One touch of your hand to mine O boy, reach'd up as you lay on
    the ground,
Then onward I sped in the battle, the even-contested battle,   5
Till late in the night reliev'd to the place at last again I made my
    way,
Found you in death so cold dear comrade, found your body son of
    responding kisses, (never again on earth responding,)

Bared your face in the starlight, curious the scene, cool blew the
    moderate night-wind,
Long there and then in vigil I stood, dimly around me the battle-
    field spreading,
Vigil wondrous and vigil sweet there in the fragrant silent night,
But not a tear fell, not even a long-drawn sigh, long, long I gazed,
Then on the earth partially reclining sat by your side leaning my
    chin in my hands,
Passing sweet hours, immortal and mystic hours with you dearest
    comrade—not a tear, not a word,
Vigil of silence, love and death, vigil for you my son and my
    soldier,
As onward silently stars aloft, eastward new ones upward stole,
Vigil final for you brave boy, (I could not save you, swift was your
    death,
I faithfully loved you and cared for you living, I think we shall
    surely meet again,)
Till at latest lingering of the night, indeed just as the dawn
    appear'd,
My comrade I wrapt in his blanket, envelop'd well his form,
Folded the blanket well, tucking it carefully over head and carefully
    under feet,
And there and then and bathed by the rising sun, my son in his
    grave, in his rude-dug grave I deposited,
Ending my vigil strange with that, vigil of night and battle-field
    dim,
Vigil for boy of responding kisses, (never again on earth re-
    sponding,)
Vigil for comrade swiftly slain, vigil I never forget, how as day
    brighten'd,
I rose from the chill ground and folded my soldier well in his
    blanket,
And buried him where he fell.

LONG, TOO LONG AMERICA

Long, too long America,
Traveling roads all even and peaceful you learn'd from joys and
    prosperity only,

But now, ah now, to learn from crises of anguish, advancing,
    grappling with direst fate and recoiling not,
And now to conceive and show to the world what your children
    enmasse really are,
(For who except myself has yet conceiv'd what your children
    enmasse really are?)   5

LOOK DOWN FAIR MOON

Look down fair moon and bathe this scene,
Pour softly down night's nimbus floods on faces ghastly, swollen,
    purple,
On the dead on their backs with arms toss'd wide,
Pour down your unstinted nimbus sacred moon.

RECONCILIATION

Word over all, beautiful as the sky,
Beautiful that war and all its deeds of carnage must in time be
    utterly lost,
That the hands of the sisters Death and Night incessantly softly
    wash again, and ever again, this soil'd world;
For my enemy is dead, a man divine as myself is dead,
I look where he lies white-faced and still in the coffin—I draw near,   5
Bend down and touch lightly with my lips the white face in the
    coffin.

WHEN LILACS LAST IN THE DOORYARD BLOOM'D

1

When lilacs last in the dooryard bloom'd,
And the great star early droop'd in the western sky in the night,
I mourn'd, and yet shall mourn with ever-returning spring.

Ever-returning spring, trinity sure to me you bring,
Lilac blooming perennial and drooping star in the west,   5
And thought of him I love.

2

O powerful western fallen star!
O shades of night—O moody, tearful night!
O great star disappear'd—O the black murk that hides the star!
O cruel hands that hold me powerless—O helpless soul of me!   10
O harsh surrounding cloud that will not free my soul.

3

In the dooryard fronting an old farm-house near the white-wash'd
    palings,
Stands the lilac-bush tall-growing with heart-shaped leaves of rich
    green,
With many a pointed blossom rising delicate, with the perfume
    strong I love,
With every leaf a miracle—and from this bush in the dooryard,   15
With delicate-color'd blossoms and heart-shaped leaves of rich green,
A sprig with its flower I break.

4

In the swamp in secluded recesses,
A shy and hidden bird is warbling a song.

Solitary the thrush,   20
The hermit withdrawn to himself, avoiding the settlements,
Sings by himself a song.

Song of the bleeding throat,
Death's outlet song of life, (for well dear brother I know,
If thou was not granted to sing thou would'st surely die.)   25

5

Over the breast of the spring, the land, amid cities,
Amid lanes and through old woods, where lately the violets peep'd
    from the ground, spotting the gray debris,
Amid the grass in the fields each side of the lanes, passing the endless
    grass,

Passing the yellow-spear'd wheat, every grain from its shroud in
    the dark-brown fields uprisen,
Passing the apple-tree blows of white and pink in the orchards,   30
Carrying a corpse to where it shall rest in the grave,
Night and day journeys a coffin.

6

Coffin that passes through lanes and streets,
Through day and night with the great cloud darkening the land,
With the pomp of the inloop'd flags with the cities draped in black,   35
With the show of the States themselves as of crape-veil'd women
    standing,
With processions long and winding and the flambeaus of the night,
With the countless torches lit, with the silent sea of faces and the
    unbared heads,
With the waiting depot, the arriving coffin, and the sombre faces,
With dirges through the night, with the thousand voices rising
    strong and solemn,   40
With all the mournful voices of the dirges pour'd around the coffin,
The dim-lit churches and the shuddering organs—where amid these
    you journey,
With the tolling tolling bells' perpetual clang,
Here, coffin that slowly passes,
I give you my sprig of lilac.   45

7

(Nor for you, for one alone,
Blossoms and branches green to coffins all I bring,
For fresh as the morning, thus would I chant a song for you O sane
    and sacred death.

All over bouquets of roses,
O death, I cover you over with roses and early lilies,   50
But mostly and now the lilac that blooms the first,
Copious I break, I break the sprigs from the bushes,
With loaded arms I come, pouring for you,
For you and the coffins all of you O death.)

8

O western orb sailing the heaven,   55
Now I know what you must have meant as a month since I walk'd,
As I walk'd in silence the transparent shadowy night,
As I saw you had something to tell as you bent to me night after
    night,
As you droop'd from the sky low down as if to my side, (while the
    other stars all look'd on,)
As we wander'd together the solemn night, (for something I know
    not what kept me from sleep,)   60
As the night advanced, and I saw on the rim of the west how full
    you were of woe,
As I stood on the rising ground in the breeze in the cool transparent
    night,
As I watch'd where you pass'd and was lost in the netherward
    black of the night,
As my soul in its trouble dissatisfied sank, as where you sad orb,
Concluded, dropt in the night, and was gone.   65

9

Sing on there in the swamp,
O singer bashful and tender, I hear your notes, I hear your call,
I hear, I come presently, I understand you,
But a moment I linger, for the lustrous star has detain'd me,
The star my departing comrade holds and detains me.   70

10

O how shall I warble myself for the dead one there I loved?
And how shall I deck my song for the large sweet soul that has
    gone?
And what shall my perfume be for the grave of him I love?

Sea-winds blown from east and west,
Blown from the Eastern sea and blown from the Western sea, till
    there on the prairies meeting,   75

These and with these and the breath of my chant,
I'll perfume the grave of him I love.

11

O what shall I hang on the chamber walls?
And what shall the pictures be that I hang on the walls,
To adorn the burial-house of him I love?   80

Pictures of growing spring and farms and homes,
With the Fourth-month eve at sundown, and the gray smoke lucid
    and bright,
With floods of the yellow gold of the gorgeous, indolent, sinking
    sun, burning, expanding the air,
With the fresh sweet herbage under foot, and the pale green leaves
    of the trees prolific,
In the distance the flowing glaze, the breast of the river, with a
    wind-dapple here and there,   85
With ranging hills on the banks, with many a line against the sky,
    and shadows,
And the city at hand with dwellings so dense, and stacks of
    chimneys,
And all the scenes of life and the workshops, and the workmen
    homeward returning.

12

Lo, body and soul—this land,
My own Manhattan with spires, and the sparkling and hurrying
    tides, and the ships,   90
The varied and ample land, the South and the North in the light,
    Ohio's shores and flashing Missouri,
And ever the far-spreading prairies cover'd with grass and corn.

Lo, the most excellent sun so calm and haughty,
The violet and purple morn with just-felt breezes,
The gentle soft-born measureless light,   95
The miracle spreading bathing all, the fulfill'd noon,
The coming eve delicious, the welcome night and the stars,
Over my cities shining all, enveloping man and land.

13

Sing on, sing on you gray-brown bird,
Sing from the swamps, the recesses, pour your chant from the
    bushes,   100
Limitless out of the dusk, out of the cedars and pines.

Sing on dearest brother, warble your reedy song,
Loud human song, with voice of uttermost woe.

O liquid and free and tender!
O wild and loose to my soul—O wondrous singer,   105
You only I hear—yet the star holds me, (but will soon depart,)
Yet the lilac with mastering odor holds me.

14

Now while I sat in the day and look'd forth,
In the close of the day with its light and the fields of spring, and the
    farmers preparing their crops,
In the large unconscious scenery of my land with its lakes and
    forests,   110
In the heavenly aerial beauty, (after the perturb'd winds and the
    storms,)
Under the arching heavens of the afternoon swift passing, and the
    voices of children and women,
The many-moving sea-tides, and I saw the ships how they sail'd,
And the summer approaching with richness, and the fields all busy
    with labor,
And the infinite separate houses, how they all went on, each with its
    meals and minutia of daily usages,   115
And the streets how their throbbings throbb'd, and the cities pent
    —lo, then and there,
Falling upon them all and among them all, enveloping me with the
    rest,
Appear'd the cloud, appear'd the long black trail,
And I knew death, its thought, and the sacred knowledge of death.

Then with the knowledge of death as walking one side of me,   120
And the thought of death close-walking the other side of me,

And I in the middle as with companions, and as holding the hands
 of companions,
I fled forth to the hiding receiving night that talks not,
Down to the shores of the water, the path by the swamp in the
 dimness,
To the solemn shadowy cedars and ghostly pines so still.   125

And the singer so shy to the rest receiv'd me,
The gray-brown bird I know receiv'd us comrades three,
And he sang the carol of death, and a verse for him I love.

From deep secluded recesses,
From the fragrant cedars and the ghostly pines so still,   130
Came the carol of the bird.

And the charm of the carol rapt me,
As I held as if by their hands my comrades in the night,
And the voice of my spirit tallied the song of the bird.

Come lovely and soothing death,   135
Undulate round the world, serenely arriving, arriving,
In the day, in the night, to all, to each,
Sooner or later delicate death.

Prais'd be the fathomless universe,
For life and joy, and for objects and knowledge curious,   140
And for love, sweet love—but praise! praise! praise!
For the sure-enwinding arms of cool-enfolding death.

Dark mother always gliding near with soft feet,
Have none chanted for thee a chant of fullest welcome?
Then I chant it for thee, I glorify thee above all,   145
I bring thee a song that when thou must indeed come, come unfal-
 teringly.

Approach strong deliveress,
When it is so, when thou hast taken them I joyously sing the dead,
Lost in the loving floating ocean of thee,
Laved in the flood of thy bliss O death.   150

From me to thee glad serenades,
Dances for thee I propose saluting thee, adornments and feastings
 for thee,

And the sights of the open landscape and the high-spread sky are
    fitting,
And life and the fields, and the huge and thoughtful night.

The night in silence under many a star,   155
The ocean shore and the husky whispering wave whose voice I
    know,
And the soul turning to thee O vast and well-veil'd death,
And the body gratefully nestling close to thee.

Over the tree-tops I float thee a song,
Over the rising and sinking waves, over the myriad fields and the
    prairies wide,   160
Over the dense-pack'd cities all and the teeming wharves and ways,
I float this carol with joy, with joy to thee O death.

15

To the tally of my soul,
Loud and strong kept up the gray-brown bird,
With pure deliberate notes spreading filling the night.   165

Loud in the pines and cedars dim,
Clear in the freshness moist and the swamp-perfume,
And I with my comrades there in the night.

While my sight that was bound in my eyes unclosed,
As to long panoramas of visions.   170

And I saw askant the armies,
I saw as in noiseless dreams hundreds of battle-flags,
Borne through the smoke of the battles and pierc'd with missiles I
    saw them,
And carried hither and yon through the smoke, and torn and bloody,
And at last but a few shreds left on the staffs, (and all in silence,) 175
And the staffs all splinter'd and broken.

I saw battle-corpses, myriads of them,
And the white skeletons of young men, I saw them,
I saw the debris and debris of all the slain soldiers of the war,
But I saw they were not as was thought,   180
They themselves were fully at rest, they suffer'd not,
The living remain'd and suffer'd, the mother suffer'd,

And the wife and the child and the musing comrade suffer'd,
And the armies that remain'd suffer'd.

16

Passing the visions, passing the night,   185
Passing, unloosing the hold of my comrade's hands,
Passing the song of the hermit bird and the tallying song of my
    soul,
Victorious song, death's outlet song, yet varying ever-altering song,
As low and wailing, yet clear the notes, rising and falling, flooding
    the night,
Sadly sinking and fainting, as warning and warning, and yet again
    bursting with joy,   190
Covering the earth and filling the spread of the heaven,
As that powerful psalm in the night I heard from recesses,
Passing, I leave thee lilac with heart-shaped leaves,
I leave thee there in the door-yard, blooming, returning with spring.

I cease from my song for thee,   195
From my gaze on thee in the west, fronting the west, communing
    with thee,
O comrade lustrous with silver face in the night.

Yet each to keep and all, retrievements out of the night,
The song, the wondrous chant of the gray-brown bird,
And the tallying chant, the echo arous'd in my soul,   200
With the lustrous and drooping star with the countenance full of
    woe,
With the holders holding my hand nearing the call of the bird,
Comrades mine and I in the midst, and their memory ever to keep,
    for the dead I loved so well,
For the sweetest, wisest soul of all my days and lands—and this for
    his dear sake,
Lilac and star and bird twined with the chant of my soul,   205
There in the fragrant pines and the cedars dusk and dim.

THERE WAS A CHILD WENT FORTH

There was a child went forth every day,
And the first object he look'd upon, that object he became,

And that object became part of him for the day or a certain part of
 the day,
Or for many years or stretching cycles of years.

The early lilacs became part of this child,   5
And grass and white and red morning-glories, and white and red
 clover, and the song of the phœbe-bird,
And the Third-month lambs and the sow's pink-faint litter, and
 the mare's foal and the cow's calf,
And the noisy brood of the barnyard or by the mire of the pond-
 side,
And the fish suspending themselves so curiously below there, and
 the beautiful curious liquid,
And the water-plants with their graceful flat heads, all became part
 of him.   10

The field-sprouts of Fourth-month and Fifth-month became part
 of him,
Winter-grain sprouts and those of the light-yellow corn, and the
 esculent roots of the garden,
And the apple-trees cover'd with blossoms and the fruit afterward,
 and wood-berries, and the commonest weeds by the road,
And the old drunkard staggering home from the outhouse of the
 tavern whence he had lately risen,
And the schoolmistress that pass'd on her way to the school,   15
And the friendly boys that pass'd, and the quarrelsome boys,
And the tidy and fresh-cheek'd girls, and the barefoot negro boy
 and girl,
And all the changes of city and country wherever he went.

His own parents, he that had father'd him and she that had
 conceiv'd him in her womb and birth'd him,
They gave this child more of themselves than that,   20
They gave him afterward every day, they became part of him.

The mother at home quietly placing the dishes on the supper-table,
The mother with mild words, clean her cap and gown, a whole-
 some odor falling off her person and clothes as she walks by,
The father, strong, self-sufficient, manly, mean, anger'd, unjust,
The blow, the quick loud word, the tight bargain, the crafty lure,   25
The family usages, the language, the company, the furniture, the
 yearning and swelling heart,

Affection that will not be gainsay'd, the sense of what is real, the thought if after all it should prove unreal,

The doubts of day-time and the doubts of night-time, the curious whether and how,

Whether that which appears so is so, or is it all flashes and specks?

Men and women crowding fast in the streets, if they are not flashes and specks what are they?   30

The streets themselves and the façades of houses, and goods in the windows,

Vehicles, teams, the heavy-plank'd wharves, the huge crossing at the ferries,

The village on the highland seen from afar at sunset, the river between,

Shadows, aureola and mist, the light falling on roofs and gables of white or brown two miles off,

The schooner near by sleepily dropping down the tide, the little boat slack-tow'd astern,   35

The hurrying tumbling waves, quick-broken crests, slapping,

The strata of color'd clouds, the long bar of maroon-tint away solitary by itself, the spread of purity it lies motionless in,

The horizon's edge, the flying sea-crow, the fragrance of salt marsh and shore mud,

These became part of that child who went forth every day, and who now goes, and will always go forth every day.

THE CITY DEAD-HOUSE

By the city dead-house by the gate,

As idly sauntering wending my way from the clangor,

I curious pause, for lo, an outcast form, a poor dead prostitute brought,

Her corpse they deposit unclaim'd, it lies on the damp brick pavement,

The divine woman, her body, I see the body, I look on it alone,   5

That house once full of passion and beauty, all else I notice not,

Nor stillness so cold, nor running water from faucet, nor odors morbific impress me,

But the house alone—that wondrous house—that delicate fair house—that ruin!

That immortal house more than all the rows of dwellings ever built!
Or white-domed capitol with majestic figure surmounted, or all the
    old high-spired cathedrals,
That little house alone more than them all—poor, desperate house!
Fair, fearful wreck—tenement of a soul—itself a soul,
Unclaim'd, avoided house—take one breath from my tremulous
    lips,
Take one tear dropt aside as I go for thought of you,
Dead house of love—house of madness and sin, crumbled, crush'd.
House of life, erewhile talking and laughing—but ah, poor house,
    dead even then,
Months, years, an echoing garnish'd house—but dead, dead, dead.

OTHERS MAY PRAISE WHAT THEY LIKE

Others may praise what they like;
But I, from the banks of the running Missouri, praise nothing in
    art or aught else,
Till it has well inhaled the atmosphere of this river, also the western
    prairie-scent,
And exudes it all again.

THE TORCH

On my Northwest coast in the midst of the night a fishermen's
    group stands watching,
Out on the lake that expands before them, others are spearing
    salmon,
The canoe, a dim shadowy thing, moves across the black water,
Bearing a torch ablaze at the prow.

PASSAGE TO INDIA

1

Singing my days,
Singing the great achievements of the present,

Singing the strong light works of engineers,
Our modern wonders, (the antique ponderous Seven outvied,)
In the Old World the east the Suez canal,   5
The New by its mighty railroad spann'd,
The seas inlaid with eloquent gentle wires;
Yet first to sound, and ever sound, the cry with thee O soul,
The Past! the Past! the Past!

The Past—the dark unfathom'd retrospect!   10
The teeming gulf—the sleepers and the shadows!
The past—the infinite greatness of the past!
For what is the present after all but a growth out of the past?
(As a projectile form'd, impell'd, passing a certain line, still keeps
    on,
So the present, utterly form'd, impell'd by the past.)   15

                            2

Passage O soul to India!
Eclaircise the myths Asiatic, the primitive fables.

Not you alone proud truths of the world,
Nor you alone ye facts of modern science,
But myths and fables of eld, Asia's, Africa's fables,   20
The far-darting beams of the spirit, the unloos'd dreams,
The deep diving bibles and legends,
The daring plots of the poets, the elder religions;
O you temples fairer than lilies pour'd over by the rising sun!
O you fables spurning the known, eluding the hold of the known,
    mounting to heaven!   25
You lofty and dazzling towers, pinnacled, red as roses, burnish'd
    with gold!
Towers of fables immortal fashion'd from mortal dreams!
You too I welcome and fully the same as the rest!
You too with joy I sing.

Passage to India!   30
Lo, soul, seest thou not God's purpose from the first?
The earth to be spann'd, connected by network,
The races, neighbors, to marry and be given in marriage,

    17. *Eclaircise:* to clarify.

The oceans to be cross'd, the distant brought near,
The lands to be welded together.   3

A worship new I sing,
You captains, voyagers, explorers, yours,
You engineers, you architects, machinists, yours,
You, not for trade or transportation only,
But in God's name, and for thy sake O soul.   4

3

Passage to India!
Lo soul for thee of tableaus twain,
I see in one the Suez canal initiated, open'd,
I see the procession of steamships, the Empress Eugenie's leading the
    van,
I mark from on deck the strange landscape, the pure sky, the level
    sand in the distance,   4
I pass swiftly the picturesque groups, the workmen gather'd,
The gigantic dredging machines.

In one again, different, (yet thine, all thine, O soul, the same,)
I see over my own continent the Pacific railroad surmounting every
    barrier,
I see continual trains of cars winding along the Platte carrying
    freight and passengers,   5
I hear the locomotives rushing and roaring, and the shrill steam-
    whistle,
I hear the echoes reverberate through the grandest scenery in the
    world,
I cross the Laramie plains, I note the rocks in grotesque shapes, the
    buttes,
I see the plentiful larkspur and wild onions, the barren, colorless,
    sage-deserts,
I see in glimpses afar or towering immediately above me the great
    mountains, I see the Wind river and the Wahsatch mountains,   55
I see the Monument mountain and the Eagle's Nest, I pass the
    Promontory, I ascend the Nevadas,
I scan the noble Elk mountain and wind around its base,
I see the Humboldt range, I thread the valley and cross the river,
I see the clear waters of lake Tahoe, I see forests of majestic pines,

Or crossing the great desert, the alkaline plains, I behold enchanting
    mirages of waters and meadows,   60
Marking through these and after all, in duplicate slender lines,
Bridging the three or four thousand miles of land travel,
Tying the Eastern to the Western sea,
The road between Europe and Asia.

(Ah Genoese thy dream! thy dream!   65
Centuries after thou art laid in thy grave,
The shore thou foundest verifies thy dream.)

4

Passage to India!
Struggles of many a captain, tales of many a sailor dead,
Over my mood stealing and spreading they come,   70
Like clouds and cloudlets in the unreach'd sky.

Along all history, down the slopes,
As a rivulet running, sinking now, and now again to the surface
    rising,
A ceaseless thought, a varied train—lo, soul, to thee, thy sight,
    they rise,
The plans, the voyages again, the expeditions,   75
Again Vasco de Gama sails forth,
Again the knowledge gain'd, the mariner's compass,
Lands found and nations born, thou born America,
For purpose vast, man's long probation fill'd,
Thou rondure of the world at last accomplish'd.   80

5

O vast Rondure, swimming in space,
Cover'd all over with visible power and beauty,
Alternate light and day and the teeming spiritual darkness,
Unspeakable high processions of sun and moon and countless stars
    above,
Below, the manifold grass and waters, animals, mountains, trees,   85
With inscrutable purpose, some hidden prophetic intention,
Now first it seems my thought begins to span thee.

    76. *de Gama*: Whitman errs; correct spelling is "da Gama."

Down from the gardens of Asia descending radiating,
Adam and Eve appear, then their myriad progeny after them,
Wandering, yearning, curious, with restless explorations,   90
With questionings, baffled, formless, feverish, with never-happy
     hearts,
With that sad incessant refrain, *Wherefore unsatisfied soul?* and
     Whither O mocking life?

Ah who shall soothe these feverish children?
Who justify these restless explorations?
Who speak the secret of impassive earth?   95
Who bind it to us? what is this separate Nature so unnatural?
What is this earth to our affections? (unloving earth, without a
     throb to answer ours,
Cold earth, the place of graves.)

Yet soul be sure the first intent remains, and shall be carried out,
Perhaps even now the time has arrived.   100

After the seas are all cross'd, (as they seem already cross'd,)
After the great captains and engineers have accomplish'd their work,
After the noble inventors, after the scientists, the chemist, the geol-
     ogist, ethnologist,
Finally shall come the poet worthy that name,
The true son of God shall come singing his songs.   105

Then not your deeds only O voyagers, O scientists and inventors,
     shall be justified,
All these hearts as of fretted children shall be sooth'd,
All affection shall be fully responded to, the secret shall be told,
All these separations and gaps shall be taken up and hook'd and
     link'd together,
The whole earth, this cold, impassive, voiceless earth, shall be com-
     pletely justified,   110
Trinitas divine shall be gloriously accomplish'd and compacted by
     the true son of God, the poet,
(He shall indeed pass the straits and conquer the mountains,
He shall double the cape of Good Hope to some purpose,)
Nature and Man shall be disjoin'd and diffused no more,
The true son of God shall absolutely fuse them.   115

6

Year at whose wide-flung door I sing!
Year of the purpose accomplish'd!
Year of the marriage of continents, climates and oceans!
(No mere doge of Venice now wedding the Adriatic,)
I see O year in you the vast terraqueous globe given and giving all,   120
Europe to Asia, Africa join'd, and they to the New World,
The lands, geographies, dancing before you, holding a festival gar-
    land,
As brides and bridegrooms hand in hand.

Passage to India!
Cooling airs from Caucasus far, soothing cradle of man,   125
The river Euphrates flowing, the past lit up again.

Lo soul, the retrospect brought forward,
The old, most populous, wealthiest of earth's lands,
The streams of the Indus and the Ganges and their many affluents,
(I my shores of America walking to-day behold, resuming all,)   130
The tale of Alexander on his warlike marches suddenly dying,
On one side China and on the other side Persia and Arabia,
To the south the great seas and the bay of Bengal,
The flowing literatures, tremendous epics, religions, castes,
Old occult Brahma interminably far back, the tender and junior
    Buddha,   135
Central and southern empires and all their belongings, possessors,
The wars of Tamerlane, the reign of Aurungzebe,
The traders, rulers, explorers, Moslems, Venetians, Byzantium, the
    Arabs, Portuguese,
The first travelers famous yet, Marco Polo, Batouta the Moor,
Doubts to be solv'd, the map incognita, blanks to be fill'd,   140
The foot of man unstay'd, the hands never at rest,
Thyself O soul that will not brook a challenge.

The mediæval navigators rise before me,
The world of 1492, with its awaken'd enterprise,
Something swelling in humanity now like the sap of the earth in
    spring,   145
The sunset splendor of chivalry declining.
And who art thou sad shade?

Gigantic, visionary, thyself a visionary,
With majestic limbs and pious beaming eyes,
Spreading around with every look of thine a golden world,   1
Enhuing it with gorgeous hues.

As the chief histrion,
Down to the footlights walks in some great scena,
Dominating the rest I see the Admiral himself,
 (History's type of courage, action, faith,)   1
Behold him sail from Palos leading his little fleet,
His voyage behold, his return, his great fame,
His misfortunes, calumniators, behold him a prisoner, chain'd,
Behold his dejection, poverty, death.

(Curious in time I stand, noting the efforts of heroes,   1
Is the deferment long? bitter the slander, poverty, death?
Lies the seed unreck'd for centuries in the ground? lo, to God's due
     occasion,
Uprising in the night, it sprouts, blooms,
And fills the earth with use and beauty.)

                                    7

Passage indeed O soul to primal thought,   1
Not lands and seas alone, thy own clear freshness,
The young maturity of brood and bloom,
To realms of budding bibles.

O soul, repressless, I with thee and thou with me,
Thy circumnavigation of the world begin,   1
Of man, the voyage of his mind's return,
To reason's early paradise,
Back, back to wisdom's birth, to innocent intuitions,
Again with fair creation.

                                    8

O we can wait no longer,   1
We too take ship O soul,

    152. *histrion:* actor.

Joyous we too launch out on trackless seas,
Fearless for unknown shores on waves of ecstasy to sail,
Amid the wafting winds, (thou pressing me to thee, I thee to me,
    O soul,)
Caroling free, singing our song of God,   180
Chanting our chant of pleasant exploration.

With laugh and many a kiss,
(Let others deprecate, let others weep for sin, remorse, humili-
    ation,)
O soul, thou pleasest me, I thee.

Ah more than any priest O soul we too believe in God,   185
But with the mystery of God we dare not dally.

O soul thou pleasest me, I thee,
Sailing these seas or on the hills, or waking in the night,
Thoughts, silent thoughts, of Time and Space and Death, like
    waters flowing,
Bear me indeed as through the regions infinite,   190
Whose air I breathe, whose ripples hear, lave me all over,
Bathe me O God in thee, mounting to thee,
I and my soul to range in range of thee.

O Thou transcendent,
Nameless, the fibre and the breath,   195
Light of the light, shedding forth universes, thou centre of them,
Thou mightier centre of the true, the good, the loving,
Thou moral, spiritual fountain—affection's source—thou reservoir,
(O pensive soul of me—O thirst unsatisfied—waitest not there?
Waitest not haply for us somewhere there the Comrade perfect?)   200
Thou pulse—thou motive of the stars, suns, systems,
That, circling, move in order, safe, harmonious,
Athwart the shapeless vastnesses of space,
How should I think, how breathe a single breath, how speak, if out
    of myself,
I could not launch, to those, superior universes?   205

Swiftly I shrivel at the thought of God,
At Nature and its wonders, Time and Space and Death,
But that I, turning, call to thee O soul, thou actual Me,
And lo, thou gently masterest the orbs,

Thou matest Time, smilest content at Death,
And fillest, swellest full the vastnesses of Space.

Greater than stars or suns,
Bounding O soul thou journeyest forth;
What love than thine and ours could wider amplify?
What aspirations, wishes, outvie thine and ours O soul?
What dreams of the ideal? what plans of purity, perfection,
    strength,
What cheerful willingness for others' sake to give up all?
For others' sake to suffer all?

Reckoning ahead O soul, when thou, the time achiev'd,
The seas all cross'd, weather'd the capes, the voyage done,
Surrounded, copest, frontest God, yieldest, the aim attain'd,
As fill'd with friendship, love complete, the Elder Brother found,
The Younger melts in fondness in his arms.

9

Passage to more than India!
Are thy wings plumed indeed for such far flights?
·O soul, voyagest thou indeed on voyages like those?
Disportest thou on waters such as those?
Soundest below the Sanscrit and the Vedas?
Then have thy bent unleash'd.

Passage to you, your shores, ye aged fierce enigmas!
Passage to you, to mastership of you, ye strangling problems!
You, strew'd with the wrecks of skeletons, that, living, never
    reach'd you.

Passage to more than India!
O secret of the earth and sky!
Of you O waters of the sea! O winding creeks and rivers!
Of you O woods and fields! of you strong mountains of my land!
Of you O prairies! of you gray rocks!
O morning red! O clouds! O rain and snows!
O day and night, passage to you!

O sun and moon and all you stars! Sirius and Jupiter!
Passage to you!

Passage, immediate passage! the blood burns in my veins!
Away O soul! hoist instantly the anchor!
Cut the hawsers—haul out—shake out every sail!
Have we not stood here like trees in the ground long enough?   245
Have we not grovel'd here long enough, eating and drinking like
    mere brutes?
Have we not darken'd and dazed ourselves with books long enough?

Sail forth—steer for the deep waters only,
Reckless O soul, exploring, I with thee, and thou with me,
For we are bound where mariner has not yet dared to go,   250
And we will risk the ship, ourselves and all.

O my brave soul!
O farther farther sail!
O daring joy, but safe! are they not all the seas of God?
O farther, farther, farther sail!   255

THE LAST INVOCATION

At the last, tenderly,
From the walls of the powerful fortress'd house,
From the clasp of the knitted locks, from the keep of the well-
    closed doors,
Let me be wafted.

Let me glide noiselessly forth;   5
With the key of softness unlock the locks—with a whisper,
Set ope the doors O soul.

Tenderly—be not impatient,
(Strong is your hold O mortal flesh,
Strong is your hold O love.)   10

AFTER THE DAZZLE OF DAY

After the dazzle of day is gone,
Only the dark, dark night shows to my eyes the stars;
After the clangor of organ majestic, or chorus, or perfect band,
Silent, athwart my soul, moves the symphony true.

A TWILIGHT SONG

As I sit in twilight late alone by the flickering oak-flame,
Musing on long-pass'd war scenes—of the countless buried un-
    known soldiers,
Of the vacant names, as unindented air's and sea's—the unreturn'd,
The brief truce after battle, with grim burial-squads, and the deep-
    fill'd trenches
Of gather'd dead from all America, North, South, East, West,
    whence they came up,
From wooded Maine, New-England's farms, from fertile Pennsyl-
    vania, Illinois, Ohio,
From the measureless West, Virginia, the South, the Carolinas,
    Texas,
(Even here in my room-shadows and half-lights in the noiseless
    flickering flames,
Again I see the stalwart ranks on-filing, rising—I hear the rhythmic
    tramp of the armies;)
You million unwrit names all, all—you dark bequest from all the
    war,
A special verse for you—a flash of duty long neglected—your
    mystic roll strangely gather'd here,
Each name recall'd by me from out the darkness and death's ashes,
Henceforth to be, deep, deep within my heart recording, for many
    a future year,
Your mystic roll entire of unknown names, or North or South,
Embalm'd with love in this twilight song.

℃ EMILY DICKINSON spent her life in Amherst, Massachusetts. Her father was a prominent lawyer, legislator, and treasurer of Amherst College. He was also particularly eager for his children to remain near him; Emily and her younger sister Lavinia never married, and they lived with their father until he died in 1874. Their one brother, William Austin, did marry, but he moved no farther than next door. Emily was well educated, considering the usual practice for women in the nineteenth century. She finished the course at Amherst Academy and

Emily Dickinson

[1830-1886]

went to Mount Holyoke Female Seminary for one year. After she was grown she left the tight, secure little world of Amherst only three times. In 1854 she went to be with her father in Washington, where he was a member of Congress. Ten years later she went to Boston twice for eye examinations. During a visit to Philadelphia on the return trip from Washington, she presumably had an infatuation with the Reverend Charles Wadsworth. Lack of better evidence points to this visit as the source in experience for her love poems.

Very few of Miss Dickinson's poems were published during her lifetime; to no printing did she give her consent. Her sister-in-law sent one poem to the *Springfield Republican,* which published it on February 14, 1866, and Helen Hunt Jackson sent one to G. P. Lathrop, who published it in *A Masque of Poets* in 1878. After her death, Emily's relatives and friends began to make known her sizable literary remains in a sequence of small volumes published over the years from 1890 to 1945.

Her reputation gradually rose as each volume was issued. Since the 1920's Emily Dickinson has been generally recognized as belonging in the top rank of American poets. A complete edition of her poetry, including variant readings, was published in 1955 under the editorship of Thomas H. Johnson.

SUCCESS IS COUNTED SWEETEST

Success is counted sweetest
By those who ne'er succeed.
To comprehend a nectar
Requires sorest need.

Not one of all the purple host
Who took the flag today
Can tell the definition
So clear of victory

As he defeated, dying,
On whose forbidden ear
The distant strains of triumph
Burst agonized and clear.

I NEVER HEAR THE WORD ''ESCAPE''

I never hear the word "escape"
Without a quicker blood,
A sudden expectation,
A flying attitude.

I never hear of prisons broad
By soldiers battered down
But I tug childish at my bars
Only to fail again.

SURGEONS MUST BE VERY CAREFUL

Surgeons must be very careful
When they take the knife.
Underneath their fine incisions
Stirs the culprit, *life*.

BRING ME THE SUNSET IN A CUP

Bring me the sunset in a cup,
Reckon the morning's flagons up

And say how many dew,
Tell me how far the morning leaps,
Tell me what time the weaver sleeps   5
Who spun the breadths of blue.

Write me how many notes there be
In the new robin's ecstasy
Among astonished boughs,
How many trips the tortoise makes,   10
How many cups the bee partakes,
The debauchee of dews.

Also, who laid the rainbow's piers,
Also, who leads the docile spheres
By withes of supple blue?   15
Whose fingers string the stalactite,
Who counts the wampum of the night
To see that none is due?

Who built this little alban house
And shut the windows down so close   20
My spirit cannot see?
Who'll let me out some gala day
With implements to fly away,
Passing pomposity?

19. *alban:* white.

A WOUNDED DEER LEAPS HIGHEST

A wounded deer leaps highest,
I've heard the hunter tell.
'Tis but the ecstasy of death,
And then the brake is still.

The smitten rock that gushes,   5
The trampled steel that springs!
A cheek is always redder
Just where the hectic stings.

Mirth is the mail of anguish,
In which it cautious arm   10
Lest anybody spy the blood
And "You're hurt" exclaim!

TWO SWIMMERS WRESTLED
ON THE SPAR

Two swimmers wrestled on the spar
Until the morning sun.
When one turned smiling to the land;
Oh God, the other one!

The stray ships, passing,
Spied a face
Upon the waters borne
With eyes in death still begging raised
And hands beseeching thrown.

I TASTE A LIQUOR NEVER BREWED

I taste a liquor never brewed
From tankards scooped in pearl.
Not all the Frankfort berries
Yield such an alcohol.

Inebriate of air am I
And debauchee of dew,
Reeling, thro endless summer days,
From inns of molten blue.

When "landlords" turn the drunken bee
Out of the foxglove's door,
When butterflies renounce their drams,
I shall but drink the more!

Till seraphs swing their snowy hats,
And saints to windows run
To see the little tippler
From Manzanilla come!

"HOPE" IS THE THING WITH
FEATHERS

"Hope" is the thing with feathers
That perches in the soul

And sings the tune without the words
And never stops at all,

And sweetest in the gale is heard;   5
And sore must be the storm
That could abash the little bird
That kept so many warm.

I've heard it in the chillest land
And on the strangest sea,   10
Yet never, in extremity,
It asked a crumb of me.

THERE'S A CERTAIN SLANT OF LIGHT

There's a certain slant of light,
Winter afternoons,
That oppresses, like the heft
Of cathedral tunes.

Heavenly hurt it gives us.   5
We can find no scar,
But internal difference
Where the meanings are.

None may teach it any—
'Tis the seal despair,   10
An imperial affliction
Sent us of the air.

When it comes, the landscape listens;
Shadows hold their breath.
When it goes, 'tis like the distance   15
On the look of death.

I FELT A FUNERAL IN MY BRAIN

I felt a funeral in my brain,
And mourners to and fro
Kept treading, treading, till it seemed
That sense was breaking through.

And when they all were seated,
A service like a drum
Kept beating, beating, till I thought
My mind was going numb.

And then I heard them lift a box
And creak across my soul   10
With those same boots of lead again;
Then space began to toll,

As all the Heavens were a bell,
And being but an ear,
And I and silence some strange race   15
Wrecked solitary here.

And then a plank in reason broke,
And I dropped down and down
And hit a world at every plunge,
And finished knowing then.   20

I KNOW SOME LONELY HOUSES
OFF THE ROAD

I know some lonely houses off the road
A robber'd like the look of—
Wooden barred,
And windows hanging low,
Inviting to   5
A portico,
Where two could creep;
One hand the tools,
The other peep
To make sure all's asleep—   10
Old fashioned eyes
Not easy to surprise!

How orderly the kitchen'd look by night,
With just a clock,
But they could gag the tick,   15
And mice won't bark;
And so the walls don't tell,
None will.

A pair of spectacles ajar just stir;
An almanac's aware.   20
Was it the mat winked,
Or a nervous star?
The moon slides down the stair
To see who's there.

There's plunder, where   25
Tankard or spoon,
Earring or stone,
A watch, some ancient brooch
To match the grandmama
Staid sleeping there.   30

Day rattles too;
Stealth's slow.
The sun has got as far
As the third sycamore.
Screams Chanticleer,   35
"Who's there?"

And echoes, trains away,
Sneer, "Where?"
While the old couple, just astir,
Fancy the sunrise left the door ajar.   40

THE SOUL SELECTS HER OWN SOCIETY

The soul selects her own society,
Then shuts the door—
To her divine majority
Present no more.

Unmoved she notes the chariots pausing   5
At her low gate;
Unmoved, an Emperor be kneeling
Upon her mat.

I've known her from an ample nation
Choose one,   10
Then close the valves of her attention
Like stone.

A BIRD CAME DOWN THE WALK

A bird came down the walk.
He did not know I saw.
He bit an angleworm in halves
And ate the fellow raw,

And then he drank a dew   5
From a convenient grass,
And then hopped sidewise to the wall
To let a beetle pass.

He glanced with rapid eyes
That hurried all around;   10
They looked like frightened beads, I thought;
He stirred his velvet head

Like one in danger, cautious;
I offered him a crumb,
And he unrolled his feathers   15
And rode him softer home

Than oars divide the ocean,
Too silver for a seam,
Or butterflies off banks of noon
Leap, plashless as they swim.   20

AFTER GREAT PAIN, A FORMAL
FEELING COMES

After great pain, a formal feeling comes.
The nerves sit ceremonious, like tombs.
The stiff heart questions was it he that bore,
And yesterday, or centuries before?

The feet, mechanical, go round,   5
Of ground, or air, or ought,
A wooden way
Regardless grown,
A quartz contentment, like a stone.

This is the hour of lead,   10
Remembered, if outlived,
As freezing persons recollect the snow:
First chill, then stupor, then the letting go.

IT MIGHT BE LONELIER

It might be lonelier
Without the loneliness.
I'm so accustomed to my fate,
Perhaps the other peace

Would interrupt the dark   5
And crowd the little room
Too scant by cubits to contain
The sacrament of him.

I am not used to hope.
It might intrude upon   10
Its sweet parade, blaspheme the place
Ordained to suffering.

It might be easier
To fail with land in sight
Than gain my blue peninsula   15
To perish of delight.

I DIED FOR BEAUTY

I died for beauty, but was scarce
Adjusted in the tomb
When one who died for truth was lain
In an adjoining room.

He questioned softly why I failed,   5
"For beauty," I replied.
"And I for truth. Themself are one.
We bretheren are," he said.

And so, as kinsmen, met a night,
We talked between the rooms,   10

Until the moss had reached our lips
And covered up our names.

I HEARD A FLY BUZZ WHEN I DIED

I heard a fly buzz when I died.
The stillness in the room
Was like the stillness in the air
Between the heaves of storm.

The eyes around had wrung them dry,   5
And breaths were gathering firm
For that last onset when the king
Be witnessed in the room.

I willed my keepsakes, signed away
What portion of me be   10
Assignable; and then it was
There interposed a fly

With blue uncertain stumbling buzz
Between the light and me;
And then the windows failed; and then   15
I could not see to see.

'TWAS WARM AT FIRST, LIKE US

'Twas warm at first, like us,
Until there crept upon
A chill, like frost upon a glass,
Till all the scene be gone.

The forehead copied stone.   5
The fingers grew too cold
To ache, and like a skater's brook,
The busy eyes congealed.

It straightened, that was all;
It crowded cold to cold.   10
It multiplied indifference,
As pride were all it could.

And even when with cords,
'Twas lowered, like a weight,
It made no signal, nor demurred,   15
But dropped like adamant.

I TOOK MY POWER IN MY HAND

I took my power in my hand
And went against the world;
'Twas not so much as David had,
But I was twice as bold.

I aimed my pebble, but myself   5
Was all the one that fell.
Was it Goliah was too large
Or was myself too small?

I'VE SEEN A DYING EYE

I've seen a dying eye
Run round and round a room
In search of something as it seemed,
Then cloudier become,
And then obscure with fog,   5
And then be soldered down
Without disclosing what it be
'Twere blessed to have seen.

I GAVE MYSELF TO HIM

I gave myself to him,
And took himself for pay.
The solemn contract of a life
Was ratified this way.

The wealth might disappoint,   5
Myself a poorer prove
Than this great purchaser suspect,
The daily own of love

Depreciate the vision;
But till the merchant buy,   10
Still fable in the Isles of Spice
The subtle cargoes lie.

At least 'tis mutual risk,
Some found it mutual gain,
Sweet debt of life each night to owe,   15
Insolvent every noon.

I LIKE TO SEE IT LAP THE MILES

I like to see it lap the miles
And lick the valleys up,
And stop to feed itself at tanks
And then prodigious step

Around a pile of mountains,   5
And supercilious peer
In shanties by the sides of roads,
And then a quarry pare

To fit its sides
And crawl between   10
Complaining all the while
In horrid, hooting stanza,
Then chase itself down hill

And neigh like Boanerges,
Then prompter than a star,   15
Stop, docile and omnipotent,
At its own stable door.

PAIN HAS AN ELEMENT OF BLANK

Pain has an element of blank.
It cannot recollect
When it begun or if there were
A time when it was not.

It has no future but itself;   5
Its infinite contain
Its past, enlightened to perceive
New periods of pain.

THEY SAY THAT "TIME ASSUAGES"

They say that "Time assuages."
Time never did assuage.
An actual suffering strengthens
As sinews do, with age.

Time is a test of trouble   5
But not a remedy.
If such it prove, it prove too
There was no malady.

BECAUSE I COULD NOT STOP FOR DEATH

Because I could not stop for Death,
He kindly stopped for me.
The carriage held but just ourselves
And immortality.

We slowly drove. He knew no haste,   5
And I had put away
My labor and my leisure too,
For his civility.

We passed the school where children strove
At recess in the ring.   10
We passed the fields of gazing grain;
We passed the setting sun—

Or rather, he passed us.
The dews drew quivering and chill,
For only gossamer my gown,   15
My tippet only tulle.

We paused before a house that seemed
A swelling of the ground.
The roof was scarcely visible,
The cornice in the ground.   2(

Since then 'tis centuries, and yet
Feels shorter than the day
I first surmised the horses' heads
Were toward Eternity.

SHE ROSE TO HIS REQUIREMENT

She rose to his requirement—dropped
The playthings of her life
To take the honorable work
Of woman and of wife.

If aught she missed in her new day   !
Of amplitude or awe,
Or first prospective, or the gold
In using wear away,

It lay unmentioned as the sea
Develop pearl and weed,   1(
But only to himself be known
The fathoms they abide.

5. *aught*: manuscript reads "ought."

REMORSE IS MEMORY AWAKE

Remorse is memory awake,
Her parties all astir,
A presence of departed acts
At window and at door.

Its past set down before the soul   !
And lighted with a match,
Perusal to facilitate
And help belief to stretch.

Remorse is cureless—the disease
Not even God can heal,   1(

For 'tis his institution and
The adequate of Hell.

THE WIND BEGUN TO KNEAD
THE GRASS

The wind begun to knead the grass
As women do a dough;
He flung a handful at the plain,
A handful at the sky.
The leaves unhooked themselves from trees   5
And started all abroad;
The dust did scoop itself like hands
And throw away the road.
The wagons quickened on the street;
The thunders gossiped low;   10
The lightning showed a yellow head
And then a livid toe.
The birds put up the bars to nests;
The cattle flung to barns.
Then came one drop of giant rain;   15
And then, as if the hands
That held the dams had parted hold,
The waters wrecked the sky,
But overlooked my father's house,
Just quartering a tree.   20

AMPLE MAKE THIS BED

Ample make this bed;
Make this bed with awe.
In it wait till judgment break
Excellent and fair.

Be its mattress straight;   5
Be its pillow round;
Let no sunrise' yellow noise
Interrupt this ground.

WE OUTGROW LOVE LIKE
OTHER THINGS

We outgrow love, like other things,
And put it in the drawer,
Till it an antique fashion shows
Like costumes grandsires wore.

A NARROW FELLOW IN THE GRASS

A narrow fellow in the grass
Occasionally rides.
You may have met him—did you not?
His notice sudden is.

The grass divides as with a comb,
A spotted shaft is seen,
And then it closes at your feet
And opens further on.

He likes a boggy acre,
A floor too cool for corn;
Yet when a boy and barefoot,
I more than once at noon

Have passed, I thought, a whip-lash
Unbraiding in the sun;
When, stooping to secure it,
It wrinkled and was gone.

Several of nature's people
I know, and they know me;
I feel for them a transport
Of cordiality;

But never met this fellow,
Attended or alone,
Without a tighter breathing
And zero at the bone.

I NEVER SAW A MOOR

I never saw a moor;
I never saw the sea.
Yet know I how the heather looks
And what a billow be.

I never spoke with God,   5
Nor visited in Heaven.
Yet certain am I of the spot
As if the checks were given.

THE LAST NIGHT THAT SHE LIVED

The last night that she lived,
It was a common night
Except the dying—this to us
Made nature different.

We noticed smallest things,   5
Things overlooked before,
By this great light upon our minds
Italicized, as 'twere.

As we went out and in
Between her final room   10
And rooms where those to be alive
Tomorrow were, a blame

That others could exist
While she must finish quite,
A jealousy for her arose   15
So nearly infinite.

We waited while she passed;
It was a narrow time.
Too jostled were our souls to speak.
At length the notice came.   20

She mentioned, and forgot;
Then lightly as a reed
Bent to the water, struggled scarce,
Consented, and was dead.

And we, we placed the hair   2
And drew the head erect;
And then an awful leisure was
Belief to regulate.

IMMORTAL IS AN AMPLE WORD

Immortal is an ample word
When what we need is by,
But when it leaves us for a time
'Tis a necessity.

Of Heaven above the firmest proof   5
We fundamental know,
Except for its marauding hand
It had been Heaven below.

AS IMPERCEPTIBLY AS GRIEF

As imperceptibly as grief
The summer lapsed away,
Too imperceptible at last
To seem like perfidy.
A quietness distilled   5
As twilight long begun,
Or nature spending with herself
Sequestered afternoon.
The dusk drew earlier in.
The morning foreign shone,   10
A courteous, yet harrowing grace,
As guest, that would be gone.
And thus, without a wing
Or service of a keel
Our summer made her light escape   15
Into the beautiful.

OF GOD WE ASK ONE FAVOR

Of God we ask one favor,
That we may be forgiven—
For what, he is presumed to know;
The crime from us is hidden.
Immured the whole of life   5
Within a magic prison,
We reprimand the happiness
That too competes with Heaven.

MY LIFE CLOSED TWICE BEFORE
ITS CLOSE

My life closed twice before its close;
It yet remains to see
If immortality unveil
A third event to me,

So huge, so hopeless to conceive   5
As these that twice befell.
Parting is all we know of heaven,
And all we need of hell.

❧ GERARD MANLEY HOPKINS is more commonly dissociated from his own age than any other Victorian poet. Because his poems were not published until 1918, well after his death, he had no impact on such contemporaries as Tennyson, Browning, Hardy, and Pater. His influence during his lifetime extended little farther than his own circle of friends, including notably Robert Bridges, English poet laureate (1913) who later supervised the publication of Hopkins' work. In addition, the twentieth-century reader finds Hopkins strikingly modern. Actually he should be understood as a product of the revival of medievalism in Victorian England.

Gerard Manley Hopkins

[1844-1889]

Hopkins was born in Stratford, Essex; a pious mother and an intellectual father cultivated the arts and saw to the careful education of their children. Gerard went, in 1863, to Ballilol College, Oxford, where he took a first-class Honors degree and distinguished himself as the best scholar in the college. At Oxford he became acquainted with the theologians who were particularly concerned with establishing the authority and catholicity of the English church. At first he was a follower of E. B. Pusey, the great defender of the Anglican *via media*. Ultimately, however, Hopkins found greater satisfaction in the Catholic church and was received there by John Henry Newman in 1866. After a short term as a teacher, Hopkins determined to enter the priesthood and became a novice in the Society of Jesus in 1868. At this point he burned all of his manuscripts that he could find, and resolved to turn his mind from poetry forever. As he continued his medieval studies he was much influenced by the philosopher Duns Scotus; undoubtedly these medieval studies also influenced his emerging ideas about poetry, for when he resumed writing he was deeply concerned to recapture the strength of the four-beat lines of early medieval English poetry. The poetry of Hopkins which survives was produced between 1875 and his death. It is not surprising to find many religious themes in his poems; their genius, however, results from his vision of the beauties of this world in a dramatic and theological context.

HEAVEN-HAVEN

A Nun Takes the Veil

I have desired to go
   Where springs not fail,
To fields where flies no sharp and sided hail
   And a few lilies blow.

And I have asked to be   5
   Where no storms come,
Where the green swell is in the havens dumb,
   And out of the swing of the sea.

THE HABIT OF PERFECTION

Elected Silence, sing to me
And beat upon my whorlèd ear,
Pipe me to pastures still and be
The music that I care to hear.

Shape nothing, lips; be lovely-dumb: 5
It is the shut, the curfew sent
From there where all surrenders come
Which only makes you eloquent.

Be shellèd, eyes, with double dark
And find the uncreated light: 10
This ruck and reel which you remark
Coils, keeps, and teases simple sight.

Palate, the hutch of tasty lust,
Desire not to be rinsed with wine:
The can must be so sweet, the crust   15
So fresh that come in fasts divine!

Nostrils, your careless breath that spend
Upon the stir and keep of pride,
What relish shall the censers send
Along the sanctuary side!   20

O feel-of-primrose hands, O feet
That want the yield of plushy sward,
But you shall walk the golden street
And you unhouse and house the Lord.

And, Poverty, be thou the bride   25
And now the marriage feast begun,
And lily-colored clothes provide
Your spouse not labored-at nor spun.

GOD'S GRANDEUR

The world is charged with the grandeur of God.
  It will flame out, like shining from shook foil;
  It gathers to a greatness, like the ooze of oil
Crushed. Why do men then now not reck his rod?
Generations have trod, have trod, have trod;   5
  And all is seared with trade; bleared, smeared with toil;
  And wears man's smudge and shares man's smell: the soil
Is bare now, nor can foot feel, being shod.

And for all this, nature is never spent;
  There lives the dearest freshness deep down things;   10
And though the last lights off the black West went
  Oh, morning, at the brown brink eastward, springs—
Because the Holy Ghost over the bent
  World broods with warm breast and with ah! bright wings.

SPRING

Nothing is so beautiful as spring—
  When weeds, in wheels, shoot long and lovely and lush;
  Thrush's eggs look little low heavens, and thrush
Through the echoing timber does so rinse and wring
The ear, it strikes like lightnings to hear him sing;   5
  The glassy peartree leaves and blooms, they brush
  The descending blue; that blue is all in a rush
With richness; the racing lambs too have fair their fling.

What is all this juice and all this joy?
   A strain of the earth's sweet being in the beginning   10
In Eden garden.——Have, get, before it cloy,
   Before it cloud, Christ, lord, and sour with sinning,
Innocent mind and Mayday in girl and boy,
   Most, O maid's child, thy choice and worthy the winning.

THE WINDHOVER

To Christ Our Lord

I caught this morning morning's minion, king-
   dom of daylight's dauphin, dapple-dawn-drawn Falcon, in his
      riding
Of the rolling level underneath him steady air, and striding
High there, how he rung upon the rein of a wimpling wing
In his ecstasy! then off, off forth on swing,   5
   As a skate's heel sweeps smooth on a bow-bend: the hurl and
      gliding
Rebuffed the big wind. My heart in hiding
Stirred for a bird,——the achieve of, the mastery of the thing!

Brute beauty and valor and act, oh, air, pride, plume here
   Buckle! AND the fire that breaks from thee then, a billion   10
Times told lovelier, more dangerous, O my chevalier!

   No wonder of it: shéer plód makes plough down sillion
Shine, and blue-bleak embers, ah my dear,
   Fall, gall themselves, and gash gold-vermilion.

   12. *sillion:* obsolete form of *selion,* the ridge between two furrows.

PIED BEAUTY

   Glory be to God for dappled things——
      For skies of couple-color as a brinded cow;
         For rose-moles all in stipple upon trout that swim;
   Fresh-firecoal chestnut-falls; finches' wings;
      Landscape plotted and pieced——fold, fallow, and plough;   5
         And áll trádes, their gear and tackle and trim.

   2. *brinded:* streaked, spotted, brindled.

All things counter, original, spare, strange;
  Whatever is fickle, freckled (who knows how?)
    With swift, slow; sweet, sour; adazzle, dim;
He fathers-forth whose beauty is past change: 1•
          Praise him.

THE LOSS OF THE EURYDICE

Foundered March 24, 1878

The Eurydice—it concerned thee, O Lord:
Three hundred souls, O alas! on board,
    Some asleep unawakened, all un-
warned, eleven fathoms fallen

Where she foundered! One stroke
Felled and furled them, the hearts of oak!
    And flockbells off the aerial
Downs' forefalls beat to the burial.

For did she pride her, freighted fully, on
Bounden bales or a hoard of bullion?—   1
    Precious passing measure,
Lads and men her lade and treasure.

She had come from a cruise, training seamen—
Men, boldboys soon to be men: 1
    Must it, worst weather,
Blast bole and bloom together?

No Atlantic squall overwrought her
Or rearing billow of the Biscay water:
    Home was hard at hand   2
And the blow bore from land.

And you were a liar, O blue March day.
Bright sun lanced fire in the heavenly bay;
    But what black Boreas wrecked her? he
Came equipped, deadly-electric,

A beetling baldbright cloud thorough England   2
Riding: there did storms not mingle? and
    Hailropes hustle and grind their
Heavengravel? wolfsnow, worlds of it, wind there?

Now Carisbrook keep goes under in gloom;
Now it overvaults Appledurcombe;   30
   Now near by Ventnor town
It hurls, hurls off Boniface Down.

Too proud, too proud, what a press she bore!
Royal, and all her royals wore.
   Sharp with her, shorten sail!   35
Too late; lost; gone with the gale.

This was that fell capsize,
As half she had righted and hoped to rise
   Death teeming in by her portholes
Raced down decks, round messes of mortals.   40

Then a lurch forward, frigate and men;
"All hands for themselves" the cry ran then;
   But she who had housed them thither
Was around them, bound them or wound them with her.

Marcus Hare, high her captain,   45
Kept to her—care-drowned and wrapped in
   Cheer's death, would follow
His charge through the champ-white water-in-a-wallow,

All under Channel to bury in a beach her
Cheeks: Right, rude of feature,   50
   He thought he heard say
"Her commander! and thou too, and thou this way."

It is even seen, time's something server,
In mankind's medley a duty-swerver,
   At downright "No or yes?"   55
Doffs all, drives full for righteousness.

Sydney Fletcher, Bristol-bred,
(Low lie his mates now on watery bed)
   Takes to the seas and snows
As sheer down the ship goes.   60

Now her afterdraught gullies him too down;
Now he wrings for breath with the deathgush brown;
   Till a lifebelt and God's will
Lend him a lift from the sea-swill.

Now he shoots short up to the round air;   65
Now he gasps, now he gazes everywhere;
    But his eye no cliff, no coast or
Mark makes in the rivelling snowstorm.

Him, after an hour of wintry waves,
A schooner sights, with another, and saves,   70
    And he boards her in Oh! such joy
He has lost count what came next, poor boy.——

They say who saw one sea-corpse cold
He was all of lovely manly mould,
    Every inch a tar,   75
Of the best we boast our sailors are.

Look, foot to forelock, how all things suit! he
Is strung by duty, is strained to beauty,
    And brown-as-dawning-skinned
With brine and shine and whirling wind.   80

O his nimble finger, his gnarled grip!
Leagues, leagues of seamanship
    Slumber in these forsaken
Bones, this sinew, and will not waken.

He was but one like thousands more,   85
Day and night I deplore
    My people and born own nation,
Fast foundering own generation.

I might let bygones be——our curse
Of ruinous shrine no hand or, worse,   90
    Robbery's hand is busy to
Dress, hoar-hallowèd shrines unvisited;

Only the breathing temple and fleet
Life, this wildworth blown so sweet,
    These daredeaths, ay this crew, in   95
Unchrist, all rolled in ruin——

Deeply surely I need to deplore it,
Wondering why my master bore it,
    The riving off that race
So at home, time was, to his truth and grace   100

68. *rivelling*: entangling.

That a starlight-wender of ours would say
The marvellous Milk was Walsingham Way
      And one—but let be, let be:
More, more than was will yet be.——

O well wept, mother have lost son;   105
Wept, wife; wept, sweetheart would be one:
      Though grief yield them no good
Yet shed what tears sad truelove should.

But to Christ lord of thunder
Crouch; lay knee by earth low under: 110
      "Holiest, loveliest, bravest,
Save my hero, O Hero savest.

And the prayer thou hearst me making
Have, at the awful overtaking,
      Heard; have heard and granted   115
Grace that day grace was wanted."

Not that hell knows redeeming,
But for souls sunk in seeming
      Fresh, till doomfire burn all,
Prayer shall fetch pity eternal.   120

AT THE WEDDING MARCH

God with honor hang your head,
Groom, and grace you, bride, your bed
With lissome scions, sweet scions,
Out of hallowed bodies bred.

Each be other's comfort kind: 5
Déep, déeper than divined,
Divine charity, dear charity,
Fast you ever, fast bind.

Then let the march tread our ears:
I to him turn with tears   10
Who to wedlock, his wonder wedlock,
Déals tríumph and immortal years.

FELIX RANDAL

Felix Randal the farrier, O he is dead then? my duty all ended,
Who have watched his mould of man, big-boned and hardy-
    handsome
Pining, pining, till time when reason rambled in it and some
Fatal four disorders, fleshed there, all contended?

Sickness broke him. Impatient he cursed at first, but mended
Being anointed and all; though a heavenlier heart began some
Months earlier, since I had our sweet reprieve and ransom
Tendered to him. Ah well, God rest him all road ever he offended!

This seeing the sick endears them to us, us too it endears.
My tongue had taught thee comfort, touch had quenched thy tears,   1
Thy tears that touched my heart, child, Felix, poor Felix Randal;

How far from then forethought of, all thy more boisterous years,
When thou at the random grim forge, powerful amidst peers,
Didst fettle for the great grey drayhorse his bright and battering
    sandal!

BROTHERS

How lovely the elder brother's
Life all laced in the other's,
Lóve-laced!—what once I well
Witnessed; so fortune fell.
When Shrovetide, two years gone,
Our boys' plays brought on
Part was picked for John,
Young Jóhn; then fear, then joy
Ran revel in the elder boy.
Their night was come now; all   1
Our company thronged the hall;
Henry, by the wall,
Beckoned me beside him:
I came where called, and eyed him
By meanwhiles; making mý play   1

Turn most on tender byplay.
For, wrung all on love's rack,
My lad, and lost in Jack,
Smiled, blushed, and bit his lip;
Or drove, with a diver's dip,   20
Clutched hands down through clasped knees—
Truth's tokens tricks like these,
Old telltales, with what stress
He hung on the imp's success.
Now the other was bráss-bóld: 25
Hé had no work to hold
His heart up at the strain;
Nay, roguish ran the vein.
Two tedious acts were past;
Jack's call and cue at last: 30
When Henry, heart-forsook,
Dropped eyes and dared not look.
Eh, how áll rúng!
Young dog, he did give tongue!
But Harry—in his hands he has flung   35
His tear-tricked cheeks of flame
For fond love and for shame.
    Ah Nature, framed in fault,
There's comfort then, there's salt;
Nature, bad, base, and blind,   40
Dearly thou canst be kind;
There dearly thén, deárly,
I'll cry thou canst be kind.

SPRING AND FALL

To a Young Child

Márgarét, are you gríeving
Over Goldengrove unleaving?
Leáves, líke the things of man, you
With your fresh thoughts care for, can you?
Áh! ás the heart grows older   5
It will come to such sights colder

By and by, nor spare a sigh
Though worlds of wanwood leafmeal lie;
And yet you wíll weep and know why.
Now no matter, child, the name:
Sórrow's spríngs áre the same.
Nor mouth had, no nor mind, expressed
What heart heard of, ghost guessed:
It ís the blight man was born for,
It is Margaret you mourn for.

INVERSNAID

This darksome burn, horseback brown,
His rollrock highroad roaring down,
In coop and in comb the fleece of his foam
Flutes and low to the lake falls home.

A windpuff-bonnet of fáwn-fróth
Turns and twindles over the broth
Of a pool so pitchblack, féll-frówning,
It rounds and rounds Despair to drowning.

Degged with dew, dappled with dew
Are the groins of the braes that the brook treads through,
Wiry heathpacks, flitches of fern,
And the beadbonny ash that sits over the burn.

What would the world be, once bereft
Of wet and of wildness? Let them be left,
O let them be left, wildness and wet;
Long live the weeds and the wilderness yet.

6. *twindles*: twists.

(CARRION COMFORT)

Not, I'll not, carrion comfort, Despair, not feast on thee;
Not untwist—slack they may be—these last strands of man
In me ór, most weary, cry *I can no more*. I can;
Can something, hope, wish day come, not choose not to be.
But ah, but O thou terrible, why wouldst thou rude on me

Thy wring-world right foot rock? lay a lionlimb against me? scan
With darksome devouring eyes my bruisèd bones? and fan,
O in turns of tempest, me heaped there; me frantic to avoid thee and
    flee?

  Why? That my chaff might fly; my grain lie, sheer and clear.
Nay in all that toil, that coil, since (seems) I kissed the rod,   10
Hand rather, my heart lo! lapped strength, stole joy, would laugh,
    chéer.
Cheer whom though? the hero whose heaven-handling flung me,
    fóot tród
Me? or me that fought him? O which one? is it each one? That
    night, that year
Of now done darkness I wretch lay wrestling with (my God!) my
    God.

NO WORST, THERE IS NONE

No worst, there is none. Pitched past pitch of grief,
More pangs will, schooled at forepangs, wilder wring.
Comforter, where, where is your comforting?
Mary, mother of us, where is your relief?
My cries heave, herds-long; huddle in a main, a chief   5
Woe, wórld-sorrow; on an áge-old anvil wince and sing—
Then lull, then leave off. Fury had shrieked "No ling-
ering! Let me be fell: force I must be brief."

  O the mind, mind has mountains; cliffs of fall
Frightful, sheer, no-man-fathomed. Hold them cheap   10
May who ne'er hung there. Nor does long our small
Durance deal with that steep or deep. Here! creep,
Wretch, under a comfort serves in a whirlwind: all
Life death does end and each day dies with sleep.

TO SEEM THE STRANGER LIES MY
LOT, MY LIFE

  To seem the stranger lies my lot, my life
  Among strangers. Father and mother dear,
  Brothers and sisters are in Christ not near

And he my peace my parting, sword and strife.
   England, whose honor O all my heart woos, wife   5
To my creating thought, would neither hear
Me, were I pleading, plead nor do I: I wear-
y of idle a being but by where wars are rife.

   I am in Ireland now; now I am at a thírd
Remove. Not but in all removes I can   10
Kind love both give and get. Only what word
Wisest my heart breeds dark heaven's baffling ban
Bars or hell's spell thwarts. This to hoard unheard,
Heard unheeded, leaves me a lonely began.

I WAKE AND FEEL THE FELL OF DARK, NOT DAY

I wake and feel the fell of dark, not day.
What hours, O what black hoürs we have spent
This night! what sights you, heart, saw; ways you went!
And more must, in yet longer light's delay.
    With witness I speak this. But where I say   5
Hours I mean years, mean life. And my lament
Is cries countless, cries like dead letters sent
To dearest him that lives alas! away.

   I am gall, I am heartburn. God's most deep decree
Bitter would have me taste: my taste was me;   10
Bones built in me, flesh filled, blood brimmed the curse.
   Selfyeast of spirit a dull dough sours. I see
The lost are like this, and their scourge to be
As I am mine, their sweating selves; but worse.

PATIENCE, HARD THING!

Patience, hard thing! the hard thing but to pray,
But bid for, Patience is! Patience who asks
Wants war, wants wounds; weary his times, his tasks;
To do without, take tosses, and obey.
   Rare patience roots in these, and, these away,   5
Nowhere. Natural heart's ivy, Patience masks

Our ruins of wrecked past purpose. There she basks
Purple eyes and seas of liquid leaves all day.

We hear our hearts grate on themselves: it kills
To bruise them dearer. Yet the rebellious wills   10
Of us we do bid God bend to him even so.
And where is he who more and more distils
Delicious kindness?   —   He is patient. Patience fills
His crisp combs, and that comes those ways we know.

❡ WILLIAM BUTLER YEATS was taken by his parents from Dublin to London shortly after his birth, but Ireland remained his spiritual home. As a child he visited his maternal grandparents in Sligo, and early developed a fascination with Irish legends, folk tales, and mannerisms of speech. When Yeats was sixteen his family returned to Dublin, where he finished high school. Soon after, he fell in with a group of artists and mystics, including George William Russell (known by his pseudonym "A.E.") and various theosophists and spiritualists who introduced the young Yeats to oriental lore. Yeats began his career as a writer with *Mosada* (1886), a dramatic

William Butler Yeats

[1865-1939]

poem. After this rather mild beginning, Yeats went to London, became acquainted with a fairly wide circle of friends, coauthored an interpretation of the poems of William Blake (1893), and published a volume of folk stories, *The Celtic Twilight* (1893), as well as *Poems* (1895). Subsequent volumes, *The Secret Rose* (1897) and *Wind Among the Reeds* (1899), marked his continued interest in Irish themes as well as the influence of London poets of the time.

In 1899 Yeats was invited to help form an Irish theater. This institution, now the famous Abbey Theatre, tied Yeats permanently to the Dublin literary world. His Protestantism was not always easily received by his public, but his interest in verse drama remained strong. Yeats' fame increased with *Responsibilities* (1914), *The Wild Swans at Coole* (1917), and *A Vision* (1925), the latter a private system of mystic philosophy which supplies some of the imagery of the poems. During the formation of the Irish Free State Yeats was offered a position as senator, in spite of his religion. In 1923 he was awarded the Nobel Prize for literature. Even at the peak of his political activity and world-wide fame, his literary productivity remained high; *The Tower* (1928) and *The Winding Stair* (1929) represent, for many, the height of his poetic accomplishment. Yeats' last years were occupied with lecture tours and continued public honors. Even at his death in 1939 his intellectual interests were keen and wide.

DOWN BY THE SALLEY GARDENS

Down by the salley gardens my love and I did meet;
She passed the salley gardens with little snow-white feet.
She bid me take love easy, as the leaves grow on the tree;
But I, being young and foolish, with her would not agree.
In a field by the river my love and I did stand,   5
And on my leaning shoulder she laid her snow-white hand.
She bid me take life easy, as the grass grows on the weirs;
But I was young and foolish, and now am full of tears.

1. *salley:* willow.

THE LAKE ISLE OF INNISFREE

I will arise and go now, and go to Innisfree,
And a small cabin build there, of clay and wattles made:
Nine bean-rows will I have there, a hive for the honeybee,
And live alone in the bee-loud glade.

And I shall have some peace there, for peace comes dropping slow,   5
Dropping from the veils of the morning to where the cricket sings;
There midnight's all a glimmer, and noon a purple glow,
And evening full of the linnet's wings.

I will arise and go now, for always night and day
I hear lake water lapping with low sounds by the shore;   10
While I stand on the roadway, or on the pavements grey,
I hear it in the deep heart's core.

THE PITY OF LOVE

A pity beyond all telling
Is hid in the heart of love:
The folk who are buying and selling,
The clouds on their journey above,
The cold wet winds ever blowing,   5
And the shadowy hazel grove
Where mouse-grey waters are flowing,
Threaten the head that I love.

THE SORROW OF LOVE

The brawling of a sparrow in the eaves,
The brilliant moon and all the milky sky,
And all that famous harmony of leaves,
Had blotted out man's image and his cry.

A girl arose that had red mournful lips
And seemed the greatness of the world in tears,
Doomed like Odysseus and the labouring ships
And proud as Priam murdered with his peers;

Arose, and on the instant clamorous eaves,
A climbing moon upon an empty sky,
And all that lamentation of the leaves,
Could but compose man's image and his cry.

WHEN YOU ARE OLD

When you are old and grey and full of sleep,
And nodding by the fire, take down this book,
And slowly read, and dream of the soft look
Your eyes had once, and of their shadows deep;

How many loved your moments of glad grace,
And loved your beauty with love false or true,
But one man loved the pilgrim soul in you,
And loved the sorrows of your changing face;

And bending down beside the glowing bars,
Murmur, a little sadly, how Love fled
And paced upon the mountains overhead
And hid his face amid a crowd of stars.

A DREAM OF DEATH

I dreamed that one had died in a strange place
Near no accustomed hand;
And they had nailed the boards above her face.
The peasants of that land,

Wondering to lay her in that solitude,   5
And raised above her mound
A cross they had made out of two bits of wood,
And planted cypress round;
And left her to the indifferent stars above
Until I carved these words: 10
She was more beautiful than thy first love,
But now lies under boards.

TO A FRIEND WHOSE WORK HAS COME TO NOTHING

Now all the truth is out,
Be secret and take defeat
From any brazen throat,
For how can you compete,
Being honour bred, with one   5
Who, were it proved he lies,
Were neither shamed in his own
Nor in his neighbours' eyes?
Bred to a harder thing
Than Triumph, turn away   10
And like a laughing string
Whereon mad fingers play
Amid a place of stone,
Be secret and exult,
Because of all things known   15
That is most difficult.

THE MAGI

Now as at all times I can see in the mind's eye,
In their stiff, painted clothes, the pale unsatisfied ones
Appear and disappear in the blue depth of the sky
With all their ancient faces like rain-beaten stones,
And all their helms of silver hovering side by side,   5
And all their eyes still fixed, hoping to find once more,
Being by Calvary's turbulence unsatisfied,
The uncontrollable mystery on the bestial floor.

AN IRISH AIRMAN FORESEES
HIS DEATH

I know that I shall meet my fate
Somewhere among the clouds above;
Those that I fight I do not hate,
Those that I guard I do not love;
My country is Kiltartan Cross,
My countrymen Kiltartan's poor,
No likely end could bring them loss
Or leave them happier than before.
Nor law, nor duty bade me fight,
Nor public men, nor cheering crowds.   1
A lonely impulse of delight
Drove to this tumult in the clouds;
I balanced all, brought all to mind,
The years to come seemed waste of breath,
A waste of breath the years behind   1
In balance with this life, this death.

THE SCHOLARS

Bald heads forgetful of their sins,
Old, learned, respectable bald heads
Edit and annotate the lines
That young men, tossing on their beds,
Rhymed out in love's despair
To flatter beauty's ignorant ear.

All shuffle there; all cough in ink;
All wear the carpet with their shoes;
All think what other people think;
All know the man their neighbour knows.   1
Lord, what would they say
Did their Catullus walk that way?

A DEEP–SWORN VOW

Others because you did not keep
That deep-sworn vow have been friends of mine;
Yet always when I look death in the face,
When I clamber to the heights of sleep,
Or when I grow excited with wine,   5
Suddenly I meet your face.

EASTER 1916

I have met them at close of day
Coming with vivid faces
From counter or desk among grey
Eighteenth-century houses.
I have passed with a nod of the head   5
Or polite meaningless words,
Or have lingered awhile and said
Polite meaningless words,
And thought before I had done
Of a mocking tale or a gibe   10
To please a companion
Around the fire at the club,
Being certain that they and I
But lived where motley is worn:
All changed, changed utterly: 15
A terrible beauty is born.

That woman's days were spent
In ignorant good-will,
Her nights in argument
Until her voice grew shrill.   20
What voice more sweet than hers
When, young and beautiful,
She rode to harriers?
This man had kept a school
And rode our wingèd horse;   25
This other his helper and friend
Was coming into his force;

He might have won fame in the end,
So sensitive his nature seemed,
So daring and sweet his thought.   30
This other man I had dreamed
A drunken, vainglorious lout.
He had done most bitter wrong
To some who are near my heart,
Yet I number him in the song;   35
He, too, has resigned his part
In the casual comedy;
He, too, has been changed in his turn,
Transformed utterly:
A terrible beauty is born.   40

Hearts with one purpose alone
Through summer and winter seem
Enchanted to a stone
To trouble the living stream.
The horse that comes from the road,   45
The rider, the birds that range
From cloud to tumbling cloud,
Minute by minute they change;
A shadow of cloud on the stream
Changes minute by minute;   50
A horse-hoof slides on the brim,
And a horse plashes within it;
The long-legged moor-hens dive,
And hens to moor-cocks call;
Minute by minute they live: 55
The stone's in the midst of all.

Too long a sacrifice
Can make a stone of the heart.
O when may it suffice?
That is Heaven's part, our part   60
To murmur name upon name,
As a mother names her child
When sleep at last has come
On limbs that had run wild.
What is it but nightfall?   65

No, no, not night but death;
Was it needless death after all?
For England may keep faith
For all that is done and said.
We know their dream; enough   70
To know they dreamed and are dead;
And what if excess of love
Bewildered them till they died?
I write it out in a verse—
MacDonagh and MacBride   75
And Connolly and Pearse
Now and in time to be,
Wherever green is worn,
Are changed, changed utterly:
A terrible beauty is born.   80

THE SECOND COMING

Turning and turning in the widening gyre
The falcon cannot hear the falconer;
Things fall apart; the centre cannot hold;
Mere anarchy is loosed upon the world,
The blood-dimmed tide is loosed, and everywhere   5
The ceremony of innocence is drowned;
The best lack all conviction, while the worst
Are full of passionate intensity.

Surely some revelation is at hand;
Surely the Second Coming is at hand.   10
The Second Coming! Hardly are those words out
When a vast image of *Spiritus Mundi*
Troubles my sight: somewhere in sands of the desert
A shape with lion body and the head of a man,
A gaze blank and pitiless as the sun,   15
Is moving its slow thighs, while all about it
Reel shadows of the indignant desert birds.
The darkness drops again; but now I know
That twenty centuries of stony sleep

12. *Spiritus Mundi*: the spirit of the world.

Were vexed to nightmare by a rocking cradle,
And what rough beast, its hour come round at last,
Slouches towards Bethlehem to be born?

SAILING TO BYZANTIUM

1

That is no country for old men. The young
In one another's arms, birds in the trees
—Those dying generations—at their song,
The salmon-falls, the mackerel-crowded seas,
Fish, flesh, or fowl, commend all summer long
Whatever is begotten, born, and dies.
Caught in that sensual music all neglect
Monuments of unageing intellect.

2

An aged man is but a paltry thing,
A tattered coat upon a stick, unless
Soul clap its hands and sing, and louder sing
For every tatter in its mortal dress,
Nor is there singing school but studying
Monuments of its own magnificence;
And therefore I have sailed the seas and come
To the holy city of Byzantium.

3

O sages standing in God's holy fire
As in the gold mosaic of a wall,
Come from the holy fire, perne in a gyre,
And be the singing-masters of my soul.
Consume my heart away; sick with desire
And fastened to a dying animal
It knows not what it is; and gather me
Into the artifice of eternity.

19. *perne:* revolve.

4

Once out of nature I shall never take   25
My bodily form from any natural thing,
But such a form as Grecian goldsmiths make
Of hammered gold and gold enamelling
To keep a drowsy Emperor awake;
Or set upon a golden bough to sing   30
To lords and ladies of Byzantium
Of what is past, or passing, or to come.

TWO SONGS FROM A PLAY

1

I saw a staring virgin stand
Where holy Dionysus died,
And tear the heart out of his side,
And lay the heart upon her hand
And bear that beating heart away;   5
And then did all the Muses sing
Of Magnus Annus at the spring,
As though God's death were but a play.

Another Troy must rise and set,
Another lineage feed the crow,   10
Another Argo's painted prow
Drive to a flashier bauble yet.
The Roman Empire stood appalled:
It dropped the reigns of peace and war
When that fierce virgin and her Star   15
Out of the fabulous darkness called.

2

In pity for man's darkening thought
He walked that room and issued thence
In Galilean turbulence;

7. *Magnus Annus*: the great year.

The Babylonian starlight brought   2c
A fabulous, formless darkness in;
Odour of blood when Christ was slain
Made all Platonic tolerance vain
And vain all Doric discipline.

Everything that man esteems   25
Endures a moment or a day.
Love's pleasure drives his love away,
The painter's brush consumes his dreams;
The herald's cry, the soldier's tread
Exhaust his glory and his might: 3c
Whatever flames upon the night
Man's own resinous heart has fed.

LEDA AND THE SWAN*

A sudden blow: the great wings beating still
Above the staggering girl, her thighs caressed
By the dark webs, her nape caught in his bill,
He holds her helpless breast upon his breast.

How can those terrified vague fingers push   5
The feathered glory from her loosening thighs?
And how can body, laid in that white rush,
But feel the strange heart beating where it lies?

A shudder in the loins engenders there
The broken wall, the burning roof and tower   10
And Agamemnon dead.
                        Being so caught up,
So mastered by the brute blood of the air,
Did she put on his knowledge with his power
Before the indifferent beak could let her drop?

* The legends about Leda and the swan differ significantly. Leda, the wife of
Tyndareus, King of Sparta, was sexually assaulted by Zeus, who came to her in
the form of a swan. Yeats refers to the version which names Helen as the product of
this union; Clytæmnestra, her fraternal twin sister, was presumably the result of
a union with Tyndareus. From this birth follows the Trojan War (caused by the
abduction of the divinely beautiful Helen) and the downfall of the Mycenæans
(marked by the murder of their leader, Agamemnon, by his wife, Clytæmnestra,
and the paramour whom she acquired while her husband was fighting at Troy).

AMONG SCHOOL CHILDREN

1

I walk through the long schoolroom questioning;
A kind old nun in a white hood replies;
The children learn to cipher and to sing,
To study reading-books and history,
To cut and sew, be neat in everything   5
In the best modern way—the children's eyes
In momentary wonder stare upon
A sixty-year-old smiling public man.

2

I dream of a Ledaean body, bent
Above a sinking fire, a tale that she   10
Told of a harsh reproof, or trivial event
That changed some childish day to tragedy—
Told, and it seemed that our two natures blent
Into a sphere from youthful sympathy,
Or else, to alter Plato's parable,   15
Into the yolk and white of the one shell.

3

And thinking of that fit of grief or rage
I look upon one child or t'other there
And wonder if she stood so at that age—
For even daughters of the swan can share   20
Something of every paddler's heritage—
And had that colour upon cheek or hair,
And thereupon my heart is driven wild:
She stands before me as a living child.

4

Her present image floats into the mind—   25
Did Quattrocento finger fashion it

Hollow of cheek as though it drank the wind
And took a mess of shadows for its meat?
And I though never of Ledaean kind
Had pretty plumage once—enough of that,   30
Better to smile on all that smile, and show
There is a comfortable kind of old scarecrow.

5

What youthful mother, a shape upon her lap
Honey of generation had betrayed,
And that must sleep, shriek, struggle to escape   35
As recollection or the drug decide,
Would think her son, did she but see that shape
With sixty or more winters on its head,
A compensation for the pang of his birth,
Or the uncertainty of his setting forth?   40

6

Plato thought nature but a spume that plays
Upon a ghostly paradigm of things;
Solider Aristotle played the taws
Upon the bottom of a king of kings;
World-famous golden-thighed Pythagoras   45
Fingered upon a fiddle-stick or strings
What a star sang and careless Muses heard:
Old clothes upon old sticks to scare a bird.

7

Both nuns and mothers worship images,
But those the candles light are not as those   50
That animate a mother's reveries,
But keep a marble or a bronze repose.
And yet they too break hearts—O Presences
That passion, piety or affection knows,
And that all heavenly glory symbolise—   55
O self-born mockers of man's enterprise;

8

Labour is blossoming or dancing where
The body is not bruised to pleasure soul,
Nor beauty born out of its own despair,
Nor blear-eyed wisdom out of midnight oil.   60
O chestnut-tree, great-rooted blossomer,
Are you the leaf, the blossom or the bole?
O body swayed to music, O brightening glance,
How can we know the dancer from the dance?

BYZANTIUM

The unpurged images of day recede;
The Emperor's drunken soldiery are abed;
Night resonance recedes, night-walkers' song
After great cathedral gong;
A starlit or a moonlit dome disdains   5
All that man is,
All mere complexities,
The fury and the mire of human veins.

Before me floats an image, man or shade,
Shade more than man, more image than a shade;   10
For Hades' bobbin bound in mummy-cloth
May unwind the winding path;
A mouth that has no moisture and no breath
Breathless mouths may summon;
I hail the superhuman;   15
I call it death-in-life and life-in-death.

Miracle, bird or golden handiwork,
More miracle than bird or handiwork,
Planted on the star-lit golden bough,
Can like the cocks of Hades crow,   20
Or, by the moon embittered, scorn aloud
In glory of changeless metal
Common bird or petal
And all complexities of mire or blood.

At midnight on the Emperor's pavement flit   25
Flames that no faggot feeds, nor steel has lit,
Nor storm disturbs, flames begotten of flame,
Where blood-begotten spirits come
And all complexities of fury leave,
Dying into a dance,   30
An agony of trance,
An agony of flame that cannot singe a sleeve.

Astraddle on the dolphin's mire and blood,
Spirit after spirit! The smithies break the flood,
The golden smithies of the Emperor!   35
Marbles of the dancing floor
Break bitter furies of complexity,
Those images that yet
Fresh images beget,
That dolphin-torn, that gong-tormented sea.   40

CRAZY JANE AND JACK THE
JOURNEYMAN

I know, although when looks meet
I tremble to the bone,
The more I leave the door unlatched
The sooner love is gone,
For love is but a skein unwound   5
Between the dark and dawn.

A lonely ghost the ghost is
That to God shall come;
I—love's skein upon the ground,
My body in the tomb—   10
Shall leap into the light lost
In my mother's womb.

But were I left to lie alone
In an empty bed,
The skein so bound us ghost to ghost   15
When he turned his head
Passing on the road that night,
Mine must walk when dead.

CRAZY JANE ON GOD

That lover of a night
Came when he would,
Went in the dawning light
Whether I would or no;
Men come, men go,   5
All things remain in God.

Banners choke the sky;
Men-at-arms tread;
Armoured horses neigh
Where the great battle was   10
In the narrow pass:
All things remain in God.

Before their eyes a house
That from childhood stood
Uninhabited, ruinous,   15
Suddenly lit up
From door to top:
All things remain in God.

I had wild Jack for a lover;
Though like a road   20
That men pass over
My body makes no moan
But sings on:
All things remain in God.

CRAZY JANE TALKS WITH THE BISHOP

I met the Bishop on the road
And much said he and I.
"Those breasts are flat and fallen now,
Those veins must soon be dry;
Live in a heavenly mansion,   5
Not in some foul sty."

"Fair and foul are near of kin,
And fair needs foul," I cried.
"My friends are gone, but that's a truth
Nor grave nor bed denied,   10
Learned in bodily lowliness
And in the heart's pride.

"A woman can be proud and stiff
When on love intent;
But Love has pitched his mansion in   15
The place of excrement;
For nothing can be sole or whole
That has not been rent."

AFTER LONG SILENCE

Speech after long silence; it is right,
All other lovers being estranged or dead,
Unfriendly lamplight hid under its shade,
The curtains drawn upon unfriendly night,
That we descant and yet again descant   5
Upon the supreme theme of Art and Song:
Bodily decrepitude is wisdom; young
We loved each other and were ignorant.

A FIRST CONFESSION

I admit the briar
Entangled in my hair
Did not injure me;
My blenching and trembling,
Nothing but dissembling,   5
Nothing but coquetry.

I long for truth, and yet
I cannot stay from that
My better self disowns,
For a man's attention   10
Brings such satisfaction
To the craving in my bones.

Brightness that I pull back
From the Zodiac,
Why those questioning eyes   15
That are fixed upon me?
What can they do but shun me
If empty night replies?

A LAST CONFESSION

What lively lad most pleasured me
Of all that with me lay?
I answered that I gave my soul
And loved in misery,
But had great pleasure with a lad   5
That I loved bodily.

Flinging from his arms I laughed
To think his passion such
He fancied that I gave a soul
Did but our bodies touch,   10
And laughed upon his breast to think
Beast gave beast as much.

I gave what other women gave
That stepped out of their clothes,
But when this soul, its body off,   15
Naked to naked goes,
He it has found shall find therein
What none other knows,

And give his own and take his own
And rule in his own right;   20
And though it loved in misery
Close and cling so tight,
There's not a bird of day that dare
Extinguish that delight.

LAPIS LAZULI

I have heard that hysterical women say
They are sick of the palette and fiddle-bow,

Of poets that are always gay,
For everybody knows or else should know
That if nothing drastic is done
Aeroplane and Zeppelin will come out,
Pitch like King Billy bomb-balls in
Until the town lie beaten flat.

All perform their tragic play,
There struts Hamlet, there is Lear,   1
That's Ophelia, that Cordelia;
Yet they, should the last scene be there,
The great stage curtain about to drop,
If worthy their prominent part in the play,
Do not break up their lines to weep.   1
They know that Hamlet and Lear are gay;
Gaiety transfiguring all that dread.
All men have aimed at, found and lost;
Black out; Heaven blazing into the head:
Tragedy wrought to its uttermost.   2
Though Hamlet rambles and Lear rages,
And all the drop-scenes drop at once
Upon a hundred thousand stages,
It cannot grow by an inch or an ounce.

On their own feet they came, or on shipboard,   2
Camel-back, horse-back, ass-back, mule-back,
Old civilisations put to the sword.
Then they and their wisdom went to rack:
No handiwork of Callimachus,
Who handled marble as if it were bronze,   3
Made draperies that seemed to rise
When sea-wind swept the corner. stands;
His long lamp-chimney shaped like the stem
Of a slender palm, stood but a day;
All things fall and are built again,   3
And those that build them again are gay.

Two Chinamen, behind them a third,
Are carved in lapis lazuli,

29. *Callimachus*: Athenian sculptor of the late fifth century B.C. who was
widely recognized for his fine draperies; he is also credited with the design of the
Corinthian column.

Over them flies a long-legged bird,
A symbol of longevity;   40
The third, doubtless a serving-man,
Carries a musical instrument.

Every discoloration of the stone,
Every accidental crack or dent,
Seems a water-course or an avalanche,   45
Or lofty slope where it still snows
Though doubtless plum or cherry-branch
Sweetens the little half-way house
Those Chinamen climb towards, and I
Delight to imagine them seated there;   50
There, on the mountain and the sky,
On all the tragic scene they stare.
One asks for mournful melodies;
Accomplished fingers begin to play.
Their eyes mid many wrinkles, their eyes,   55
Their ancient, glittering eyes, are gay.

POLITICS

"In our time the destiny of man presents its meaning in political terms."
—Thomas Mann

How can I, that girl standing there,
My attention fix
On Roman or on Russian
Or on Spanish politics?
Yet here's a travelled man that knows   5
What he talks about,
And there's a politician
That has read and thought,
And maybe what they say is true
Of war and war's alarms,   10
But O that I were young again
And held her in my arms!

℄ ROBERT FROST, the poet who made the New England scene familiar to the twentieth-century reading public, was born and spent his boyhood in San Francisco. When his father died in 1885, Robert returned with his mother to her home in Lawrence, Massachusetts. He graduated from high school there, but his college career at Dartmouth was cut short because of his reluctance to be dependent on his grandfather. After 1890 he regularly submitted poems for publication, but he had little success. In 1895 he married, and two years later he accepted his grandfather's help to go to Harvard. Subsequently, his grandfather set him up with a farm in New Hampshire. In 1912, after a checkered career of farming, teaching, and other endeavors, Frost sold his farm and took his wife and four children to England. His first volume, *A Boy's Will*, was published there in 1913; English critics hailed it as a work of genuine merit. His second volume, *North of Boston*, appeared the following year; both were republished soon in America, and Frost returned to New England to stay.

Robert Frost

[1874-1963]

In 1916, which saw the publication of *Mountain Interval*, Frost became poet in residence at Amherst College; he was associated with the college as Professor of English from 1923 to 1938. In 1920 he helped form the famous Breadloaf School of English. Frost won the first of his four Pulitzer Prizes for *New Hampshire* in 1924. His fame now grew quickly. *West Running Brook* (1928) sold well, as did the first *Collected Poems* in 1931. In 1936 he was named Charles Eliot Norton Professor of Poetry at Harvard; later (1939–1942) he served there as Ralph Waldo Emerson Fellow in Poetry. *A Further Range* (1936) and *A Witness Tree* (1942), both of which won Pulitzer Prizes, and the various editions of his *Collected Poems* (particularly those of 1939 and 1949) made Frost the most famous living poet in America. Almost alone among twentieth-century poets, Frost became an important figure for large segments of the American population. He read one of his poems, "The Gift Outright," at the Presidential inauguration in 1961, scarcely two years before he died on January 29, 1963.

MENDING WALL

Something there is that doesn't love a wall,
That sends the frozen-ground-swell under it,
And spills the upper boulders in the sun;
And makes gaps even two can pass abreast.
The work of hunters is another thing: 5
I have come after them and made repair
Where they have left not one stone on a stone,
But they would have the rabbit out of hiding,
To please the yelping dogs. The gaps I mean,
No one has seen them made or heard them made,   10
But at spring mending-time we find them there.
I let my neighbor know beyond the hill;
And on a day we meet to walk the line
And set the wall between us once again.
We keep the wall between us as we go.   15
To each the boulders that have fallen to each.
And some are loaves and some so nearly balls
We have to use a spell to make them balance:
"Stay where you are until our backs are turned!"
We wear our fingers rough with handling them.   20
Oh, just another kind of outdoor game,
One on a side. It comes to little more:
There where it is we do not need the wall:
He is all pine and I am apple orchard.
My apple trees will never get across   25
And eat the cones under his pines, I tell him.
He only says, "Good fences make good neighbors."
Spring is the mischief in me, and I wonder
If I could put a notion in his head:
"*Why* do they make good neighbors? Isn't it   30
Where there are cows? But here there are no cows.
Before I built a wall I'd ask to know
What I was walling in or walling out,
And to whom I was like to give offense.
Something there is that doesn't love a wall,   35
That wants it down." I could say "Elves" to him,
But it's not elves exactly, and I'd rather

He said it for himself. I see him there
Bringing a stone grasped firmly by the top
In each hand, like an old-stone savage armed.
He moves in darkness as it seems to me,
Not of woods only and the shade of trees
He will not go behind his father's saying,
And he likes having thought of it so well
He says again, "Good fences make good neighbors."

THE DEATH OF THE HIRED MAN

Mary sat musing on the lamp-flame at the table
Waiting for Warren. When she heard his step,
She ran on tip-toe down the darkened passage
To meet him in the doorway with the news
And put him on his guard. "Silas is back."
She pushed him outward with her through the door
And shut it after her. "Be kind," she said.
She took the market things from Warren's arms
And set them on the porch, then drew him down
To sit beside her on the wooden steps.

"When was I ever anything but kind to him?
But I'll not have the fellow back," he said.
"I told him so last haying, didn't I?
If he left then, I said, that ended it.
What good is he? Who else will harbor him
At his age for the little he can do?
What help he is there's no depending on.
Off he goes always when I need him most.
He thinks he ought to earn a little pay,
Enough at least to buy tobacco with,
So he won't have to beg and be beholden.
'All right,' I say, 'I can't afford to pay
Any fixed wages, though I wish I could.'
'Someone else can.' 'Then someone else will have to.'
I shouldn't mind his bettering himself
If that was what it was. You can be certain,
When he begins like that, there's someone at him
Trying to coax him off with pocket-money,—

In haying time, when any help is scarce.
In winter he comes back to us. I'm done." 30

"Sh! not so loud: he'll hear you," Mary said.

"I want him to: he'll have to soon or late."

"He's worn out. He's asleep beside the stove.
When I came up from Rowe's I found him here,
Huddled against the barn-door fast asleep, 35
A miserable sight, and frightening, too—
You needn't smile—I didn't recognize him—
I wasn't looking for him—and he's changed.
Wait till you see."
                    "Where did you say he'd been?"

"He didn't say. I dragged him to the house, 40
And gave him tea and tried to make him smoke.
I tried to make him talk about his travels.
Nothing would do: he just kept nodding off."

"What did he say? Did he say anything?"

"But little."

                    "Anything? Mary, confess 45
He said he'd come to ditch the meadow for me."

"Warren!"

                    "But did he? I just want to know."

"Of course he did. What would you have him say?
Surely you wouldn't grudge the poor old man
Some humble way to save his self-respect. 50
He added, if you really care to know,
He meant to clear the upper pasture, too.
That sounds like something you have heard before?
Warren, I wish you could have heard the way
He jumbled everything. I stopped to look 55
Two or three times—he made me feel so queer—
To see if he was talking in his sleep.
He ran on Harold Wilson—you remember—
The boy you had in haying four years since.
He's finished school, and teaching in his college. 60

Silas declares you'll have to get him back.
He says they two will make a team for work:
Between them they will lay this farm as smooth!
The way he mixed that in with other things.
He thinks young Wilson a likely lad, though daft   6
On education—you know how they fought
All through July under the blazing sun,
Silas up on the cart to build the load,
Harold along beside to pitch it on."

"Yes, I took care to keep well out of earshot."   7

"Well, those days trouble Silas like a dream.
You wouldn't think they would. How some things linger!
Harold's young college boy's assurance piqued him.
After so many years he still keeps finding
Good arguments he sees he might have used.   7
I sympathize. I know just how it feels
To think of the right thing to say too late.
Harold's associated in his mind with Latin.
He asked me what I thought of Harold's saying
He studied Latin like the violin   8
Because he liked it—that an argument!
He said he couldn't make the boy believe
He could find water with a hazel prong—
Which showed how much good school had ever done him.
He wanted to go over that. But most of all   8
He thinks if he could have another chance
To teach him how to build a load of hay—"

"I know, that's Silas' one accomplishment.
He bundles every forkful in its place,
And tags and numbers it for future reference,   9
So he can find and easily dislodge it
In the unloading. Silas does that well.
He takes it out in bunches like big birds' nests.
You never see him standing on the hay
He's trying to lift, straining to lift himself."   9

"He thinks if he could teach him that, he'd be
Some good perhaps to someone in the world.
He hates to see a boy the fool of books.

Poor Silas, so concerned for other folk,
And nothing to look backward to with pride,   100
And nothing to look forward to with hope,
So now and never any different."

Part of a moon was falling down the west,
Dragging the whole sky with it to the hills.
Its light poured softly in her lap. She saw it   105
And spread her apron to it. She put out her hand
Among the harp-like morning-glory strings,
Taut with the dew from garden bed to eaves,
As if she played unheard some tenderness
That wrought on him beside her in the night.   110
"Warren," she said, "he has come home to die:
You needn't be afraid he'll leave you this time."

"Home," he mocked gently.

                            "Yes, what else but home?
It all depends on what you mean by home.
Of course he's nothing to us, any more   115
Than was the hound that came a stranger to us
Out of the woods, worn out upon the trail."

"Home is the place where, when you have to go there,
They have to take you in."

                            "I should have called it
Something you somehow haven't to deserve."   120

Warren leaned out and took a step or two,
Picked up a little stick, and brought it back
And broke it in his hand and tossed it by.
"Silas has better claim on us you think
Than on his brother? Thirteen little miles   125
As the road winds would bring him to his door.
Silas has walked that far no doubt today.
Why doesn't he go there? His brother's rich,
A somebody—director in the bank."

"He never told us that."

                            "We know it though."   130

"I think his brother ought to help, of course.
I'll see to that if there is need. He ought of right
To take him in, and might be willing to—
He may be better than appearances.
But have some pity on Silas. Do you think   135
If he had any pride in claiming kin
Or anything he looked for from his brother,
He'd keep so still about him all this time?"

"I wonder what's between them."

                              "I can tell you.
Silas is what he is—we wouldn't mind him—   140
But just the kind that kinsfolk can't abide.
He never did a thing so very bad.
He don't know why he isn't quite as good
As anybody. Worthless though he is,
He won't be made ashamed to please his brother."   145

"*I* can't think Si ever hurt anyone."

"No, but he hurt my heart the way he lay
And rolled his old head on that sharp-edged chair-back.
He wouldn't let me put him on the lounge.
You must go in and see what you can do.   150
I made the bed up for him there tonight.
You'll be surprised at him—how much he's broken.
His working days are done; I'm sure of it."

"I'd not be in a hurry to say that."

"I haven't been. Go, look, see for yourself.   155
But, Warren, please remember how it is:
He's come to help you ditch the meadow.
He has a plan. You mustn't laugh at him.
He may not speak of it, and then he may.
I'll sit and see if that small sailing cloud   160
Will hit or miss the moon."

                              It hit the moon.
Then there were three there, making a dim row,
The moon, the little silver cloud, and she.

Warren returned—too soon, it seemed to her,
Slipped to her side, caught up her hand and waited. 165

"Warren?" she questioned.

"Dead," was all he answered.

AFTER APPLE–PICKING

My long two-pointed ladder's sticking through a tree
Toward heaven still,
And there's a barrel that I didn't fill
Beside it, and there may be two or three
Apples I didn't pick upon some bough. 5
But I am done with apple-picking now.
Essence of winter sleep is on the night,
The scent of apples: I am drowsing off.
I cannot rub the strangeness from my sight
I got from looking through a pane of glass 10
I skimmed this morning from the drinking trough
And held against the world of hoary grass.
It melted, and I let it fall and break.
But I was well
Upon my way to sleep before it fell, 15
And I could tell
What form my dreaming was about to take.
Magnified apples appear and disappear,
Stem end and blossom end,
And every fleck of russet showing clear. 20
My instep arch not only keeps the ache,
It keeps the pressure of a ladder-round.
I feel the ladder sway as the boughs bend.
And I keep hearing from the cellar bin
The rumbling sound 25
Of load on load of apples coming in.
For I have had too much
Of apple-picking: I am overtired
Of the great harvest I myself desired.
There were ten thousand thousand fruit to touch, 30
Cherish in hand, lift down, and not let fall.
For all

That struck the earth,
No matter if not bruised or spiked with stubble,
Went surely to the cider-apple heap   35
As of no worth.
One can see what will trouble
This sleep of mine, whatever sleep it is.
Were he not gone,
The woodchuck could say whether it's like his   40
Long sleep, as I describe its coming on,
Or just some human sleep.

THE ROAD NOT TAKEN

Two roads diverged in a yellow wood,
And sorry I could not travel both
And be one traveler, long I stood
And looked down one as far as I could
To where it bent in the undergrowth;   5

Then took the other, as just as fair,
And having perhaps the better claim,
Because it was grassy and wanted wear;
Though as for that the passing there
Had worn them really about the same,   10

And both that morning equally lay
In leaves no step had trodden black.
Oh, I kept the first for another day!
Yet knowing how way leads on to way,
I doubted if I should ever come back.   15

I shall be telling this with a sigh
Somewhere ages and ages hence:
Two roads diverged in a wood, and I—
I took the one less traveled by,
And that has made all the difference.   20

MEETING AND PASSING

As I went down the hill along the wall
There was a gate I had leaned at for the view

And had just turned from when I first saw you
As you came up the hill. We met. But all
We did that day was mingle great and small 5
Footprints in summer dust as if we drew
The figure of our being less than two
But more than one as yet. Your parasol
Pointed the decimal off with one deep thrust.
And all the time we talked you seemed to see 10
Something down there to smile at in the dust.
(Oh, it was without prejudice to me!)
Afterward I went past what you had passed
Before we met and you what I had passed.

THE OVEN BIRD

There is a singer everyone has heard,
Loud, a mid-summer and a mid-wood bird,
Who makes the solid tree trunks sound again.
He says that leaves are old and that for flowers
Mid-summer is to spring as one to ten. 5
He says the early petal-fall is past
When pear and cherry bloom went down in showers
On sunny days a moment overcast;
And comes that other fall we name the fall.
He says the highway dust is over all. 10
The bird would cease and be as other birds
But that he knows in singing not to sing.
The question that he frames in all but words
Is what to make of a diminished thing.

BIRCHES

When I see birches bend to left and right
Across the lines of straighter darker trees,
I like to think some boy's been swinging them.
But swinging doesn't bend them down to stay
As ice-storms do. Often you must have seen them 5
Loaded with ice a sunny winter morning
After a rain. They click upon themselves

As the breeze rises, and turn many-colored
As the stir cracks and crazes their enamel.
Soon the sun's warmth makes them shed crystal shells   10
Shattering and avalanching on the snow-crust—
Such heaps of broken glass to sweep away
You'd think the inner dome of heaven had fallen.
They are dragged to the withered bracken by the load,
And they seem not to break; though once they are bowed   15
So low for long, they never right themselves:
You may see their trunks arching in the woods
Years afterwards, trailing their leaves on the ground
Like girls on hands and knees that throw their hair
Before them over their heads to dry in the sun.   20
But I was going to say when Truth broke in
With all her matter-of-fact about the ice-storm
I should prefer to have some boy bend them
As he went out and in to fetch the cows—
Some boy too far from town to learn baseball,   25
Whose only play was what he found himself,
Summer or winter, and could play alone.
One by one he subdued his father's trees
By riding them down over and over again
Until he took the stiffness out of them,   30
And not one but hung limp, not one was left
For him to conquer. He learned all there was
To learn about not launching out too soon
And so not carrying the tree away
Clear to the ground. He always kept his poise   35
To the top branches, climbing carefully
With the same pains you use to fill a cup
Up to the brim, and even above the brim.
Then he flung outward, feet first, with a swish,
Kicking his way down through the air to the ground.   40
So was I once myself a swinger of birches.
And so I dream of going back to be.
It's when I'm weary of considerations,
And life is too much like a pathless wood
Where your face burns and tickles with the cobwebs   45
Broken across it, and one eye is weeping
From a twig's having lashed across it open.

I'd like to get away from earth awhile
And then come back to it and begin over.
May no fate willfully misunderstand me   50
And half grant what I wish and snatch me away
Not to return. Earth's the right place for love:
I don't know where it's likely to go better.
I'd like to go by climbing a birch tree,
And climb black branches up a snow-white trunk   55
Toward heaven, till the tree could bear no more,
But dipped its top and set me down again.
That would be good both going and coming back.
One could do worse than be a swinger of birches.

THE HILL WIFE

Loneliness

Her Word

One ought not to have to care
    So much as you and I
Care when the birds come round the house
    To seem to say good-by;

Or care so much when they come back   5
    With whatever it is they sing;
The truth being we are as much
    Too glad for the one thing

As we are too sad for the other here—
    With birds that fill their breasts   10
But with each other and themselves
    And their built or driven nests.

House Fear

Always—I tell you this they learned—
Always at night when they returned
To the lonely house from far away
To lamps unlighted and fire gone gray,

They learned to rattle the lock and key   5
To give whatever might chance to be
Warning and time to be off in flight:
And preferring the out- to the in-door night,
They learned to leave the house-door wide
Until they had lit the lamp inside.   10

The Smile

Her Word

I didn't like the way he went away.
That smile! It never came of being gay.
Still he smiled—did you see him?—I was sure!
Perhaps because we gave him only bread
And the wretch knew from that that we were poor.   5
Perhaps because he let us give instead
Of seizing from us as he might have seized.
Perhaps he mocked at us for being wed,
Or being very young (and he was pleased
To have a vision of us old and dead).   10
I wonder how far down the road he's got.
He's watching from the woods as like as not.

The Oft-Repeated Dream

She had no saying dark enough
    For the dark pine that kept
Forever trying the window-latch
    Of the room where they slept.

The tireless but ineffectual hands   5
    That with every futile pass
Made the great tree seem as a little bird
    Before the mystery of glass!

It never had been inside the room,
    And only one of the two   10
Was afraid in an oft-repeated dream
    Of what the tree might do.

The Impulse

It was too lonely for her there,
   And too wild,
And since there were but two of them,
   And no child,

And work was little in the house,   5
   She was free,
And followed where he furrowed field,
   Or felled tree.

She rested on a log and tossed
   The fresh chips,   10
With a song only to herself
   On her lips.

And once she went to break a bough
   Of black alder.
She strayed so far she scarcely heard   15
   When he called her—

And didn't answer—didn't speak—
   Or return.
She stood, and then she ran and hid
   In the fern.   20

He never found her, though he looked
   Everywhere,
And he asked at her mother's house
   Was she there.

Sudden and swift and light as that   25
   The ties gave,
And he learned of finalities
   Besides the grave.

FIRE AND ICE

Some say the world will end in fire,
Some say in ice.
From what I've tasted of desire

I hold with those who favor fire.
But if it had to perish twice,   5
I think I know enough of hate
To say that for destruction ice
Is also great
And would suffice.

STOPPING BY WOODS ON A
SNOWY EVENING

Whose woods these are I think I know.
His house is in the village though;
He will not see me stopping here
To watch his woods fill up with snow.

My little horse must think it queer   5
To stop without a farmhouse near
Between the woods and frozen lake
The darkest evening of the year.

He gives his harness bells a shake
To ask if there is some mistake.   10
The only other sound's the sweep
Of easy wind and downy flake.

The woods are lovely, dark and deep,
But I have promises to keep,
And miles to go before I sleep,   15
And miles to go before I sleep.

PLOWMEN

A plow, they say, to plow the snow.
They cannot mean to plant it, no—
Unless in bitterness to mock
At having cultivated rock.

ONCE BY THE PACIFIC

The shattered water made a misty din.
Great waves looked over others coming in,

And thought of doing something to the shore
That water never did to land before.
The clouds were low and hairy in the skies,   5
Like locks blown forward in the gleam of eyes.
You could not tell, and yet it looked as if
The shore was lucky in being backed by cliff,
The cliff in being backed by continent;
It looked as if a night of dark intent   10
Was coming, and not only a night, an age.
Someone had better be prepared for rage.
There would be more than ocean-water broken
Before God's last *Put out the Light* was spoken.

BEREFT

Where had I heard this wind before
Change like this to a deeper roar?
What would it take my standing there for,
Holding open a restive door,
Looking down hill to a frothy shore?   5
Summer was past and day was past.
Somber clouds in the west were massed.
Out in the porch's sagging floor,
Leaves got up in a coil and hissed,
Blindly struck at my knee and missed.   10
Something sinister in the tone
Told me my secret must be known:
Word I was in the house alone
Somehow must have gotten abroad,
Word I was in my life alone,   15
Word I had no one left but God.

ACQUAINTED WITH THE NIGHT

I have been one acquainted with the night.
I have walked out in rain—and back in rain.
I have outwalked the furthest city light.

I have looked down the saddest city lane.

I have passed by the watchman on his beat   5
And dropped my eyes, unwilling to explain.

I have stood still and stopped the sound of feet
When far away an interrupted cry
Came over houses from another street,

But not to call me back or say good-by;   10
And further still at an unearthly height,
One luminary clock against the sky

Proclaimed the time was neither wrong nor right.
I have been one acquainted with the night.

TWO TRAMPS IN MUD TIME

Out of the mud two strangers came
And caught me splitting wood in the yard.
And one of them put me off my aim
By hailing cheerily "Hit them hard!"
I knew pretty well why he dropped behind   5
And let the other go on a way.
I knew pretty well what he had in mind:
He wanted to take my job for pay.

Good blocks of oak it was I split,
As large around as the chopping block;   10
And every piece I squarely hit
Fell splinterless as a cloven rock.
The blows that a life of self-control
Spares to strike for the common good
That day, giving a loose to my soul,   15
I spent on the unimportant wood.

The sun was warm but the wind was chill.
You know how it is with an April day
When the sun is out and the wind is still,
You're one month on in the middle of May.   20
But if you so much as dare to speak,
A cloud comes over the sunlit arch,
A wind comes off a frozen peak,
And you're two months back in the middle of March.

A bluebird comes tenderly up to alight 25
And turns to the wind to unruffle a plume
His song so pitched as not to excite
A single flower as yet to bloom.
It is snowing a flake: and he half knew
Winter was only playing possum. 30
Except in color he isn't blue,
But he wouldn't advise a thing to blossom.

The water for which we may have to look
In summertime with a witching-wand,
In every wheelrut's now a brook, 35
In every print of a hoof a pond.
Be glad of water, but don't forget
The lurking frost in the earth beneath
That will steal forth after the sun is set
And show on the water its crystal teeth. 40

The time when most I loved my task
These two must make me love it more
By coming with what they came to ask.
You'd think I never had felt before
The weight of an ax-head poised aloft, 45
The grip on earth of outspread feet.
The life of muscles rocking soft
And smooth and moist in vernal heat.

Out of the woods two hulking tramps
(From sleeping God knows where last night, 50
But not long since in the lumber camps).
They thought all chopping was theirs of right
Men of the woods and lumberjacks,
They judged me by their appropriate tool.
Except as a fellow handled an ax, 55
They had no way of knowing a fool.

Nothing on either side was said.
They knew they had but to stay their stay
And all their logic would fill my head:
As that I had no right to play 60
With what was another man's work for gain.
My right might be love but theirs was need.

And where the two exist in twain
Theirs was the better right—agreed.

But yield who will to their separation,   65
My object in living is to unite
My avocation and my vocation
As my two eyes make one in sight.
Only where love and need are one,
And the work is play for mortal stakes,   70
Is the deed ever really done
For Heaven and the future's sakes.

DESERT PLACES

Snow falling and night falling fast, oh, fast
In a field I looked into going past,
And the ground almost covered smooth in snow,
But a few weeds and stubble showing last.

The woods around it have it—it is theirs.   5
All animals are smothered in their lairs.
I am too absent-spirited to count;
The loneliness includes me unawares.

And lonely as it is that loneliness
Will be more lonely ere it will be less—   10
A blanker whiteness of benighted snow
With no expression, nothing to express.

They cannot scare me with their empty spaces
Between stars—on stars where no human race is.
I have it in me so much nearer home   15
To scare myself with my own desert places.

THE STRONG ARE SAYING NOTHING

The soil now gets a rumpling soft and damp,
And small regard to the future of any weed.
The final flat of the hoe's approval stamp
Is reserved for the bed of a few selected seed.

There is seldom more than a man to a harrowed piece.   5
Men work alone, their lots plowed far apart,
One stringing a chain of seed in an open crease,
And another stumbling after a halting cart.

To the fresh and black of the squares of early mold
The leafless bloom of a plum is fresh and white;   10
Though there's more than a doubt if the weather is not too cold
For the bees to come and serve its beauty aright.

Wind goes from farm to farm in wave on wave,
But carries no cry of what is hoped to be.
There may be little or much beyond the grave,   15
But the strong are saying nothing until they see.

COME IN

As I came to the edge of the woods,
Thrush music—hark!
Now if it was dusk outside,
Inside it was dark.

Too dark in the woods for a bird   5
By sleight of wing
To better its perch for the night,
Though it still could sing.

The last of the light of the sun
That had died in the west   10
Still lived for one song more
In a thrush's breast.

Far in the pillared dark
Thrush music went—
Almost like a call to come in   15
To the dark and lament.

But no, I was out for stars:
I would not come in.
I meant not even if asked,
And I hadn't been.   20

A SEMI–REVOLUTION

I advocate a semi-revolution.
The trouble with a total revolution
(Ask any reputable Rosicrucian)
Is that it brings the same class up on top.
Executives of skillful execution   5
Will therefore plan to go halfway and stop.
Yes, revolutions are the only salves,
But they're one thing that should be done by halves.

REVELATION

We make ourselves a place apart
   Behind light words that tease and flout,
But oh, the agitated heart
   Till someone really find us out.

'Tis pity if the case require   5
   (Or so we say) that in the end
We speak the literal to inspire
   The understanding of a friend.

But so with all, from babes that play
   At hide-and-seek to God afar,   10
So all who hide too well away
   Must speak and tell us where they are.

¶ T. S. ELIOT was born in St. Louis, Missouri, and was educated at Harvard, where he received his M.A. degree in 1910. Immediately thereafter, he went to the University of Paris, where he heard lectures by Henri Bergson and others. The next year marked his return to Harvard to study oriental philosophy and ancient Indian languages. His studies were further enriched by sojourns in Germany in 1914 and at Merton College, Oxford, in 1915. After his marriage, in 1915, he taught in British academies for a few years, bringing to completion his first volume of poetry, *Prufrock, and Other Observations,* which was published in 1917.

Thomas
Stearns
Eliot

[1888-1965]

Eliot supported himself from 1918 to 1924 in Lloyd's Bank, London; during this time he published two more volumes, *Poems* (1920), of which the chief poem was "Gerontion," and *The Wasteland* (1922). His first book of criticism was also brought out in 1920: *The Sacred Wood.* In 1925, Eliot became permanently associated with the English publishing house Faber and Faber. In this position he was able to bring his literary work more closely in alliance with his means of financial support. Throughout the 1920's, he remained unusually active. He edited *The Criterion,* an influential London literary quarterly, from 1923 to 1929. He published four volumes of criticism: *Homage to John Dryden* (1924), *Shakespeare and the Stoicism of Seneca* (1928), *For Lancelot Andrewes* (1928), and *Dante* (1929). These volumes were in addition to a third volume of poetry, *The Hollow Men* (1925), and the first collected edition of his works, *Poems, 1909– 1925.* In the 1930's, Eliot published seven more volumes of critical essays and four new volumes of poems: *Ash Wednesday* (1930), *Sweeney Agonistes* (1932), *The Rock* (1934), and *Old Possum's Book of Practical Cats* (1939). Eliot also turned for the first time to poetic dramas. *Murder in the Cathedral,* widely recognized as a classic, was first published in 1935 and *The Family Reunion* four years later. Since 1940 Eliot's chief publications have been *Four Quartets* (1939–1942), the verse dramas *The Cocktail Party* (1950) and *The Confidential Clerk* (1954), and a volume of essays, *Notes Toward the Definition of Culture* (1949).

THE LOVE SONG OF
J. ALFRED PRUFROCK

S'io credesse che mia risposta fosse
A persona che mai tornasse al mondo,
Questa fiamma staria senza piu scosse.
Ma perciocche giammai di questo fondo
Non torno vivo alcun, s'i'odo il vero,
*Senza tema d'infamia ti rispondo.**

Let us go then, you and I,
When the evening is spread out against the sky
Like a patient etherised upon a table;
Let us go, through certain half-deserted streets,
The muttering retreats
Of restless nights in one-night cheap hotels
And sawdust restaurants with oyster-shells:
Streets that follow like a tedious argument
Of insidious intent
To lead you to an overwhelming question. . .
Oh, do not ask, "What is it?"
Let us go and make our visit.

In the room the women come and go
Talking of Michelangelo.

The yellow fog that rubs its back upon the window-panes,
The yellow smoke that rubs its muzzle on the window-panes
Licked its tongue into the corners of the evening,
Lingered upon the pools that stand in drains,
Let fall upon its back the soot that falls from chimneys,
Slipped by the terrace, made a sudden leap,

* The epigraph is from Dante's *Inferno*, XXVII, 61–66; a shade is speaking
to Dante. A translation of this passage is printed by permission of the translator,
Mark Musa, and the Indiana University Press:

> If I suspected I were speaking to one
>   Who someday might return to see the world,
>   Certainly this flame would cease to flicker;
> But since no one, if I have heard the truth,
>   Ever returns alive from this deep pit,
>   Without fear of dishonor I answer you.

And seeing that it was a soft October night,
Curled once about the house, and fell asleep.

And indeed there will be time
For the yellow smoke that slides along the street,
Rubbing its back upon the window-panes;   25
There will be time, there will be time
To prepare a face to meet the faces that you meet;
There will be time to murder and create,
And time for all the works and days of hands
That lift and drop a question on your plate;   30
Time for you and time for me,
And time yet for a hundred indecisions,
And for a hundred visions and revisions,
Before the taking of a toast and tea.

In the room the women come and go   35
Talking of Michelangelo.

And indeed there will be time
To wonder, "Do I dare?" and, "Do I dare?"
Time to turn back and descend the stair,
With a bald spot in the middle of my hair—   40
[They will say: "How his hair is growing thin!"]
My morning coat, my collar mounting firmly to the chin,
My necktie rich and modest, but asserted by a simple pin—
[They will say: "But how his arms and legs are thin!"]
Do I dare   45
Disturb the universe?
In a minute there is time
For decisions and revisions which a minute will reverse.

For I have known them all already, known them all:—
Have known the evenings, mornings, afternoons,   50
I have measured out my life with coffee spoons;
I know the voices dying with a dying fall
Beneath the music from a farther room.
  So how should I presume?

And I have known the eyes already, known them all—   55
The eyes that fix you in a formulated phrase,
And when I am formulated, sprawling on a pin,

When I am pinned and wriggling on the wall,
Then how should I begin
To spit out all the butt-ends of my days and ways?
    And how should I presume?

And I have known the arms already, known them all—
Arms that are braceleted and white and bare
[But in the lamplight, downed with light brown hair!]
Is it perfume from a dress
That makes me so digress?
Arms that lie along a table, or wrap about a shawl.
    And should I then presume?
    And how should I begin?

.   .   .   .   .

Shall I say, I have gone at dusk through narrow streets
And watched the smoke that rises from the pipes
Of lonely men in shirt-sleeves, leaning out of windows? . . .

I should have been a pair of ragged claws
Scuttling across the floors of silent seas.

.   .   .   .   .

And the afternoon, the evening, sleeps so peacefully!
Smoothed by long fingers,
Asleep . . . tired . . . or it malingers,
Stretched on the floor, here beside you and me.
Should I, after tea and cakes and ices,
Have the strength to force the moment to its crisis?
But though I have wept and fasted, wept and prayed,
Though I have seen my head [grown slightly bald] brought in
      upon a platter,
I am no prophet—and here's no great matter;
I have seen the moment of my greatness flicker,
And I have seen the eternal Footman hold my coat, and snicker,
And in short, I was afraid.

And would it have been worth it, after all,
After the cups, the marmalade, the tea,
Among the porcelain, among some talk of you and me,
Would it have been worth while,

To have bitten off the matter with a smile,
To have squeezed the universe into a ball
To roll it toward some overwhelming question,
To say: "I am Lazarus, come from the dead,
Come back to tell you all, I shall tell you all"——   95
If one, settling a pillow by her head,
    Should say: "That is not what I meant at all.
    That is not it, at all."

And would it have been worth it, after all,
Would it have been worth while,   100
After the sunsets and the dooryards and the sprinkled streets,
After the novels, after the teacups, after the skirts that trail along
    the floor——
And this, and so much more?——
It is impossible to say just what I mean!
But as if a magic lantern threw the nerves in patterns on a screen: 105
Would it have been worth while
If one, settling a pillow or throwing off a shawl,
And turning toward the window, should say:
    "That is not it at all,
    That is not what I meant, at all."   110

     .   .   .   .   .

No! I am not Prince Hamlet, nor was meant to be;
Am an attendant lord, one that will do
To swell a progress, start a scene or two,
Advise the prince; no doubt, an easy tool,
Deferential, glad to be of use,   115
Politic, cautious, and meticulous;
Full of high sentence, but a bit obtuse;
At times, indeed, almost ridiculous——
Almost, at times, the Fool.

I grow old . . . I grow old . . .   120
I shall wear the bottoms of my trousers rolled.

Shall I part my hair behind? Do I dare to eat a peach?
I shall wear white flannel trousers, and walk upon the beach.
I have heard the mermaids singing, each to each.

I do not think that they will sing to me.   125

I have seen them riding seaward on the waves
Combing the white hair of the waves blown back
When the wind blows the water white and black.

We have lingered in the chambers of the sea
By sea-girls wreathed with seaweed red and brown
Till human voices wake us, and we drown.

AUNT HELEN

Miss Helen Slingsby was my maiden aunt,
And lived in a small house near a fashionable square
Cared for by servants to the number of four.
Now when she died there was silence in heaven
And silence at her end of the street.
The shutters were drawn and the undertaker wiped his feet—
He was aware that this sort of thing had occurred before.
The dogs were handsomely provided for,
But shortly afterwards the parrot died too.
The Dresden clock continued ticking on the mantelpiece,
And the footman sat upon the dining-table
Holding the second housemaid on his knees—
Who had always been so careful while her mistress lived.

COUSIN NANCY

Miss Nancy Ellicott
Strode across the hills and broke them,
Rode across the hills and broke them—
The barren New England hills—
Riding to hounds
Over the cow-pasture.

Miss Nancy Ellicott smoked
And danced all the modern dances;
And her aunts were not quite sure how they felt about it,
But they knew that it was modern.

Upon the glazen shelves kept watch
Matthew and Waldo, guardians of the faith,
The army of unalterable law.

GERONTION

Thou hast nor youth nor age
But as it were an after dinner sleep
*Dreaming of both.**

Here I am, an old man in a dry month,
Being read to by a boy, waiting for rain.
I was neither at the hot gates
Nor fought in the warm rain
Nor knee deep in the salt marsh, heaving a cutlass,   5
Bitten by flies, fought.
My house is a decayed house,
And the jew squats on the window sill, the owner,
Spawned in some estaminet of Antwerp,
Blistered in Brussels, patched and peeled in London.   10
The goat coughs at night in the field overhead;
Rocks, moss, stonecrop, iron, merds.
The woman keeps the kitchen, makes tea,
Sneezes at evening, poking the peevish gutter.
                              I an old man,
A dull head among windy spaces.   15

Signs are taken for wonders. "We would see a sign!"
The word within a word, unable to speak a word,
Swaddled with darkness. In the juvescence of the year
Came Christ the tiger

In depraved May, dogwood and chestnut, flowering judas,   20
To be eaten, to be divided, to be drunk
Among whispers; by Mr. Silvero
With caressing hands, at Limoges
Who walked all night in the next room;

By Hakagawa, bowing among the Titians;   25
By Madame de Tornquist, in the dark room
Shifting the candles; Fräulein von Kulp
Who turned in the hall, one hand on the door.
    Vacant shuttles
Weave the wind. I have no ghosts,   30

* The epigraph is from Shakespeare's *Measure for Measure*, III, 2.

An old man in a draughty house
Under a windy knob.

After such knowledge, what forgiveness? Think now
History has many cunning passages, contrived corridors
And issues, deceives with whispering ambitions,   3
Guides us by vanities. Think now
She gives when our attention is distracted
And what she gives, gives with such supple confusions
That the giving famishes the craving. Gives too late
What's not believed in, or if still believed,   4
In memory only, reconsidered passion. Gives too soon
Into weak hands, what's thought can be dispensed with
Till the refusal propagates a fear. Think
Neither fear nor courage saves us. Unnatural vices
Are fathered by our heroism. Virtues   4
Are forced upon us by our impudent crimes.
These tears are shaken from the wrath-bearing tree.

The tiger springs in the new year. Us he devours.
    Think at last
We have not reached conclusion, when I   5
Stiffen in a rented house. Think at last
I have not made this show purposelessly
And it is not by any concitation
Of the backward devils
I would meet you upon this honestly.   5
I that was near your heart was removed therefrom
To lose beauty in terror, terror in inquisition.
I have lost my passion: why should I need to keep it
Since what is kept must be adulterated?
I have lost my sight, smell, hearing, taste and touch: 6
How should I use them for your closer contact?

These with a thousand small deliberations
Protract the profit of their chilled delirium,
Excite the membrane, when the sense has cooled,
With pungent sauces, multiply variety   6
In a wilderness of mirrors. What will the spider do,
Suspend its operations, will the weevil
Delay? De Bailhache, Fresca, Mrs. Cammel, whirled

Beyond the circuit of the shuddering Bear
In fractured atoms. Gull against the wind, in the windy straits   70
Of Belle Isle, or running on the Horn,
White feathers in the snow, the Gulf claims,
And an old man driven by the Trades
To a sleepy corner.

                              Tenants of the house,
Thoughts of a dry brain in a dry season.   75

WHISPERS OF IMMORTALITY

Webster was much possessed by death
And saw the skull beneath the skin;
And breastless creatures under ground
Leaned backward with a lipless grin.

Daffodil bulbs instead of balls   5
Stared from the sockets of the eyes!
He knew that thought clings round dead limbs
Tightening its lusts and luxuries.

Donne, I suppose, was such another
Who found no substitute for sense,   10
To seize and clutch and penetrate;
Expert beyond experience,

He knew the anguish of the marrow
The ague of the skeleton;
No contact possible to flesh   15
Allayed the fever of the bone.

          .   .   .   .   .

Grishkin is nice: her Russian eye
Is underlined for emphasis;
Uncorseted, her friendly bust
Gives promise of pneumatic bliss.   20

The couched Brazilian jaguar
Compels the scampering marmoset
With subtle effluence of cat;
Grishkin has a maisonette;

The sleek Brazilian jaguar
Does not in its arboreal gloom
Distil so rank a feline smell
As Grishkin in a drawing-room.

And even the Abstract Entities
Circumambulate her charm;
But our lot crawls between dry ribs
To keep our metaphysics warm.

SWEENEY AMONG THE NIGHTINGALES

ὤμοι, πέπληγμαι καιρίαν πληγὴν ἔσω.*

Apeneck Sweeney spreads his knees
Letting his arms hang down to laugh,
The zebra stripes along his jaw
Swelling to maculate giraffe.

The circles of the stormy moon
Slide westward toward the River Plate,
Death and the Raven drift above
And Sweeney guards the hornèd gate.

Gloomy Orion and the Dog
Are veiled; and hushed the shrunken seas;
The person in the Spanish cape
Tries to sit on Sweeney's knees

Slips and pulls the table cloth
Overturns a coffee-cup,
Reorganised upon the floor
She yawns and draws a stocking up;

The silent man in mocha brown
Sprawls at the window-sill and gapes;
The waiter brings in oranges
Bananas figs and hothouse grapes;

The silent vertebrate in brown
Contracts and concentrates, withdraws;

* The epigraph is from Aeschylus' *Agamemnon*, 1343: "Alas, I am struck
a blow at my heart within."

Rachel *née* Rabinovitch
Tears at the grapes with murderous paws;

She and the lady in the cape   25
Are suspect, thought to be in league;
Therefore the man with heavy eyes
Declines the gambit, shows fatigue,

Leaves the room and reappears
Outside the window, leaning in,   30
Branches of wistaria
Circumscribe a golden grin;

The host with someone indistinct
Converses at the door apart,
The nightingales are singing near   35
The Convent of the Sacred Heart,

And sang within the bloody wood
When Agamemnon cried aloud,
And let their liquid siftings fall
To stain the stiff dishonoured shroud.   40

THE HOLLOW MEN

A penny for the Old Guy *

1

We are the hollow men
We are the stuffed men
Leaning together
Headpiece filled with straw. Alas!
Our dried voices, when   5
We whisper together
Are quiet and meaningless
As wind in dry grass
Or rats' feet over broken glass
In our dry cellar   10

* A traditional phrase used by begging urchins on Guy Fawkes Day.

Shape without form, shade without colour,
Paralysed force, gesture without motion;

Those who have crossed
With direct eyes, to death's other Kingdom
Remember us—if at all—not as lost
Violent souls, but only
As the hollow men
The stuffed men.

2

Eyes I dare not meet in dreams
In death's dream kingdom
These do not appear:
There, the eyes are
Sunlight on a broken column
There, is a tree swinging
And voices are
In the wind's singing
More distant and more solemn
Than a fading star.

Let me be no nearer
In death's dream kingdom
Let me also wear
Such deliberate disguises
Rat's coat, crowskin, crossed staves
In a field
Behaving as the wind behaves
No nearer—

Not that final meeting
In the twilight kingdom

3

This is the dead land
This is cactus land
Here the stone images
Are raised, here they receive

The supplication of a dead man's hand
Under the twinkle of a fading star.

Is it like this   45
In death's other kingdom
Waking alone
At the hour when we are
Trembling with tenderness
Lips that would kiss   50
Form prayers to broken stone.

4

The eyes are not here
There are no eyes here
In this valley of dying stars
In this hollow valley   55
This broken jaw of our lost kingdoms

In this last of meeting places
We grope together
And avoid speech
Gathered on this beach of the tumid river   60

Sightless, unless
The eyes reappear
As the perpetual star
Multifoliate rose
Of death's twilight kingdom   65
The hope only
Of empty men.

5

Here we go round the prickly pear
Prickly pear prickly pear
Here we go round the prickly pear   70
At five o'clock in the morning.

Between the idea
And the reality
Between the motion

And the act
Falls the Shadow

For Thine is the Kingdom

Between the conception
And the creation
Between the emotion
And the response
Falls the Shadow

Life is very long

Between the desire
And the spasm
Between the potency
And the existence
Between the essence
And the descent
Falls the Shadow

For Thine is the Kingdom

For Thine is
Life is
For Thine is the

This is the way the world ends
This is the way the world ends
This is the way the world ends
Not with a bang but a whimper.

JOURNEY OF THE MAGI

'A cold coming we had of it,
Just the worst time of the year
For a journey, and such a long journey:
The ways deep and the weather sharp,
The very dead of winter.'
And the camels galled, sore-footed, refractory,
Lying down in the melting snow.
There were times we regretted
The summer palaces on slopes, the terraces,
And the silken girls bringing sherbet.

Then the camel men cursing and grumbling
And running away, and wanting their liquor and women,
And the night-fires going out, and the lack of shelters,
And the cities hostile and the towns unfriendly
And the villages dirty and charging high prices: 15
A hard time we had of it.
At the end we preferred to travel all night,
Sleeping in snatches,
With the voices singing in our ears, saying
That this was all folly.   20

Then at dawn we came down to a temperate valley,
Wet, below the snow line, smelling of vegetation;
With a running stream and a water-mill beating the darkness,
And three trees on the low sky,
And an old white horse galloped away in the meadow.   25
Then we came to a tavern with vine-leaves over the lintel,
Six hands at an open door dicing for pieces of silver,
And feet kicking the empty wine-skins.
But there was no information, and so we continued
And arrived at evening, not a moment too soon   30
Finding the place; it was (you may say) satisfactory.

All this was a long time ago, I remember,
And I would do it again, but set down
This set down
This: were we led all that way for   35
Birth or Death? There was a Birth, certainly,
We had evidence and no doubt. I had seen birth and death,
But had thought they were different; this Birth was
Hard and bitter agony for us, like Death, our death.
We returned to our places, these Kingdoms,   40
But no longer at ease here, in the old dispensation,
With an alien people clutching their gods.
I should be glad of another death.